Frontiers of Research in Economic Theory

The Nancy L. Schwartz Memorial Lectures, 1983–1997

"Leading economists presenting fundamentally important issues in economic theory" is the theme of the Nancy L. Schwartz Memorial Lecture series held annually at the J. L. Kellogg Graduate School of Management of Northwestern University. This collection of essays, drawn from the lectures delivered in the years 1983 through 1997, discusses economic behavior at the individual and group levels and the implications to the performance of economic systems.

Using nontechnical language, the speakers present theoretical, experimental, and empirical analysis of topics such as decision making under uncertainty and under full and bounded rationality, the influence of economic incentives and habits, and the effects of learning and evolution on dynamic choice. Perfect competition, economic development, social insurance and social mobility, and negotiation and economic survival are other major economic subjects analyzed, advancing our understanding of economic behavior.

Econometric Society Monographs No. 29

Editors:
Peter Hammond, Stanford University
Alberto Holly, University of Lausanne

The Econometric Society is an international society for the advancement of economic theory in relation to statistics and mathematics. The Econometric Society Monograph Series is designed to promote the publication of original research contributions of high quality in mathematical economics and theoretical and applied econometrics.

Other titles in the series:
G. S. Maddala *Limited-dependent and qualitative variables in econometrics*,
   0 521 33825 5
Gerard Debreu *Mathematical economics: Twenty papers of Gerard Debreu*,
   0 521 33561 2
Jean-Michel Grandmont *Money and value: A reconsideration of classical and neoclassical monetary economics*, 0 521 31364 3
Franklin M. Fisher *Disequilibrium foundations of equilibrium economics*, 0 521 37856 7
Andreu Mas-Colell *The theory of general economic equilibrium: A differentiable approach*, 0 521 26514 2, 0 521 38870 8
Cheng Hsiao *Analysis of panel data*, 0 521 38933 X
Truman F. Bewley, Editor *Advances in econometrics – Fifth World Congress (Volume I)*,
   0 521 46726 8
Truman F. Bewley, Editor *Advances in econometrics – Fifth World Congress (Volume II)*,
   0 521 46725 X
Herve Moulin *Axioms of cooperative decision making*, 0 521 36055 2, 0 521 42458 5
L. G. Godfrey *Misspecification tests in econometrics: The Lagrange multiplie principle and other approaches*, 0 521 42459 3
Tony Lancaster *The econometric analysis of transition data*, 0 521 43789 X
Alvin E. Roth and Marilda A. Oliviera Sotomayor, Editors *Two-sided matching: A study in game-theoretic modeling and analysis*, 0 521 43788 1
Wolfgang Härdle, *Applied nonparametric regression*, 0 521 42950 1
Jean-Jacques Laffont, Editor *Advances in economic theory – Sixth World Congress (Volume I)*, 0 521 48459 6
Jean-Jacques Laffont, Editor *Advances in economic theory – Sixth World Congress (Volume II)*, 0 521 48460 X
Halbert White *Estimation, inference and specification*, 0 521 25280 6, 0 521 57446 3
Christopher Sims, Editor *Advances in econometrics – Sixth World Congress (Volume I)*,
   0 521 56610 X
Christopher Sims, Editor *Advances in econometrics – Sixth World Congress (Volume II)*,
   0 521 56609 6
Roger Guesnerie *A contribution to the pure theory of taxation*, 0 521 23689 4,
   0 521 62956 X
David M. Kreps and Kenneth F. Wallis, Editors *Advances in economics and econometrics – Seventh World Congress (Volume I)*, 0 521 58011 0, 0 521 58983 5
David M. Kreps and Kenneth F. Wallis, Editors *Advances in economics and econometrics – Seventh World Congress (Volume II)*, 0 521 58012 9, 0 521 58982 7
David M. Kreps and Kenneth F. Wallis, Editors *Advances in economics and econometrics – Seventh World Congress (Volume III)*, 0 521 58013 7, 0 521 58981 9

Nancy L. Schwartz (Photo courtesy Northwestern University Archives)

Frontiers of Research in Economic Theory

The Nancy L. Schwartz Memorial Lectures, 1983–1997

Edited by

DONALD P. JACOBS

EHUD KALAI

MORTON I. KAMIEN

CAMBRIDGE
UNIVERSITY PRESS

CAMBRIDGE
UNIVERSITY PRESS

University Printing House, Cambridge CB2 8BS, United Kingdom

Cambridge University Press is part of the University of Cambridge.

It furthers the University's mission by disseminating knowledge in the pursuit of
education, learning and research at the highest international levels of excellence.

www.cambridge.org
Information on this title: www.cambridge.org/9780521632225

© Donald P. Jacobs, Ehud Kalai, and Morton I. Kamien 1998

First published 1998

A catalogue record for this publication is available from the British Library

Library of Congress Cataloguing in Publication data

Frontiers of research in economic theory: the Nancy L. Schwartz
Memorial Lectures, 1983–1997 / edited by Donald P. Jacobs, Ehud
Kalai, Morton I. Kamien.
p. cm. – (Econometric Society monographs ; no. 29)
"Include[s] the lectures previously published by the Kellogg
school in pamphlet form between 1983 and 1991, and again between
1993 and 1997, in the Econometric Society Monograph series" –
Foreword.
Includes bibliographical references.
ISBN 0-521-63222-6. – ISBN 0-521-63538-1 (pbk.)
1. Economics. I. Schwartz, Nancy Lou. II. Jacobs, Donald P.
III. Kalai, Ehud, 1942– . IV. Kamien, Morton I. V. J. L. Kellogg
Graduate School of Management. VI. Series.
HB 171.F783   1998
330 – dc21

                                                    98–6159
                                                    CIP

ISBN 978-0-521-63222-5 Hardback
ISBN 978-0-521-63538-7 Paperback

Contents

Editors' Foreword

A dedicated scholar and teacher, Nancy Lou Schwartz was the Morrison Professor of Decision Sciences, the first female faculty member to be appointed to an endowed chair at the J. L. Kellogg Graduate School of Management of Northwestern University. She joined Kellogg in 1970, chaired the Department of Managerial Economics and Decision Sciences, and served as director of the school's doctoral program until her death in 1981. Unwavering in her dedication to academic excellence, she published more than 40 papers and coauthored two books. At the time of her death she was associate editor of *Econometrica*, on the board of editors of the *American Economic Review*, and on the governing councils of the American Economic Association and the Institute of Management Sciences.

The Nancy L. Schwartz Memorial Lecture series was established by her family, colleagues, and friends in tribute to her memory. The lectures present issues of fundamental importance in economic theory.

The editors are most pleased to include the lectures previously published by the Kellogg school in pamphlet form between 1983 and 1991, and again between 1993 and 1997, in the Econometric Society Monograph series. Regretfully, circumstances did not permit the inclusion of the 1992 lecture by Kenneth J. Arrow entitled "Information and Returns to Scale." The editors are grateful to the Econometric Society and to the acquiring editor, Avinash Dixit, for publishing this book, and to Scott Parris from Cambridge University Press for his outstanding help.

The Schwartz Lecturers

Biographical sketches are listed in chronological order of delivery of the lectures.

Hugo Sonnenschein has served as president of The University of Chicago since 1993. He received his A.B. degree in mathematics from the University of Rochester in 1961 and his M.S. and Ph.D. degrees in economics from Purdue University in 1964. His previous faculty positions include the University of Minnesota from 1964 to 1970, Northwestern University from 1973 to 1976, Princeton University from 1976 to 1987 and again from 1991 to 1993, when he served as provost, and the University of Pennsylvania, where he served as dean and professor from 1991 to 1993. Dr. Sonnenschein held a Guggenheim Fellowship in 1976–7, and is a Fellow of the American Academy of Arts and Sciences and a member of the National Academy of Sciences.

Dr. Sonnenschein was editor of *Econometrica* from 1977 to 1984 and president of the Econometric Society in 1988–9. He has been on the board of editors of the *Journal of Mathematical Economics* since 1974, coedited the series *Fundamentals of Pure and Applied Economics*, and coedited Volume IV of the *Handbook of Mathematical Economics*. He has published more than 60 articles in major economics journals.

Andreu Mas-Colell has served as professor of economics at Pompeu Fabra University in Barcelona, Spain, since 1995. He completed his undergraduate education at the University of Barcelona and the Universidad de Valladolid in Spain. He came to the United States in 1968 to do graduate work, earning a Ph.D. from the University of Minnesota in 1972. Before joining the faculty as professor of economics at Harvard from 1981 to 1995, he was on the economics and mathematics faculties at the University of California at Berkeley.

Professor Mas-Colell is a Fellow of the Econometric Society and has been a member of its council: he is or has been an associate editor of *Econometrica*, the *Journal of Mathematical Economics*, the *Journal of Economic Theory*, the journal *Games and Economic Behavior*, and the *SIAM Journal of Applied Mathematics*. He is coauthor of the textbook *Microeconomic Theory* (1995). He has published more than 60 articles on economic theory and mathematical economics.

Menahem E. Yaari is a professor of economics at the Hebrew University of Jerusalem, where he holds the Schonbrunn Chair in Mathematical Economics. His undergraduate degree, in economics and philosophy, was granted by the Hebrew University in 1958. From 1958 to 1962, he was a graduate student at Stanford University, earning a Ph.D. in economics and statistics. From 1962 to 1965, he was assistant professor and then associate professor at Yale University and a member of the Cowles Foundation for Research in Economics.

Professor Yaari has been on the faculty of the Hebrew University since 1967 and has served as president of the Open University in Tel Aviv. He served as coeditor of *Econometrica* from 1968 to 1975 and was elected a Fellow of the Econometric Society in 1970. Professor Yaari's research has been mainly in the economics of uncertainty, in consumer theory, and in economic justice.

Robert J. Aumann is a professor of mathematics at the Hebrew University of Jerusalem, where he has been teaching since 1956. He holds a B.S. from the City College of New York and M.S. and Ph.D. degrees from M.I.T. Professor Aumann has held visiting positions at Princeton, Yale, Tel-Aviv University, the University of California–Berkeley, CORE, Stanford University, the University of Minnesota, MSRI, and SUNY–Stony Brook. Winner of the 1984 Harvey Prize and the 1994 Israel prize, he is a Fellow of the Econometric Society, a Foreign Honorary Member of the American Academy of Arts and Sciences and the American Economic Association, and a Member of the U.S. National Academy of Sciences and the Israel Academy of Sciences and Humanities.

Professor Aumann is a leader in the development of game theory and its applications to economics. His research has made fundamental advances in several areas of mathematical economics and cooperative and noncooperative game theory. He is the author of 4 books and more than 60 research articles, and has supervised a dozen Ph.D. students who have become major contributors to the field.

Robert E. Lucas, Jr., received the Nobel Memorial Prize in Economic Science in 1995 and is the John Dewey Distinguished Professor of Economics at the University of Chicago, where he has taught since 1974. He received his B.A. in history (1959) and his Ph.D. in economics (1964) from the University of Chicago and taught at Carnegie-Mellon University from 1963 to 1974. He has been a Fellow of the Econometric Society since 1976, a Fellow of the American Academy of Arts and Sciences since 1980, and a member of the National Academy of Sciences since 1981.

Professor Lucas is an editor of the *Journal of Political Economy* and an associate editor of the *Journal of Monetary Economics*. He has served as president of the Econometric Society from 1996 to 1997 and on the executive committee of the American Economic Association, of which he has also been vice president. He is the author of over 40 articles and books on economics.

Truman F. Bewley is the Alfred Cowles Professor of Economics at Yale University, where he has been teaching since 1982. He holds a B.A. in history from Cornell University (1963) and Ph.D.s in economics and mathematics from the University of California–Berkeley (1970 and 1971, respectively). He has previously taught at Harvard University, the University of Bonn, and Northwestern University. In 1978 he was elected to become a Fellow of the Econometric Society and has served on its council since 1987.

Professor Bewley was awarded numerous grants from the National Science Foundation as well as a Guggenheim Fellowship. He is on the editorial boards of the *Journal of Mathematical Economics*, *Econometrica*, and *Economic Letters*. He served as the program chairman of the 1985 World Congress of the Econometric Society. Professor Bewley has published extensively in the areas of economics theory, game theory, and mathematics.

Reinhard Selten received the Nobel Memorial Prize in Economic Science in 1994 and is a professor of economics at the University of Bonn, where he has been teaching since 1984. He holds a master's degree in mathematics from the Johann-Wolfgang-Goethe University in Frankfurt (1957) and a doctorate in mathematics from Frankfurt University (1961). He received his habilitation for economics at Frankfurt University (1968).

Professor Selten has previously taught at Frankfurt University, the University of California–Berkeley, The Free University of Berlin, and the University of Bielefeld. He is a Fellow of the Econometric Society and a member of the Northrhine-Westfalian Academy of Sciences. He has served on the editorial boards of several game theory and economics journals and has been the chief editor of the *International Journal of Game Theory*. Professor Selten's research interests are in the areas of game theory, oligopoly theory, and experimental economics. He is author of 4 books and more than 60 articles in these areas.

Vernon L. Smith is Regents' Professor of Economics and research director of the Economic Science Laboratory at the University of Arizona. He is author of more than 100 articles and books on capital theory, finance, natural resource economics, and the application of experimental methods in economic analysis, and has served on the board of editors of the *American Economic Review*, the *Cato Journal, Journal of Economic Behavior and Organization*, the *Journal of Risk and Uncertainty*, and *Science*.

Professor Smith is past president of the Public Choice Society, the Economic Science Association, and the Western Economic Association. His previous faculty appointments include Purdue University, Brown University, and the University of Massachusetts. He has been a Ford Foundation Faculty Research Fellow, Fellow of the Center for Advanced Study in the Behavioral Sciences, and a Sherman Fairchild Distinguished Scholar at the California Institute of Technology. Professor Smith was awarded numerous grants from the National Science Foundation and other organizations. He has received an honorary doctor of management degree from Purdue University and is a Fellow of the Econometric Society.

Gary S. Becker received the Nobel Memorial Prize in Economic Science in 1992 and is University Professor of the University of Chicago, where he has taught sociology and economics since 1969. Previously, he taught at Columbia University, where he was the Arthur Lehman Professor of Economics. He holds an A.B. degree from Princeton University, and M.M. and Ph.D. degrees from the University of Chicago as well as several honorary doctorates from U.S. and European universities.

Professor Becker is a columnist for *Business Week* and has served as a member, consultant, and fellow of boards and major committees for academic institutions and government ministries. He has been elected Member and Fellow of several distinguished academic societies, including the National Academy of Sciences, the American Philosophical Society, the American Statistical Association, the Econometric Society, the National Academy of Education, and the American Academy of Arts and Sciences. He has served as the president of the American Economic Association and the Mont Pelerin Society, and is the winner of several prestigious academic awards, including the John Bates Clark Medal.

With a strong interest in theories of human capital, Professor Becker has written several books and over 60 journal articles dealing with major economic, political, and sociological issues.

Peter A. Diamond is the Paul A. Samuelson Professor of Economics at the Massachusetts Institute of Technology, where he has been teaching since 1966. He holds a B.A. in Mathematics from Yale University (1960), a Ph.D. in Economics from M.I.T. (1963), and has previously taught at the University of California–Berkeley. He was elected Fellow of the Econometric Society (1968), Fellow of the American Academy of Arts and Sciences (1978), and member of the National Academy of Sciences (1984). He is a founding member of the National Academy of Social Insurance (1988) and was the inaugural winner of the Erwin Nemmers Prize (1994).

Professor Diamond has been a member of government and congressional panels and commissions. He was president of the Econometric Society and vice president of the American Economic Association. He served on the editorial boards of the *Journal of Economic Theory*, the *Journal of Public Economics*, and the *American Economic Review*.

Professor Diamond's research interests are in micro- and macroeconomic theory. He is the author of over 80 journal and book articles that made fundamental contributions to a variety of areas, including government debt and capital accumulation, capital markets and risk sharing, optimal taxation, search and matching in labor markets, and social insurance.

Robert B. Wilson is the Atholl McBean Professor of Economics at the Graduate School of Business of Stanford University, where he has been teaching since 1964. He holds A.B. (1959), M.B.A. (1961), and D.B.A. (1963) degrees from Harvard University and an honorary Doctor of Economics (1986) from the Norwegian School of Economics.

Professor Wilson is the author of *Nonlinear Pricing* (1993) and more than 90 journal articles and book chapters dealing with issues in game theory and economics. He is also a member of the National Academy of Sciences, a Fellow of the Econometric Society (1976), and a vice president of the society (1996–7).

Roy Radner is professor of economics and information systems at the Stern School of Business, New York University. His previous affiliations include the University of Chicago, Yale University, the University of California–Berkeley, and AT&T Bell Laboratories. He holds B.S., M.S., and Ph.D. degrees from the University of Chicago.

Professor Radner is the author of 10 books and has published more than 90 research articles in economics, statistics, and operations management. Within economic theory, he pioneered research in the areas of team theory, growth theory, rational expectations equilibrium, and structures of markets and organizations as they relate to issues of decentralization and computation, bargaining and regulation, incentives, information, and moral hazard.

Professor Radner's honors include memberships, fellowships, or distinguished fellowships in the National Academy of Sciences, the American Academy of Arts and Sciences, the Econometric Society, the American Economic Association, and the American Association for the Advancement of Science. He is a past president of the Econometric Society and the current chair of the Economics Section of the National Academy of Sciences. Professor Radner has served as an editor for numerous scientific journals, including: *Management Science, Econometrica, Journal of Economic Theory, Journal of Mathematical Economics, American Economic Review, Games and Economic Behavior, Economic Theory, Economic Design,* and *Review of Accounting Studies.*

Nancy L. Stokey is a professor of economics at the University of Chicago, where she has been teaching since 1990. She holds a B.A. in economics from the University of Pennsylvania (1972) and a Ph.D. in economics (1978) from Harvard University. Her previous teaching affiliations include the Kellogg Graduate School of Management of Northwestern University, where she was the Harold L. Stuart Professor of Managerial Economics, and the departments of economics at the University of Minnesota and Harvard University. She was elected Fellow of the Econometric Society (1988) and a Fellow of the American Academy of Arts and Science (1993). She is a member of the Council of the Econometric Society and is vice president of the American Economic Association.

Professor Stokey has been awarded numerous research grants from the National Science Foundation and has served on committees and panels of this foundation. She has been an associate editor for the *Journal of Economic Theory, Econometrica, Games and Economic Behavior,* and the *Journal of Economic Growth.*

The research contributions of Professor Stokey cover a wide variety of topics in microeconomics, macroeconomics, and game theory. Her papers have been published by the leading economic journals, and her book, *Recursive Methods in Economic Dynamics* (coauthored with R. E. Lucas and E. C. Prescott), was published in 1989.

David M. Kreps is the Paul E. Holden Professor of Economics at the
Graduate School of Business at Stanford University, where he has been
teaching since 1975. His other research and teaching affiliations include
the universities of Tel Aviv, Cambridge, Yale, Harvard, Oxford, Paris, and
Bocconi, the Hebrew University, and the Catholic University of Louvain.
He received his A.B. degree, summa cum laude with the highest distinc-
tion in mathematics, from Dartmouth College (1972), and his M.A. and
Ph.D. degrees (1975) from Stanford University.

Professor Kreps is a Fellow of the American Academy of Arts and
Sciences and a Fellow of the Econometric Society, for which he also
served as a member of the Executive Council. He was a Sloan
Foundation Fellow, a Guggenheim Foundation Fellow, and the 1989
recipient of the John Bates Clark Medal. In 1990 he was the Clarendon
Lecturer in Economics at Oxford University and delivered the Fisher-
Schultz Lecture to the Fifth World Congress of the Econometric Society.
His services to the profession include being coeditor of *Econometrica*,
panel member of the NSF Program in Economics, and cochair of the
Seventh World Congress of the Econometric Society. For his excellence
in teaching, he received the Distinguished Teacher Award from his institution in 1991.

The author of 3 books and more than 40 papers and articles, Professor
Kreps is considered one of the major contributors to the modern areas
of decision theory, economics, game theory, finance, and management.
His papers have been published by the top journals of these fields.

Nancy L. Schwartz

MORTON I. KAMIEN

Nancy Lou Schwartz began her academic career in 1964 at Carnegie-Mellon University's Graduate School of Industrial Administration. She was part of the wave of young faculty that Dick Cyert, the school's dean, hired between 1963 and 1965. They included Tren Dolbear, Mel Hinich, Bob Kaplan, Lester Lave, John Ledyard, Mike Lovell, Bob Lucas, Ken MacCrimmon, Tim McGuire, Dick Roll, and Tom Sargent. By the time she left Carnegie-Mellon in 1970 for Northwestern University she was a tenured associate professor and had been awarded a Ford Foundation Faculty Research Fellowship.

Nancy had come to Carnegie-Mellon fresh out of Purdue University's fabled economics department. Ed Ames, Lance Davis, George Horwich, Chuck Howe, John Hughes, Jim Quirk, Stan Reiter, Nate Rosenberg, Rubin Saposnik, and Vernon Smith were among her teachers, while Pat Henderschott, Tom Muench, Don Rice, Gene Silberberg, and Hugo Sonnenschein were among her classmates. Her Ph.D. dissertation, supervised by Chuck Howe and Stan Reiter, dealt with the optimal scheduling of towboats and barges along a river with multiple branches. It involved a generalization of the standard transportation problem in which a single conveyance is employed to haul cargo to two complementary conveyances. The optimal coordination of the two conveyances adds a layer of computational complexity to this transportation problem. Nancy developed a simulation routine to approximate its optimal solution.

Nancy was a first-rate graduate student by all the conventional measures, such as grades, passing of qualifying examinations, and timely writing of a dissertation. The outstanding characteristic for which she was known to her teachers and classmates was an uncanny ability to spot logical flaws in an argument. And the manner in which she would point out the flaw was also special in that it always came in the way of a seemingly innocent clarifying question. Nancy was too shy and too polite to point out a flaw directly. However, in time, her instructors and classmates came to realize that when she claimed not to understand a step in an argument, typically a critical one, it meant almost certainly that it was wrong. All this, of course, created a certain amount of dread among the instructors when her hand went up to ask a question, and some merriment among her classmates.

When Nancy joined Northwestern's graduate school of management in 1970 as a full professor, after considerable coaxing by John Hughes and Stan Reiter, it was hardly the world-class institution it eventually came to be. The physical facilities were abysmal. There was no dedicated management school building on the Evanston campus, and the bulk of the masters program teaching was on the Chicago campus. Office space consisted of wooden partitions in the old library building that did not reach the ceiling. The Department of Managerial Economics and Decision Sciences, MEDS, did not yet exist. Its predecessor was a combination of three departments: Managerial Economics, Quantitative Methods, and Operations Management. There were a few bright young faculty already there, including Dave Baron, Rich Khilstrom, Mark Walker, Tony Camacho, and Matt Tuite, but there remained a lot to be done. And so Nancy became one of the three senior faculty members instrumental in building the department. She participated in the hiring of John Roberts, Mark Satterthwaite, Arik Tamir, Ted Groves, Bala Balachandran, Roger Myerson, Ehud Kalai, Eitan Zemel, Bob Weber, Nancy Stokey, Paul Milgrom, Bengt Holmstrom, Yair Tauman, and Dov Samet.

Nancy headed up the department's Ph.D. program and chaired the department from 1977 to 1979 and then became the director of the entire school's Ph.D. program. She was involved in guiding numerous students through their Ph.D. dissertations, including Raffi Amit, Raymond DeBondt, Eitan Muller, Jennifer Reinganum, and Esther Gal-Or. In addition to attending to these internal administrative responsibilities, Nancy served on the Council of the Institute of Management Sciences, on the editorial board of *American Economic Review*, and as an associate editor of *Econometrica*. In 1981 Don Jacobs appointed her the Morrison Professor of Managerial Economics and Decision Sciences. She was the first woman to hold a chaired professorship at the school of management.

Nancy's research beyond her dissertation was focused on theoretical issues in industrial organization. The earliest was inspired by J. R. Hicks's theory of induced technical advance, in which he claimed that firms directed their research efforts toward reducing the employment of a relatively more expensive factor of production. This theory was criticized on two grounds. The first was that it ignored the relative costs of achieving each type of technical advance. The second was that it was more relative factor shares than relative factor prices that induced the direction of technical advance.

Nancy was involved in a series of papers that dealt with all these issues through the analysis of the behavior of a firm seeking to maximize profits over time by choosing both the levels of its factors of production and the focus of its research efforts, taking all costs into account. The analyses suggested that both relative factor prices and relative factor shares played a role in inducing the direction of technical advance. In the long run, technical advance tended toward neutrality; no one factor was targeted for reduction relative to the others.

Nancy's next major research project dealt with how rapidly firms developed new products or methods of production in the presence of rivals. This work eventually led to the theory of patent races. It was inspired by Yoram Barzel's claim that the quest to be the first to innovate led firms to overinvest in research and development from society's standpoint. This claim appeared to challenge the conventional wisdom that firms tended to underinvest in research and development from society's standpoint because they could not capture all the benefits. Barzel's result was driven by the assumption that the winner of the race to innovate would capture all the realizable profits and that the quest to edge out rivals would force the firm to accelerate development to the zero profit point. This would lead to higher than optimal investment in research and development in which the marginal cost of advancing development only slightly equals the marginal benefit of earlier access to the profit stream. Barzel supposed that each innovator knew who the rivals were. The critical feature of the work in which Nancy was involved was the opposite assumption, namely, that the innovator did not know at all who the rivals were. However, the innovator knew that they were out there and took account of them through the hazard rate, the conditional probability of a rival's introduction of a similar invention at the next instant of time given that it had not yet been introduced. In this model the innovating firm faced a sea of anonymous rivals, any one of whom might introduce a similar invention in the very next instant of time. The large number of rivals assumption meant that the individual firm's level of expenditure on research and development did not elicit an expenditure reaction from its unknown rivals, to whom it, too, was unknown. Rival imitation was allowed in this model and it was shown that when it was immediate, investment in research and development would cease in conformity with the conventional wisdom. Moreover, increasing intensity of competition in the form of a higher hazard rate could not force a firm to accelerate development of its innovation to the break-even point, as the decline in the probability of winning would cause firms to drop out of the race short of it. Thus, the model allowed for increases in a firm's research and development expenditure with increasing intensity of rivalry up to a certain point and a decline thereafter, a feature consistent with empirical findings that industries in which the intensity of competition is intermediate between monopoly and perfect competition are the ones with the most research intensity. It was precisely this feature of the model that led to Loury's first formal patent race paper, in which the hazard rate became endogenously determined by Cournot-type interactions among the rival firms through their research expenditures. Lee and Wilde's paper followed, then the Dasgupta and Stiglitz papers, and then Reinganum's fully dynamic patent race model.

The works on the timing of innovations in the presence of rivals naturally led to the question of how a successful innovator might adopt a price strategy to retard rival entry and to the next major project in which Nancy was involved. The major theories of entry retardation at that time were the limit pricing ones proposed by Bain and by Sylos-Labini, as synthesized by Modigliani. The crux of this theory is that the incumbent firm sets a price and supplies the corresponding quantity demanded so that the residual demand function faced by the potential entrant just allows him or her to realize no more than a normal profit. Implementation of this limit pricing strategy requires that the incumbent know the average cost function of each potential entrant. The project in which Nancy participated involved dropping this assumption and replacing it with the supposition that the conditional probability of entry given that no entry had yet occurred, the hazard rate, was a monotonically increasing function of the incumbent's current market price. This assumption led to the formulation of the incumbent firm's problem as an optimal control problem with the probability of entry on or before the present time the state variable and the current price the control variable. The firm's objective was to maximize the present value of expected profits, where its pre-entry profits are at least as high as its post-entry profits, which are determined by whatever market structure emerges after entry. It was implicitly assumed that by lowering its price, the firm sought to divert a potential entrant to entry into another industry. The analysis of this model disclosed that the incumbent firm optimally chose a price below its immediate monopoly price but above the price it would take to deter entry altogether. In other words, it is optimal for the firm to delay entry rather than postpone it indefinitely. It is in this sense that the incumbent firm engages in limit pricing.

This model of limit pricing under uncertainty eventually led to Esther Gal-Or's dissertation and the Milgrom–Roberts paper in which the incumbent firm's current price is used to signal a potential entrant about the type of competitor he or she will face after entry. Its original vision as a game among incumbents seeking to divert entrants away from themselves was realized in Bagwell's work.

Beyond these major projects, Nancy was involved in a number of less prolonged excursions. There was a widely cited paper on the optimal maintenance and sale date of a machine subject to an uncertain time of failure. There were analyses of a growth model involving an essential exhaustible resource and endogenous development of a technology to replace it; of whether competition leads firms to produce more durable products; of the effect of health maintenance organizations on the delivery of care services; of the consequences for a firm seeking to maximize profits over time by producing a durable good by means of labor and capital, of the irreversibility of capital investment; of a firm's adoption of new technology when it anticipates further improvements in technology; of the consequences of technical advance for international trade; of the consistency of conjectural variations; and of the role of exclusion costs on the provision of public goods.

Apart from the individual articles, Nancy coauthored two books: *Dynamic Optimization: Calculus of Variations and Optimal Control in Economics and Management Science* and *Market Structure and Innovation*. The first was the outgrowth of an intense use of techniques for optimization over time in many of the analyses she conducted. The focus of the book was to expose to the student the tricks that were employed in the application of these techniques rather than provide a rigorous treatment of the theory behind them. The second was the culmination of all the work in technical advance in which Nancy had been involved. It was the direct result of a survey article on the same subject that she had coauthored.

Nancy led a full and successful academic life and interacted with many of the best economists in her cohort, the older generation of economists who were her teachers, and the younger generation that she taught or hired. She provided a role model for younger women who contemplated becoming academic economists. The fact that all but one of the distinguished contributors to this volume are male says all that needs to be said about the milieu in which she carved out a respected niche.

xxii   Nancy L. Schwartz

References

Bagwell, K. 1992. "A Model of Competitive Limit Pricing," *Journal of Economics and Management*, pp. 585–606.

Barzel, Y. 1968. "Optimal Timing of Innovations," *Review of Economics and Statistics*, pp. 348–55.

Dasgupta, P. and J. Stiglitz. 1980. "Industrial Structure and the Nature of Innovative Activity," *Economics Journal*, pp. 266–93.

Dasgupta, P. and J. Stiglitz. 1980. "Uncertainty, Industrial Structure and the Speed of R&D," *Bell Journal of Economics*, pp. 1–28.

Gal-Or, E. 1980. "Limit Price Entry Prevention and Its Impact on Potential Investors – A Game Theoretic Approach," Ph.D. dissertation, Northwestern University.

Hicks, J. R. 1932. *The Theory of Wages.* London: Macmillan.

Lee, T. and L. Wilde. 1980. "Market Structure and Innovation: A Reformulation," *Quarterly Journal of Economics*, pp. 429–36.

Loury, G. C. 1979. "Market Structure and Innovation," *Quarterly Journal of Economics*, pp. 395–410.

Milgrom, P. and J. Roberts. 1982. "Limit Pricing and Entry Under Incomplete Information: An Equilibrium Analysis," *Econometrica*, pp. 443–60.

Modigliani, F. 1958. "New Developments on the Oligopoly Front," *Journal of Political Economy*, pp. 215–32.

Reinganum, J. 1981. "Dynamic Games of Innovation," *Journal of Economic Theory*, pp. 21–41.

Reinganum, J. 1982. "A Dynamic Game of R&D: Patent Protection and Competitive Behavior," *Econometrica*, pp. 671–88.

Publications of Nancy L. Schwartz

ARTICLES

"Asymmetry Between Bribes and Charges," *Water Resources Research*, 1966, pp. 147–57, with M. I. Kamien and F. T. Dolbear.

"Asymmetry Between Bribes and Charges: Reply," *Water Resources Research*, 1966, pp. 856–7, with M. I. Kamien and F. T. Dolbear.

"Optimal 'Induced' Technical Change," *Econometrica*, January 1968, pp. 1–17, with M. I. Kamien.

"A Naive View of the Indicator Problem," Ch. V in *Targets and Indicators of Monetary Policy*, Karl Brunner, ed., Chandler Publishing Company, 1969, pp. 98–112, with M. I. Kamien.

"Discrete Programs for Moving Known Cargoes from Origins to Destination on Time at Minimum Bargeline Fleet Cost," *Transportation Science*, May 1968, pp. 134–45.

"Determination of Equipment Requirements for the Bargeline: Analysis and Computer Simulation," Ch. 4 in *Inland Waterway Transportation: Studies in Public and Private Management and Investment Decisions*, Charles W. Howe, ed., Resources for the Future, Inc., Johns Hopkins Press, 1969, pp. 50–72.

"Induced Factor Augmenting Technical Progress from a Macroeconomic Viewpoint," *Econometrica*, October 1969, pp. 668–84, with M. I. Kamien.

"Market Structure, Elasticity of Demand and Incentive to Invent," *Journal of Law and Economics*, April 1970, pp. 241–52, with M. I. Kamien.

"Factor Augmenting Technical Advance in a Two Sector Economy," *Oxford Economic Papers*, November 1970, pp. 338–56, with N. C. Miller.

"Revelation of Preference for Public Good with Imperfect Exclusion," *Public Choice*, Fall 1970, pp. 19–30, with M. I. Kamien.

"Expenditure Patterns for Risky R and D Projects," *Journal of Applied Probability*, March 1971, pp. 60–73, with M. I. Kamien.

"Optimal Maintenance and Sale Age for a Machine Subject to Failure," *Management Science*, April 1971, pp. B495–504, with M. I. Kamien.

"Limit Pricing and Uncertain Entry," *Econometrica*, May 1971, pp. 441–54, with M. I. Kamien.

"Sufficient Conditions in Optimal Control Theory," *Journal of Economic Theory*, June 1971, pp. 207–14, with M. I. Kamien.

"Theory of the Firm with Induced Technical Change," *Metroeconomica*, Sep.–Dec. 1971, pp. 233–56, with M. I. Kamien.

"Timing of Innovations Under Rivalry," *Econometrica*, January 1972, pp. 43–60, with M. I. Kamien.

"Market Structure, Rivals' Response and the Firm's Rate of Product Improvement," *Journal of Industrial Economics*, April 1972, pp. 159–72, with M. I. Kamien.

"A Direct Approach to Choice Under Uncertainty," *Management Science*, April 1972, pp. B470–7, with M. I. Kamien.

"Exclusion Costs and the Provision of Public Goods," *Public Choice*, Spring 1972, pp. 43–55, with M. I. Kamien.

"Some Economic Consequences of Anticipating Technical Advance," *Western Economic Journal*, June 1972, pp. 123–38, with M. I. Kamien.

"Uncertain Entry and Excess Capacity," *American Economic Review*, December 1972, pp. 918–27, with M. I. Kamien.

"Exclusion, Externalities, and Public Goods," *Journal of Public Economics*, August 1973, pp. 217–30, with M. I. Kamien and D. J. Roberts.

"Payment Plans and the Efficient Delivery of Health Care Services," *Journal of Risk and Insurance*, September 1973, pp. 427–36, with M. I. Kamien.

"Risky R&D with Rivalry," *Annals of Economic and Social Measurement*, January 1974, pp. 267–77, with M. I. Kamien.

"Patent Life and R&D Rivalry," *American Economic Review*, March 1974, pp. 183–7, with M. I. Kamien.

"Product Durability Under Monopoly and Competition," *Econometrica*, March 1974, pp. 289–301, with M. I. Kamien.

"Cournot Oligopoly and Uncertain Entry," *Review of Economic Studies*,

January 1975, pp. 125–31, with M. I. Kamien.

"Market Structure and Innovation: A Survey," *Journal of Economic Literature*, March 1975, pp. 1–37, with M. I. Kamien.

"On the Degree of Rivalry for Maximum Innovative Activity," *Quarterly Journal of Economics*, May 1976, pp. 245–60, with M. I. Kamien.

"Technology: More for Less?" in Sidney Weintraub, ed., *Modern Economic Thought*, University of Pennsylvania Press, 1977, pp. 501–15, with M. I. Kamien.

"A Note on Resource Usage and Market Structure," *Journal of Economic Theory*, August 1977, pp. 394–7, with M. I. Kamien.

"Optimal Exhaustible Resource Depletion with Endogenous Technical Change," *Review of Economic Studies*, February 1978, pp. 179–96, with M. I. Kamien.

"Optimal Capital Accumulation and Durable Goods Production," *Zeitschrift für Nationalokonomie*, Vol. 37, 1977, pp. 25–43, with M. I. Kamien.

"Potential Rivalry, Monopoly Profits, and the Pace of Inventive Activity," *Review of Economic Studies*, October 1978, pp. 547–57, with M. I. Kamien.

"Self-Financing of an R&D Project," *American Economic Review*, June 1978, pp. 252–61, with M. I. Kamien.

"Disaggregated Intertemporal Models with an Exhaustible Resource and Technical Advance," *Journal of Environmental Economics and Management*, 1977, pp. 271–88, with M. I. Kamien.

"A Generalized Hazard Rate." *Economics Letters*, Vol. 5, 1980, pp. 245–9, with M. I. Kamien.

"Technical Change Inclinations of a Resource Monopolist," in G. Horwich and J. P. Quirk, eds., *Essays in Contemporary Fields of Economics*, Purdue University Press, 1981, pp. 41–53, with M. I. Kamien.

"Role of Common Property Resources in Optimal Planning Models with Exhaustible Resources," in V. K. Smith and J. V. Krutilla, eds., *Explorations in Natural Resource Economics*, R.F.F., 1982.

"Conjectural Variations," *Canadian Journal of Economics*, 1983, pp. 191–211, with M. I. Kamien.

BOOKS

Dynamic Optimization, Elsevier North-Holland, 1981 (second edition, 1991), with M. I. Kamien.

Market Structure and Innovation, Cambridge University Press, 1981 (Spanish edition, 1988), with M. I. Kamien.

The Lectures

1983

HUGO SONNENSCHEIN
The Economics of Incentives:
An Introductory Account

I am honored to have been asked to present the first Nancy L. Schwartz Memorial Lecture. This invitation was extended without any suggestion of how I might most fittingly pay tribute to Nancy's memory. The only orders were that I present a public lecture, rather than a research seminar. It would, for example, be reasonable for me to review Nancy's scholarly contribution and to place it in perspective. When you recall that her publications included more than forty articles and two books and when you keep in mind the range of the contribution, from the mathematics of optimization to the theory of market structure, you can see that I would have had my work cut out. Alternatively, I could have chosen to present an exposition of recent research on the theory of oligopoly; as you know, Nancy was an expert in this area. But instead of either of these topics, I have decided to speak on the economics of incentives, an area that was not at the center of Nancy's research interest.

Let me begin by explaining this choice. A professor contributes to his or her university in a variety of ways. Most important, he or she is a researcher and a teacher. At a great university such as Northwestern, these tasks are more closely related than one might think. For Nancy, the education of doctoral students was an integral part of her own research, and the excellent dissertation "Dynamic Games of Research and Development with Rivalry," written by Jennifer Reinganum, is but one of many examples supporting this claim. One can see in the dissertation the guiding hands of Mort Kamien and Nancy. In addition to his or her duties as a scholar and teacher, the senior professor sometimes serves as a manager and a recruiter. This work tends to be much less well rewarded than the production of outstanding research. From 1977 to 1979, Nancy chaired the Department of Managerial Economics and Decision

Sciences, and from the time that she arrived at Northwestern in 1970 until her passing, she was a major force in shaping the MEDS department. During those years, the Kellogg School moved from "good" to "very good" to "distinguished" in the eyes of most graduate management school watchers. During the same period, the MEDS department moved from nowhere to the largest and very best department of its kind in the world – a department that Harvard, Yale, Stanford, and, I must add, my own university have repeatedly tried to raid, with but limited success, in order to stay abreast of the latest developments.

The MEDS department is by now a rather well-rounded group with broad strengths; however, it is no secret that substantial credit for the reputation it has achieved must go to the remarkable advances that have been made here in the economics of incentives.

THE ECONOMICS OF INCENTIVES*

From its infancy in the eighteenth century, the framework of economic analysis has had three major ingredients. First, it takes as axiomatic that economic agents act on their own behalf, with or without sympathy for others. It does not judge self-interested action to be immoral or unworthy of serious study. Quite the contrary, it suggests that the pursuit of one's own interest describes well economic behavior and asks us to develop its consequences. Second, the framework takes *social* equilibrium to be the concern of economic analysis. Economics is a branch of *social* science, and as such it requires at least two potent actors. The laws of physics and chemistry exist in the absence of mankind. For psychology it may be enough that there is a single human being. However, for sociology, political science, and economics, you need at least two people. Finally, the framework of economic analysis takes the goals of individual economic agents to be in conflict; it views it as the business of economics and social science to determine the extent to which this conflict does or does not result in the efficient use of resources, promote the social good, and so on.

The really big contributions to economics all fall within the framework I have outlined: economics is the study of social equilibrium that results from the acquisitive behavior of several agents with conflicting goals. Adam Smith taught us to consider carefully the possibility that selfish

*This text formed the basis for public lectures that I presented at several universities during the years 1981–83. It was originally published in *Technology, Organization and Economic Structure*, eds. Rvuzo Sato and Martin J. Beckmann, no. 210 in *Lecture Notes in Economics and Mathematical Systems*, New York: Springer-Verlag, 1983, and is reprinted here with permission from Springer-Verlag New York, Inc.

acquisitive behavior might in some way promote the social good. Marx praised the early achievements of capitalism, but he believed that the ownership of capital and its direction by a relatively small number of profit-seeking capitalists would lead to increasingly severe depressions and eventually to the collapse of capitalism itself. Smith and Marx shared a common framework, but they emphasized different issues and thus were led to different conclusions. Walras proposed a detailed mathematical theory of what it means for an agent to act on his or her own behalf, and he used this theory to explain the relative value of goods and services. Pareto helped us to understand the meaning of a socially efficient use of resources; and modern welfare economics, in particular as embodied in the work of Kenneth Arrow, provides a rigorous treatment of the relationship between the outcome of self-interested behavior, as formalized by Walras, and social efficiency, as defined by Pareto.

And to be sure, this framework does not leave out macroeconomics. The classical "big question" of macroeconomics concerns the possibility that the acquisitive behavior of individual agents may lead to unemployment or to recurrent booms and busts. Marx looked for answers to these questions in a new political and social order. Keynes looked for answers to these questions in the possibility of a role for government in the regulation of aggregate economic variables.

So, with this common framework, why is it that economists appear to disagree so very much when faced with the most basic questions? I am not speaking of disagreement that stems from differences of fact (for a while, people in macro liked to hide behind this as a basic reason for disagreement); rather, I am speaking of disagreement that implies a complete divergence of opinion on how economic processes work or can be made to work. Two engineers may disagree on whether or not a rocket will go up because of questions regarding the values of certain hard-to-measure parameters. But their difference is not a result of the fact that they subscribe to different physical theories. It is my contention that economists so often come down on both sides of the same question because they don't have a theory that is adequate to handle the issues at the heart of the question. Furthermore, I believe that, more often than not, the piece of theory that is missing would be provided in a more complete economics of incentives.

Let me be concrete by defining one of the paradigmatic problems in the economics of incentives.

> Question: Is it possible that private acquisitive behavior will lead to the construction of a socially optimal amount of sidewalks and streetlights? Or, with such joint consumption goods, that is, public goods, will selfish behavior necessarily lead to misrepre-

sentation and inefficiency? With public goods, is it *necessary* to have a benevolent planner, or an occasionally elected planner, who guesses the preferences of the populace and coerces agents into paying for the cost of new projects?

Not only is this problem at the heart of the economics of incentives, but you surely realize that it falls squarely in the center of the framework for economic analysis that I put forth at the beginning of the essay: acquisitive behavior, social equilibrium, conflicting goals.

Let me be a bit more precise. I am not asking whether the economists' stylized model of perfect competition, as put forth in any principle course, will lead to the construction of an optimal sidewalk and streetlight system. Of course it will not. As a part of the definition of selfish acquisitive behavior, I allow agents to write contracts and set up governments that enforce those contracts. Just as I can sign a paper that promises that I will deliver two tons of red winter wheat in St. Paul this August 10, I can choose to participate in a society in which a vote of the majority can force me either to move or to pay for a portion of the cost of a sidewalk and streetlight project. In short, my notion of acquisitiveness includes the possibility that I choose strategically where to live, and that I might bind myself to quite involved contracts.

When I went to graduate school, there were two accepted answers to the sidewalk and streetlight problem. The reason that there were two answers is that there were two accepted ways of looking at the problem – much as if creationism and evolutionary theory had equal status. And the reason that there were two accepted ways of looking at the problem is that there was not yet an economics of incentives. Sadly, but predictably, the answers yielded opposite conclusions.

The first answer we were taught was based on a paper by Samuelson [6]. For simplicity, assume that sidewalks and streetlights are produced at constant marginal cost; each additional unit costs the same amount. An optimal sidewalk and streetlight system (for a mid-size city) might be roughly proportional in size to the number of inhabitants. For example, it might involve an expenditure of $100 per person. For a sidewalk and streetlight system to be optimal, it is necessary for the sum of the marginal benefits to consumers, for another $100 of expenditure, to be equal to $100. One can finance the optimal sidewalk and streetlight system by charging each consumer the private marginal benefit he receives from the last $100 unit of sidewalk and streetlight times the number of $100 units provided. As the number of residents goes up, the number of units of sidewalks and streetlights goes up, and the marginal benefit of an additional $100 of sidewalks and streetlights to each resident goes down. In the example, each agent is asked to pay the same amount ($100) no matter what the size of society, but the marginal benefit to him from his expenditure goes to zero as he is imbedded in a larger and larger society.

Samuelson said that in such a case an acquisitive consumer would "free ride." Given the free choice to contribute his "fair share" (his marginal benefit times the number of units provided) to the financing of sidewalks and streetlights, he would selfishly maximize his welfare by claiming that his marginal benefit is zero. Then, his "fair share" would be zero times the number of units provided, which is zero, and he would lose only the marginal benefit of the $100 of extra sidewalks and streetlights that his contribution would provide – essentially nothing. He could in fact use the $100 he saves to buy private consumption goods, for example, chocolates, or whatever. We are left with the clear impression that a society composed of a collection of acquisitive agents will not be able to solve the problem of providing public goods in the amount that would be socially desirable.

Samuelson referred to this inadequacy as the "free-rider problem." He identified an incentive problem and said that it had no solution. The implicit policy prescription is that we must rely on the actions of a benevolent planner, who guesses (perhaps scientifically) the preferences of agents and implements socially desirable plans.

The second answer with which we were provided was based on a classic paper by Ronald Coase [2]. To be fair, it is Coase taken to an extreme, and I do not believe that it would have gone over so well on a qualifying examination. This answer comes to the opposite conclusion from the one suggested by Samuelson: one argues that the sidewalk-streetlight problem is no problem at all! For if the project proposed initially, including its financing, is not optimal, then a collection of citizens can propose an alternative plan, which will benefit some and hurt none. Clearly it will be unanimously favored. Agents, pursuing their own self-interests, will commit themselves to such a plan voluntarily. Thus, selfish behavior will lead to the optimal provision of sidewalks and streetlights. You will of course recognize that the above argument ignores the strategic aspects of group decision making. I may oppose a plan that would lead to an improvement in my welfare if I believe that the next plan on the agenda would benefit me even more. Nevertheless, the argument continues to be sold.

During the past 20 years we have made great strides in our understanding of the sidewalk and streetlight problem. We recognize Samuelson's answer as being particularly unimaginative regarding the possibility of cooperative behavior, and similarly we recognize the

Coase answer as trivializing the problem of cooperation. Economic research now almost routinely takes up the problem of whether or not there are institutions that will enforce cooperative behavior, institutions that will get the sidewalks and streetlights built in precisely the amount that is socially optimal. We now consider the possibility of "designing cooperation," just as engineers have been concerned with the problem of designing electric switches. We are very much at the stage of basic research, more physics than real engineering, but I want to argue that our success has been real, and I want to emphasize that this achievement has been at the very top of what has happened in economics during the last couple of decades.

To my mind there is no hope that economists will speak "with one tongue" until we understand the economics of incentives and the possibility of designing cooperative behavior. In order to understand unemployment you must understand the labor contract. In order to understand the labor contract you must understand the economics of incentives. When workers and managers get together, they have the opportunity to sign contracts that contain cost-of-living and severance pay clauses. The fact that they are capable of designing quite imaginative contracts has a *profound* effect on macroeconomics.

The purpose of this essay is to illustrate, by the use of simple examples, some of what we have learned. The material is quite striking, and if you are being exposed to it for the first time, then I believe you are in for a treat. The first illustration is very, very simple.

Five siblings are to inherit some land from their father, who is their surviving parent. The father is concerned that the land go to the sibling who places the highest dollar value on it. To make matters simple, assume that the siblings are at this point independently wealthy and that the father plans to leave all of his other possessions to charity. Also assume that, once inherited, the land cannot be sold. The father decides to hold a sealed-bid auction. He sits the siblings down, far away from each other, in his large drawing room, and he tells them that the sibling who bids the most gets the land for the price that he or she bids. Think of yourself as a participant in this auction. Certainly you will bid no more than you believe the land is worth to you. In fact, you would be likely to try to figure out how much your siblings might bid and to use this information in shading your own bid. You might even consider the fact that your siblings may be taking into account the fact that you are taking into account what they might bid. The result is that you have an incentive not to tell the truth. Think of what this means for the example at hand: the person who gets the land may not be the one who values it the most. And this outcome is not socially efficient, for there is then a trade that will benefit both the person who values it most and the person who got it!

This conclusion has much the same feel as Samuelson's articulation of the free-rider problem. Individuals act strategically; they don't tell the truth, and the joint outcome might be quite bad. Can this be overcome, can we design a solution?

Vickery [8] explained a resolution to this problem. The patriarch of the family should announce that the land will go to the highest bidder at the *second* highest bid. Now imagine yourself again as one of the children. I claim that you can do no better than to bid the true value that you place on the land, and of course in this case the child who gets the land is the one who values it the most. Consider two cases: (a) you tell the truth and get the land, and (b) you tell the truth and don't get the land.

In either case, even if you know exactly how your siblings bid, could you do better? Let us consider (a). You could shade your bid, but this doesn't affect what you pay. By misrepresenting your preference all you could do is lose the land, which by telling the truth you get at a price below what it is worth to you. Thus you can do no better than tell the truth. You should figure out case (b) yourself.

We have designed a situation in which in the language of game theory, truth is a dominant strategy. You can do no better than tell the truth. How about that! In this scheme it is in the interest of each agent to tell the truth, and the person who gets the land is the one who values it the most. By choosing a clever scheme we assure a socially efficient outcome. Now let's get a bit more sophisticated.

We return to the case of a public project. The project costs $1000 and there are ten agents. As a baseline proposal consider the plan that the project will be built and each agent taxed $100. Define the net benefit v_i accruing to the ith agent to be the maximum amount that the agent would be willing to pay to have the project built and receive a $100 assessment, rather than not to have the project built. Note that the net benefit to the ith agent may be positive, negative, or zero. If people would tell the truth, then a sensible scheme for deciding whether or not to build the project is first to sum the v_i's. Then, if the sum is nonnegative, the project should be built; and if the sum is negative, it shouldn't be built. With this as a basis, one might ask people to declare the net value of the project to them (let w_i be the declared value for agent i), and build the project if $\Sigma w_i \geqq 0$. But there is an obvious problem. If $v_i > 0$, then i wants the project built and he might as well declare w_i equals 3 billion dollars. Similarly, if $v_i < 0$, then i does not want the project built and he might as well declare -5 billion dollars. Clearly, it is not necessarily in each agent's interest to tell the truth.

Enter Groves and Clark, [4] and [1]. These economists independently designed a scheme that makes truth a dominant strategy and gets the project built precisely when the sum of the net benefits is nonnegative. Here is how their scheme works. As before, let w_i denote the net benefit declared by i. The project is built if and only if $\Sigma w_j \geq 0$. In addition, if the project is built i pays \$100 and receives a sidepayment of $\sum_{j \neq i} w_j$. If the project is not built, i pays nothing and receives no sidepayment.

Just as with the land auction, one shows that for each agent truth is a dominant strategy ($w_i = v_i$), by considering the following two cases: (a) i tells the truth and $\Sigma w_j \geq 0$, and (b) i tells the truth and $\Sigma w_j < 0$. Consider first (a). Since $\Sigma w_j \geq 0$, the project is built. The net benefit to i before he receives a sidepayment is v_i; after the sidepayment his net benefit is $v_i + \sum_{j \neq i} w_j$. Since we assume i tells the truth, $v_i = w_i$ and so $v_i + \sum_{j \neq i} w_j = \Sigma w_j \geq 0$. Thus i's net benefit is nonnegative if he tells the truth and the project is built. By declaring a net benefit other than v_i, the ith agent can only change his payoff ($v_i + \sum_{j \neq i} w_j$) if he chooses w_i so low that the project is not built. But then his net benefit would be zero. Thus truth is the best strategy no matter what valuations $w_j (j \neq i)$ are declared by the other agents. Again, (b) is left to the reader.

This is indeed a remarkable result; it is simple but penetrating. After seeing it, one does not so lightly say that it is not possible to design cooperation. It looks as if Samuelson was just not quite clever enough. The free-rider problem is not essential. People can read the work of Groves and Clark and bind themselves to schemes that promote the social good. The perspective is that self-interested agents will bind themselves in this way.

But it turns out that there are some delicate problems that arise if you try to apply schemes of this type generally. To give a hint, note that the government in the Groves-Clark runs a big deficit. We could correct this by adding a negative constant to the sidepayments and hope for balance on average, but this does not solve all of the problems. A more serious defect is that we must assume that the preferences of all individuals are of a special form (called the transferable utility form) in order to justify the rule that a project be built when the sum of the net benefits is positive.

In fact, there is no way to solve all of the incentive problems, and this is the conclusion of a remarkable result known as the Gibbard-Satterthwaite theorem, [3] and [7]. This is a negative result, but it must be listed among the really important contributions to social science in the last couple of decades, for it helps us to understand the limits of what is possible. Like all truly fundamental results, it is easy to explain if not to understand the details of how it is established.

Consider a set of alternatives

$$A = \left\{x^1, x^2, \ldots, x^m\right\};$$

these might be candidates for office, or alternative government budgets. We will assume that $m \geq 3$ and that there are n agents. A *social choice function* is a rule that assigns to each n-vector of rankings of A, a social choice $x \in A$. For the case of three alternatives (x,y,z) and four people, a typical point in the domain of a social choice function is

1	2	3	4
x	x	y	z
y	z	z	x
z	y	x	y

This might have associated with it the alternative x, with the interpretation that when the four agents vote as indicated, the outcome is x. For simplicity we will assume that for each alternative there is some ranking that will make that alternative the social choice.

A social choice function is *strategy-proof* if no agent can ever secure a more favored outcome by misrepresenting his preference. A social choice function is *dictatorial* if there is some agent who always gets his first choice, no matter how the other agents vote.

The Gibbard-Satterthwaite theorem tells us that any social choice function that is strategy-proof is dictatorial. In other words, the only general scheme that aggregates preferences to make social choices and is strategy-proof is the dictatorial scheme. Needless to say, the dictatorial scheme does not involve serious mediation. This argues strongly for the Samuelson side of the Samuelson-Coase difference to which we have been alluding; however, one can hardly credit Samuelson with the Gibbard-Satterthwaite insight.

The Gibbard-Satterthwaite theorem is sort of a Pandora's box. Once the result is known, there is no taking it back, and knowledgeable agents will not believe that it is in their interest to tell the truth without trying to discover the rule by which preferences are to be aggregated or how other agents are voting. This can lead to intuitively unattractive consequences, and I like to illustrate this point by recalling, in a wildly embellished form, my experience at the University of Massachusetts.

I taught at UM for three years. Department chairmen were elected for three-year terms, but for several consecutive years each chairman resigned or was dismissed at the end of nine months. The members of the department became very sophisticated at voting. In my last year there were four candidates: first, the darling of the macroeconomists in the department, John M. Keynes. We had it on good authority that JM was most anxious to come to UM because of the exciting cosmopolitan environment. The second candidate was named F. Y. Edgeworth. He was in fact my own choice, and rumor had it that he was fascinated with the architecture of our campus. Nothing against Keynes, but FY was really well plugged into the microeconomics establishment, and I felt certain that he would be a most valuable critic and appreciator of my work. Two candidates remained, John Glutz and Stu Smith. Glutz was the candidate of the provost and Smith was the candidate of the acting dean. None of us had ever heard of either of them. There was some gossip that Glutz possessed information about an indiscreet act committed by the provost during his younger days as an assistant professor at a university to our south. Blackmail was the name of the game! Later we learned that Smith was the acting dean's real name (we knew him only as dean). The acting dean had nominated himself with the hope that he could become a "real" chairman after he was finished "acting."

There were eleven macroeconomists in the department and eleven microeconomists. The former were all for JM, and the latter all favored FY. Of course, both groups favored FY and JM over the remaining candidates; they were indifferent between the nominations provided by the acting dean and provost. The voting was by rank order. List the candidates: the first choice on a ballot gets four points, the second gets three, etc. The total number of points obtained by each candidate is added, and the candidate with the largest number of points wins.

I picked up my ballot and immediately voted: FY, SS, JG, and JM. The reasoning was clear: I knew that either FY or JM would win, and I wanted to get the most distance between them. Well, it turned out that everyone was as sophisticated as I was: everyone put FY and JM first or last. SS was second on two thirds of the ballots, and this is how the acting dean became chairman of the economics department at UM. This was so intolerable that there were mass resignations.

The next day I kicked myself for being so devious. But if we had been allowed to revote, I might have done the same again. If I thought that my colleagues had "learned their lesson" and were going to vote their true preference, then it would have been in my interest to remain devious! In any case the point should be clear. If a scheme is not strategy-proof, then it may be in an agent's interest to misrepresent his preference, and this can lead to outcomes that are quite undesirable in terms of the voters' own preferences. There is no benevolent invisible hand at work here!

Let us now return to the "good news."

Faced with the difficulty of the Gibbard-Satterthwaite theorem, we ask, is there hope of designing cooperation in a general context? One direction that has been explored is to weaken the notion of social equilibrium. At the same time, it is necessary to introduce schemes that have agents choose actions from sets other than the set of all possible preferences over social outcomes. Consider for a moment the case of two agents. The first picks from the set $\{a_1, a_2, \ldots, a_n\}$ and the second picks from the set $\{b_1, b_2, \ldots, b_n\}$. A game form is an $n \times m$ matrix, where for each i and j the ij entry is the outcome if the first agent plays a_i and the second agent plays b_j. In the Groves-Clark scheme, each agent has a "best play," and it is independent of the play chosen by other players. This is the case of equilibrium in dominant strategies. Now we will require less for social equilibrium, namely, that the strategies chosen are "Nash."

The Nash equilibrium concept essentially does the following. It associates to each game form and each set of individual preferences (these define the utility payoffs of the game) a play for each agent. The assigned plays have the property that, given the plays attributed to others, no agent can improve his position by altering his own play. If you believe that all of the other agents in a game in which you are participating have read and believe the work of Nash, and if everyone has the information to determine the game in which he is playing, then the best you can do is make the play assigned by Nash. The weakness of the Nash equilibrium concept is that it requires each agent to know the preferences of all other agents. This is not true with dominant strategy equilibrium.

Great strides have been made in constructing game forms for economies with public goods so that each Nash equilibrium is associated with a good outcome. The first and perhaps the most significant of these was due to John Ledyard and Ted Groves [5]. By loosening the notion of equilibrium from dominant strategy to Nash, they were able to get around the difficulties presented by the Gibbard-Satterthwaite theorem. But a resolution via Nash equilibrium, because of its strong informational requirement, is not entirely satisfactory. It may still be in an agent's interest to misrepresent his preferences to others.

To understand this point, consider two games, I and II. The payoffs in the ij^{th} place are the utilities for A (who chooses a_1 or a_2) and B (who chooses b_1 or b_2), respectively, when the joint choice is (a_i, b_j).

	I B			II B	
	b_1	b_2		b_1	b_2
a_1	1,1	3,4	a_1	1,4	3,1
a_2	2,5	1,6	a_2	2,6	1,5

Suppose that I give the true utility payoffs and both agents know the utility numbers. A can see that if he plays a_1, then B would do best to play b_2 (since $4 > 1$). Similarly, if he plays a_2, then B would do best to play b_2 (since $6 > 5$). Thus, A can be sure that B will play the dominant strategy b_2, and on this basis A does best to play a_1. The pair (a_1,b_2) is in fact the unique Nash equilibrium for I.

But suppose that B can convince A that his utility payoffs are as indicated in II. Then, reasoning as before, A can be sure that B will play the dominant strategy b_1, and on this basis A does best to play a_2, which makes (a_2,b_1) the unique Nash equilibrium for II. But in terms of B's true preferences you will see that this outcome yields B the payoff 5, while in I, where A knew B's true preference, B only received the payoff 4. The point is clear: with Nash equilibrium it may be in an agent's interest to misrepresent his preferences in order to secure a better outcome. Furthermore, as indicated in the "voting for a chairman" example, such misrepresentation can be expected sometimes to lead to socially inferior outcomes.

But I do not want you to draw the conclusion that schemes based on Nash equilibrium are useless and teach us nothing. Rather, I would say that there are at least two features that must be taken into account in the design of mechanisms for promoting cooperative behavior. First, the informational requirements: who has to know what? Second, the incentive problems: is it in each agent's self-interest to act as we have prescribed for him to act? This classification follows the work of Leo Hurwicz, who pioneered the abstract approach to the design of schemes.

Schemes based on Nash equilibrium may sometimes have rather strenuous informational requirements (e.g., everyone's true preference is common knowledge), but we should still appreciate what they are able to do for the incentive problem: agents acting in their own behalf, but with possibly the need for substantial amounts of information, will selfishly promote the social good. Furthermore, one can always hope that by improving the design we can lessen the informational requirements. This is the direction of current research.

I will close this essay by reviewing the major points.

1. The economics of incentives is at the core of economic theory. It applies not only to public goods allocation, but also to such questions as: how can a firm owner get a manager to perform in the owner's interest? What directions should society give to the managers of a public utility?
2. It is possible to be much more inventive in the design of schemes than was foreseen by Samuelson. You now know some schemes. But this is not to say that I foresee so much progress in the

design of schemes that such ideas will replace the need for governments to indirectly estimate costs and benefits, and to proceed to construct projects that yield the largest net benefit.
3. There are limits to how far one can go with schemes that make it in each agent's interest always to tell the truth; the Gibbard-Satterthwaite helps us to precisely understand these limits.
4. Nash equilibrium provides a way around these limits, but at the cost of large informational requirements. One can substantially solve the incentives problems if each agent has a great deal of information about the agents he is participating with.

References

[1] Clark, E. H. [1971] "Multipart pricing of public goods," *Public Choice*, 19–33.
[2] Coase, R. [1960] "The problem of social cost," *Journal of Law and Economics*, 3, 1–44.
[3] Gibbard, A. [1973] "Manipulation of voting schemes: a general result," *Econometrica*, 41, 587–601.
[4] Groves, T. [1973] "Incentives in teams," *Econometrica*, 41, 617–31.
[5] Groves, T., and J. Ledyard [1977] "Optimal allocation of public goods: a solution to the 'Free Rider'," *Econometrica*, 45, 783–809.
[6] Samuelson, P. [1954] "The pure theory of public expenditures," *Review of Economics and Statistics*, 36, 387–89.
[7] Satterthwaite, M. [1975] "Strategy-proofness and Arrow's conditions: existence and correspondence theorems for voting procedures and social welfare functions," *Journal of Economic Theory*, 10, 187–217.
[8] Vickery, W. [1961] "Counterspeculation, auctions and competitive sealed tenders," *Journal of Finance*, 16, 1–17.

1984

ANDREU MAS-COLELL
On the Theory of Perfect Competition

My earliest intellectual contact with the work of Nancy Schwartz dates from my graduate-student days at Minnesota. There was an optimal growth course, taught by John Chipman, that was not to be missed. The pièce de résistance was Pontryagin's Maximum Principle, and I will always be thankful to the *Journal of Economic Theory* article by Kamien and Schwartz for helping me to get through it. It took several nights of a still-remembered week, but at the end I understood the principle. So I have a debt that is a pleasure to repay on this occasion. It is for me truly an honor to be delivering the Nancy L. Schwartz Memorial Lecture. My subject will be market competition as viewed by traditional general equilibrium theory. Nancy Schwartz made outstanding contributions to our understanding of dynamic market competition from the standpoint of industrial organization theory. I hope, therefore, that this is a fitting topic for me in this lecture.

With or without the qualification of "perfect," competition has been a central theme of economics since at least Adam Smith's times. You have all heard of the Invisible Hand, and on a clear day some of you may even have seen it doing its work. Like so much in Adam Smith, the Invisible Hand emerges from the *Wealth of Nations* as a powerful ingredient of a vision – that competition leads to a beneficial state of affairs – but not as a precise theorem. The task of getting one was undertaken by later generations of economists, and you may get the impression from my lecture that we are still at it. The development of economics has combined a decided progress in methods with the persistence of a few constantly rethought, fundamental themes. The Invisible Hand is one of these.

It is time I let the cat out of the bag and tell you precisely what I will attempt in this hour. First, I will define a rough-and-ready concept of perfect competition in the tradition of Léon Walras. I will then focus on one aspect of the definition – the absence of monopoly power. The bulk of the hour will go into a theoretical examination of what I will call the Negligibility Hypothesis, as a foundation for the absence of monopoly power and the occurrence of perfect competition. To this end I will review three somewhat linked, but nevertheless distinct, theories of perfect competition. The three, with 19th-century origins, have been extensively reconsidered in the last, say, twenty years. They all view the world as populated by economic agents in competition with each other, but differ in perceiving the way this competition takes place. They are, first, Cournot's Quantity-Setting Noncooperative Equilibrium Theory, proposed by Cournot [1838] and studied recently by Shubik [1973], Hart [1979], and Novshek and Sonnenschein [1978]; second, Edgeworth's Contract Theory, reinvented by game theorists under the name of the Core and studied by Debreu and Scarf [1963] and Aumann [1964]; and, third, Clark's Marginal Productivity Theory, resuscitated these days in a remarkable contribution of Ostroy [1980] under the name of the No-Surplus Theory. After reviewing these three theories, I will devote fifteen minutes to an extended commentary and a defense of the usefulness of the Negligibility Hypothesis in the context of general economic theory.

It is within custom, and convenient, to define a situation as perfectly competitive if it is characterized by, first, the universality of markets and, second, the absence of monopoly power. To put it in a more precise but more jargon-loaded way: perfect competition prevails if an equilibrium is reached noncooperatively, in an environment where prices are quoted in every possible market and taken as given by every economic agent. As qualified by Oskar Lange with respect to price taking and by Kenneth Arrow with respect to price quoting, this is essentially the definition of Léon Walras. As a definition, it has the advantage that more or less automatically the equilibrium turns out to be a beneficial state of the economy in the strongest sense one could hope for, given the nature of the problem, namely the sense of Pareto: with the same physical environment it is impossible to reorganize the economic activity so as to make everybody better off.

If you read, for example, the splendid historical article of Stigler [1965] on the concept of perfect competition, you will see that some conditions turn up repeatedly as preconditions of perfect competition. Before moving on, let me comment on four of those:

1) Economic agents actively pursue their selfish benefit. I am taking this for granted, and it is implicit in the notion that the economy settles at a noncooperative equilibrium.
2) Resources are freely movable across sectors. I prefer not to assume this because it really is part of the description of the environment and a concept of perfect competition should be defined (another thing is that it occurs) for any environment.
3) There are perfect knowledge and transparency of markets. This is a key implicit hypothesis in the notion of equilibrium. When acting, every individual knows precisely the ruling price system. There is no noise there.
4) There are no externalities. This requirement is captured, more or less adequately, in the principle of universality of markets. Individual cost and benefit depend only on prices and own actions. Any external influence defines a new commodity that must be ruthlessly priced out.

The second aspect of the definition concerns the absence of monopoly power. I will not in this lecture make an issue of the universality of markets. I will follow an established tradition and try to connect the absence of monopoly power with what I shall call the Negligibility Hypothesis, namely, the notion that the influence on the rest of the economy, looked at as a whole, of the actions of a single economic agent is unnoticeable and negligible. This is admittedly a vague statement, but it will be better, for the moment, to leave it at this and not to strive for a rigorous, abstract definition.

I will exposit the three theories under review in the context of a simple example. Because my emphasis is not on the universality of markets, there will not be much conceptual loss if I restrict myself to a single market where some generic good, which I shall call the "good," is exchanged for "money," standing for generalized purchasing power. Although this is an unnecessary simplification, it will facilitate matters if I assume that economic agents are naturally classified as buyers or sellers of the good. A seller may be thought of as an individually owned firm, i.e., as an agent that, for example, cares only about final holdings of money and that can produce amounts of the good according to some cost function displaying, perhaps, decreasing average cost in some region and finite capacity. A buyer can be thought of as the usual sort of consumer, coming initially into the picture with some money but no good and having preferences defined on amounts of money and good. Denoting by p the price of the good relative to money, we can construct from individual preferences an aggregate demand function, expressing the total amount of good requested by consumers when they make their demands under the hypothesis that the price is independent of their actions. Under a technical condition on individual preferences (absence of income effects), the demand function is nonincreasing in price.

The perfectly competitive equilibria in the Walras sense described previously can now be obtained in the familiar way. Construct from the seller's preferences or technologies an aggregate supply function; that is, assume that every seller maximizes profit or utility taking the announced price as given. Then the intersection of demand and supply schedules yields the equilibrium prices.

The Negligibility Hypothesis will be embodied in the assumption that there is a continuum of both buyers and sellers and that there is a uniform upper bound on the supply of good by any seller or of money by any buyer.

An economic environment is therefore perfectly well defined.

The first theory I shall review is Cournot's quantity-setting equilibrium. The characteristics of this theory are that, first, buyers and sellers are treated asymmetrically. Sellers compete actively, while buyers adapt passively, nonstrategically. Second, the Law of One Price holds; namely, every unit of the good is transacted for exactly the same amount of money. Third, and most important, we deal with quantity competition. Each firm, that is to say, each seller, fixes the quantity to be sold. The aggregate quantity is then auctioned off and absorbed by consumers at some price. This price can then be used to compute the firm's profits. We are at a quantity Cournot equilibrium if no seller could make itself better off by merely changing its production when, in principle, it correctly perceives the influence, if any, of this change in the market price.

Suppose now that the aggregate demand function can be inverted to a continuous function giving the buyer's clearing price as a function of the aggregate production. Under the Negligibility Hypothesis we then have the desired result: the Cournot quantity-setting equilibrium is identical with the Walras price-taking equilibrium. The proof is almost a tautology. Buyers take prices as given by definition, while sellers do it by construction. Every seller has an infinitesimal upper bound on how much it can sell. Therefore, no seller can influence aggregate production; hence, no seller can influence the price system. Note that the assumption according to which market prices depend continuously on aggregate quantities is used in an essential way. If an arbitrarily small expansion of production could cause a finite drop in price, then correct modeling would demand that even infinitesimal firms could have that effect. It is therefore possible, as an equilibrium phenomenon, that the economy

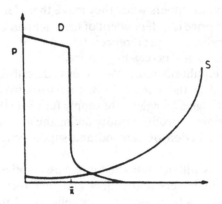

Figure 1

locks itself up at an aggregate production inferior to the Walras production. In Figure 1 this could happen at $\bar{x}$. Note that in Figure 1 the demand
function $D(p)$ is nonincreasing and therefore could have been generated
from a population of consumers with no income effects.

Everything said so far can be generalized to models with many goods
and in which buyers and sellers are treated more symmetrically. Shubik
[1973], Hart [1979], K. Roberts [1980], and Novshek and Sonnenschein
[1978] are some of the relevant names for all of this.

Interesting and suggestive as Cournot theory is, it cannot be the last
word. It has allowed us to identify an interesting condition, namely, the
continuity of market prices on quantities, but it has limitations. What is
perhaps the main limitation could be summarized by the question: why
competition through quantities? There is no answer or, rather, the
answer is that this is beyond the particular theory and that implicit in
the latter there is a given institutional and technological frame of reference that determines in each case the appropriate competition strategy.
The implicit hypothesis in the model discussed is, thus, that the strategies are quantities. It stands to reason, of course, that a broad-sensed
Cournot approach could allow for any strategy set.

Consider for example, a rather extreme case, where instead of com-
mitting to quantities firms commit to prices (and demand is split equally
among firms charging the same price). Suppose that the total mass of
firms is much larger than the mass of buyers, that firms are all identical,
and that average cost increases to infinity at some finite capacity. Then
the perfectly competitive equilibrium would have every active firm
selling at a price equal to minimum average cost. However, with price

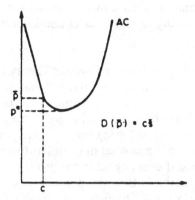

Figure 2

commitments as strategies we have that every active firm will still charge the same price, but the admissible prices include a range that extends above minimum average cost. And this even with the Negligibility Hypothesis. See Figure 2. What happens is that the incentive to undercut is severely limited by the fact that the demand forthcoming to a firm has to be supplied, up to the feasible limit, at the posted price, whatever the cost may be. This may seem bizarre but note that as was pointed out by Grossman (1981), on the face of it Cournot quantity strategies are of the same nature. They are also a commitment to supply a given quantity at whatever the price may be.

There is a sense, however, in which even this example could be understood within a generalized Cournot approach to the theory of perfect competition. I will be very vague in the sense I refer to, because all this is still conjectural. It turns out that many market-like mechanisms that differ in many respects and have different equilibria all have the property that, under the Negligibility Hypothesis, their equilibria are perfectly competitive and therefore almost independent of the details of the mechanism (the "almost" stands for the possibility of nonuniqueness of equilibrium); see Dubey, Mas-Colell, and Shubik [1980]. A key mechanism requirement for this result is, in each case, an appropriate version of the continuity condition of payoffs on individual actions, a condition that we encountered when studying the quantity-setting model and that, not surprisingly, would be violated in the previous example. The matter could be pursued axiomatically, but this would take us too far afield. Just let me emphasize that from the study of the narrow quantity-setting Cournot model we identified as important a certain continuity condition and that its importance can be confirmed by a more abstract approach not tied to particular, arbitrary-looking strategy spaces and institutional settings.

The second theory I want to review, Edgeworth's Contract Theory, or the Core, is much more parsimonious in the institutional detail that must be made explicit a priori. Edgeworth viewed a state of the economy as a constellation of contracts specifying bilateral exchanges among economic agents. Competition works in the following way. Anyone, perhaps some fictitious arbitrageur, can propose a new set of contracts to a group of people. The proposal is accepted if every agent in the group finds the proposal beneficial under the hypothesis that any preexisting contract involving the particular agent is dropped. The proposal is viable if, provided it is accepted, it is feasible; that is, a nonnegative surplus of every commodity is left. Of course, this means that the deal is profitable to the hypothetical arbitrageur. A situation is in equilibrium if no profitable deal is possible in this sense. An equivalent formulation is that an allocation of goods and resources is a Core equilibrium, or is in the Core, if there is no group of agents that can separate away and with its resources alone arrange matters so as to make every member of the group better off. This second phrasing has a more cooperative flavor than the first. But this is merely semantics. It should also be noted that the Core notion of competition is quite heavy on informational requirements. People's preferences, endowments, and technologies have to be public knowledge.

In the context of this example, I will now argue that under the Negligibility Hypothesis and with no further qualification or condition, every Core equilibrium is perfectly competitive; that is, it is a Walras price-taking equilibrium. I will reason in two steps. First, I will try to convince you that in a Core equilibrium the Law of One Price must hold. Second, I will argue that all buyers and sellers must be realizing their optimal plan at the price obtained from the first step. Needless to say, I will not be rigorous.

For the first step, try the following proof. If two units of the good are sold at different prices, then the seller of the lower-priced unit and the buyer of the higher-priced unit could gain by getting together. This is obvious but not quite a proof, because Core competition only allows entire transactions of individuals to be recontracted, not single units. No problem. The Negligibility Hypothesis comes to the rescue. Because there is a continuum of buyers and sellers, the proportion of more-than-averagely-priced buyers relative to less-than-averagely-priced sellers can always be adjusted so that the total amount of the transaction is the same in the two sides of the market. Thus, in Figure 3 the clouds of transac-

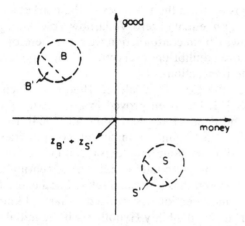

Figure 3

tions of buyers and sellers are represented, respectively, as B and S. Because of feasibility, the origin is contained in the relative interior of the convex hull of B and S. If B and S are not contained in a line through the origin, which would violate the Law of One Price, then it is intuitive that groups of buyers B' and sellers S' can be found so that their total transaction $z_{B'} + z_{S'}$ leaves a surplus of both goods and money.

For the second step, let p be the price determined from the first. Note that as long as there are transactions, the question of who sets the price is irrelevant. By the Law of One Price, the price is implicit in the trades made. If there are no transactions a special argument is needed, so I leave this case aside. Consider the optimal trades at the fixed price p of the different buyers and sellers. If those trades are the actual trades, then we are done. Suppose this is not so, that there is, for example, a group of sellers such that all members of the group are strictly better off at their p-optimal trade than at their actual trade. By continuity this remains true if the price is lowered slightly to, say, $p' < p$. All active buyers will also be better off at the p' optimal trade than at their actual trade. This is clear enough because the price has been lowered. Hence we have a group of sellers and buyers that would be better off if they could get their optimal trades at p'. By construction, and this is an important point, the optimal trades of these buyers and sellers at p' are nonzero. So at p' there are both notionally active buyers and notionally active sellers. Of course, the aggregate net demand of the group at p' need not be zero, but as we did for the Law of One Price, we can, because of the Negligibility

Hypothesis, select a subgroup from the two sides of the market so as to make the aggregate trade at p' equal to zero. Voilà, now a blocking group has been found! To get away from contradiction we must therefore conclude that at the given Core equilibrium everyone is at the optimum for the price p implicit in the transactions.

This result is known as the Core Equivalence Theorem, which goes back to Edgeworth [1881]. It has been proved in great generality by, among others, Debreu and Scarf [1963] and Aumann [1964]. Roughly speaking, as long as there is a finite number of commodities, the Equivalence Theorem holds without any extra condition, certainly without anything similar to the continuity conditions appearing in the Cournot approach. The Theorem has also been refined and extended in a multitude of directions, one direction first noticed, as far as I know, by Townsend [1983]. Under the Negligibility Hypothesis, if the initial situation is not perfectly competitive then not only can a group separate and arrange matters to be better off with its own resources (that this can be done we already know), but a group can separate and its members be better off at a Walras equilibrium of the separate economy. In a less serious wording: an economy not in perfectly competitive equilibrium can be upset not only by a cleverly designed parallel economy, but by one that is perfectly competitive (is this a theory of the underground economy?). Note that this stronger version of the Theorem is exactly what I proved, heuristically, for the example.

Parenthetically, under the Negligibility Hypothesis all the needed improving or blocking groups can be taken to be arbitrarily small. This should be intuitive enough. Simply, anything that can be done can also be done at any reduced scale. Knowing this is of interest because we could wish to require that upsetting profitable deals not be macroscopically significant. Besides being heuristically sensible in a theory of non-cooperation, this requirement would have the added advantage of destroying some peculiarities of the Core notion of competition, such as the fact that a Core equilibrium is always, with or without the Negligibility Hypothesis, an optimum.

Although distinct, the two theories covered so far, Cournot's and Edgeworth's, are similar and could be looked at as different limits of the same general picture. In both cases we have a notion of competition and a corresponding one of competitive equilibrium. In both cases the competitive equilibrium turns out to be perfectly competitive under the Negligibility Hypothesis. This is completely general for the least structured notion of competition – the Core – but it is subject to a mechanism-dependent qualification – continuity – for the concept more constrained by a structured mechanism, namely, Cournot's. One can go back to the example where, under Negligibility, Cournot failed to be perfectly competitive and see how easily the Edgeworth contract would get out of the impasse. Essentially, some sellers can recontract larger sales with some buyers without a precipitous drop of price.

The third theory I will discuss, Ostroy's No-Surplus Theory, is somewhat different. Again a notion of competition is defined. But under Ostroy's definition a competitive equilibrium is automatically a perfectly competitive equilibrium, with or without the Negligibility Hypothesis. The role of the hypothesis is now not that of assuring that the competitive equilibrium is a Walras equilibrium but rather the converse: it assumes that the Walras price-taking equilibrium, which will exist under standard conditions, is a competitive equilibrium in the sense of No-Surplus Theory. Typically, this will not be the case for the situation with only a finite number of traders, which of course implies that competitive equilibrium rarely exists in a world with nonnegligible agents. To summarize, what the Negligibility Hypothesis gives us now is the existence of a perfectly competitive equilibrium. You will have to excuse the terminological, but not conceptual, inconsistency I am falling into: I have defined perfectly competitive to mean price taking, and I've just said that price taking may not imply competitive. To avoid confusion I will minimize the use of the undefined term "competitive."

No-Surplus theory is based on the marginal productivity theory of Clark [1899]. The idea is to define a situation as perfectly competitive if all agents receive exactly what they contribute, at the margin, to the economy as a whole. This is more easily said than made precise. If we are dealing with a social production function for a generalized consumption good and agents are factor providers, then it is fairly clear how to define the marginal contribution of a single agent. It is simply the difference of what the economy can produce with or without the agent. But how to proceed for a general market system? Marginal contribution to what? Let me explain in the context of two good examples how simply Ostroy has solved this conundrum. The first requirement, and this is a serious limitation, is that the position being considered be Pareto optimal. Let it be so. Now take any particular agent t, buyer or seller, and ask what would be the minimal amount of money $m(t)$ that would need to be added to the resources of the rest of the economy if agent t were dropped from the economy but all the remaining agents were compensated so as to end up no worse off. The amount $m(t)$ should be considered normalized to the size of a single agent. Under the Negligibility Hypothesis, it has the magnitude of a derivative. If $m(t) > 0$ for some agent t, then the rest of the economy needs compensation for the loss of

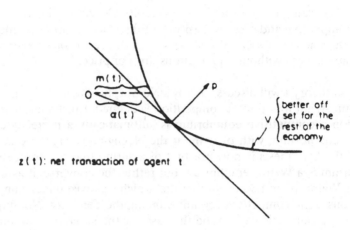

Figure 4

the agent, i.e., in net terms he or she is contributing some surplus to the rest of the economy. The agent has something extra, so to speak, to bargain for. We could say, consequently, that we are at a No-Surplus equilibrium if $m(t) = 0$ for all agents. This is precisely Ostroy's definition.

Let me argue that taking perfectly competitive equilibria to mean No-Surplus amounts to a strengthening of the definition so far; a No-Surplus equilibrium is necessarily a Walras price-taking equilibrium. This is straightforward, so I am a bit embarrassed at having to use a few symbols and Figure 4, but it will be painless and it still will take only one minute. Let p be a shadow price (in terms of money) for the good at the No-Surplus equilibrium. Remember that No-Surplus equilibria are optima by definition. For every agent t let $\alpha(t)$ be the imputed net subsidy or tax received by the agent at price p. That is, $\alpha(t)$ is the negative of the net value of his or her transaction at price p. By the definition of shadow price and the construction of $m(t)$ we have $m(t) \geq \alpha(t)$ for every t. Therefore, $\alpha(t) = 0$ for all t implies $\alpha(t) \leq 0$ for all t. But the sum of the $\alpha(t)$ over the agents adds up to zero. Therefore, $\alpha(t) = 0$ for all t and we have our proof. Incidentally, Figure 4 also helps to understand why, if there is any trade, a Walras equilibrium in an economy with a finite number of agents will not be No-Surplus. (Sorry for the double negative.) Even if $\alpha(t) = 0$, the boundary of V will typically exhibit some curvature, and so $m(t) > 0$.

Strictly speaking, even with the Negligibility Hypothesis a Walras equilibrium may fail to be No-Surplus. Consider the following example with two goods that, to emphasize symmetry, I will call apples and oranges.

There is an equal mass of two types of people. Agents of Type I own, say, 10 oranges each, but care only about apples, while the reverse is true for agents of Type II. There is a single Walras price-taking equilibrium in this example: apples and oranges are priced equally and completely exchanged among the two types in the obvious way. Of course this is also the unique Core equilibrium. From the point of view of Cournot, the model is also well behaved. The demand functions of apples in terms of oranges and of oranges in terms of apples are nicely continuous and strictly downward sloping. Nevertheless, every agent contributes a positive surplus at the Walras allocation. Drop, for example, an agent of Type I, who, remember, at the Walras allocation, consumes only apples. The rest of the economy gains 10 apples but loses 10 oranges. However, the 10 apples are useless since they cannot be used to compensate the losers of the 10 oranges (who are Type II people and do not care about apples). If everyone in the rest of the economy has to be compensated, then 10 extra oranges are needed. This is, therefore, a measure of the (nonzero) surplus contributed by the dropped agent.

What is lacking in this example is a bit of differentiability. Suppose that the Walras equilibrium has the following property: looking at the allocation of goods as a Pareto optimum, the shadow or supporting price system p is, up to normalization, uniquely determined. This, of course, fails in the example where any price system would be supporting. Under Negligibility, the desired result does then obtain. Drop an agent from the economy. Its net trade is infinitesimal from the point of view of the rest of the economy (i.e., it is entirely at the margin), and the differentiability property does therefore imply that the net compensating needs for money can be computed by evaluating the gains and losses with the price system p. Because we are at a Walras equilibrium the net value of the trade of any agent at these shadow prices is zero. Hence the compensating needs for money are zero. We are at a No-Surplus equilibrium. Summing up: Negligibility, plus some smoothness, implies the equality of price taking and No-Surplus equilibrium.

What should we make of the discussion thus far and the different equivalence results exposited? Simply put: that, perhaps subject to some continuity and smoothness restrictions one would do well to watch for, the Negligibility Hypothesis yields price-taking equilibria. There is an important proviso that need not be forgotten. As mentioned at the beginning of the lecture, the principle of universality of markets has been taken for granted. Now this principle, which cannot be dispensed with, can, will, and should in many cases interfere with the Negligibility Hypothesis, for the following reason: negligible has to mean negligible with respect to

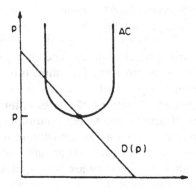

Figure 5

something. What matters for the equivalence results is that every agent's trades be negligible in the markets where he or she operates. If there are too many markets this may fail even with a continuum of agents. You only need to consider the limit case of juxtaposition of a continuum of bilateral monopolies. For the Negligibility Hypothesis to imply price-taking equilibrium, the rule of thumb is that the set of commodity types has to be small relative to the set of agents. The vagueness of this statement is somewhat inevitable, because a precise, definitive theorem is not yet available, though progress toward it has been made by Ostroy (see Gretsky and Ostroy [1985]).

Up to now I have looked at the Negligibility Hypothesis as a sufficient condition for perfectly competitive, price-taking equilibria. What about necessity? A suggestion of nonnecessity is immediately conveyed by a familiar example (see, for example, Grossman [1981]). There are two identical firms that need to incur some fixed cost if they operate. Let p be the minimum average cost and suppose that the demand function of the consumers is downward sloping and such that the demand at p, $D(p)$, can be produced by a single firm at an average cost p (see Figure 5). Suppose also, to simplify, that fixed costs are so high that no two firms can be active and make nonnegative profits. Consider then a price-taking state of the economy where the price is the minimum average cost p, one firm covers the entire demand at p, and the other produces nothing. This price-taking equilibrium is the only state in the Core. Indeed, only one firm can be active; if it were to charge more than p to some consumers, then the firm-in-waiting could offer a better deal to a group of consumers. It is also a No-Surplus equilibrium because if a firm is left out, the rest of the economy has at its disposal an exact copy to replace it. Hence any firm contributes zero surplus, which, incidentally, agrees with its getting zero profits. From the point of view of the quantity-setting Cournot model, this price-taking state is not an equilibrium, so at least this does not substantiate the perfectly competitive character of the model. But sensible amending, using price-quantity strategies, would do it.

I should confess that I do not know what to make of this example. Two big firms and perfect competition: should I be comfortable with this? I am uncertain, but something tells me that the result has to be quite model-specific and less solid than the analogous conclusion with the Negligibility Hypothesis. In the little time that I have left, I would like to make a plea for the general usefulness of the Negligibility Hypothesis in the analysis of noncooperative models. The two points I want to make are not distinct, but have different emphases.

The first point is that under the Negligibility Hypothesis the noncooperative analysis of a social system often becomes tractable. Delicate game theoretic considerations may degenerate, and strong conclusions, positive or negative, may be obtainable. Those who were present at last year's Schwartz Memorial Lecture (a tough act to follow, incidentally) may remember that Hugo Sonnenschein presented an idealized contrast between Samuelson and Coase and showed that much more was possible in the way of mechanism design for the provision of public goods than Samuelson thought possible. Not so, however, under the Negligibility Hypothesis. With the latter, Samuelson was right. If he had this hypothesis in mind, I do not know. I cannot now justify this claim, but it has been proved, in a precise setting, by J. Roberts (1976). Analytically, what the hypothesis contributes is the possibility of neglecting the impact of the actions of a single agent on the rest of the system or, at least, on most of the rest of the system. Another field where this simplifying power may be exploitable is monopolistically competitive theory, which can be looked at as a marriage of oligopoly theory and the Negligibility Hypothesis. In my view, the theory of monopolistic competition derives its theoretical importance not from being a "realistic complication of the theory of perfect competition, but from being a simplified, tractable limit of oligopoly theory. Hart [1982] has done interesting work on this.

My second point is similarly heuristic. If I look at the example of the two big firms, I cannot help feeling that the key issue is whether the firms will collude or not. Just assuming that they will not is a strong hypothesis; it amounts to leaving quite a lot out of the theory. Obviously, a justification of the noncooperation hypothesis itself should be part of a full theoretical treatment. It turns out that the Negligibility Hypothesis is here of much help, as it makes noncooperation a plausible *outcome* rather than hypothesis. The intuition is clear: if the impact of a firm on the rest of the economy is negligible, then, whatever the prevailing enforcing arrangements, the incentive for the firm to defect from the collusive arrangement will be strong. After all, it is unlikely that the firm will be found out. This sort of argument can be made rigorous, but it requires, interestingly enough, a link with the economics of imperfect information, a subject, incidentally, so strong in this center of learning that I get into these waters with some trepidation. The reason for the link can be easily explained. A complete information world is a somewhat degenerate one where it is actually possible to detect and therefore punish any deviation from collusion. But if there is some noise in the system and agents are small (in the limit negligible), then moral hazard takes over and the incentives to cheat become overwhelming. This argument was first made by Stigler [1964] and has been elaborated by Green [1980]. We have an interesting paradox here because perfect information is usually listed among the preconditions of perfect competition, and now it is noise that helps perfect competition. Perhaps, very tentatively, the reason for this is that while perfect information favors perfect competition if noncooperation is granted, the influence on the noncooperation hypothesis may go in the reverse direction: the more noise, the more difficult it is to coordinate. Obviously, if you have a duopoly and each duopolist is perfectly informed of the technology of the other, then perfect collusion can be enforced by threats. But if the knowledge is not perfect, then we may have misrepresentation of cost functions, an adverse selection problem, which will be reflected in the equilibrium not always yielding the monopoly solution. Progress in these directions has recently been made by K. Roberts [1983].

It is only fair that after sponsoring the Negligibility Hypothesis for its analytical convenience, I address the issue of its realism. It would be disingenuous for me to plead lack of time in order not to do so. As usual I shall make two observations.

The first is that, obviously, the real world is full of big traders. The federal government itself is no small fry. So a theory built on the Negligibility Hypothesis cannot hope to be the general theory. Let that be granted. But somewhere in the country where trade-off frontiers live, there is a frontier for the extent of coverage and the strength of results of theories. I bet that those built on the Negligibility Hypothesis are centrally located in this frontier. This is, however, a matter of judgment based on the conviction that mass phenomena constitute an essential part of the economic world. Everything I have said should not be of much relevance for anyone who perceives the latter as a small bunch of players playing high-stakes poker.

My second observation is that although I have been talking about a literal continuum of agents, this should be thought of only as the limit version of the Negligibility Hypothesis. It is an analytically useful limit because results come sharp and clean, unpolluted by ε's and δ's, but it is also the less realistic limit. What constitutes a useful approximation? This is a central problem technically known as the rate-of-convergence problem. Obviously, it is quite a different matter if for all practical purposes 8 agents are a continuum, rather than 8000. Although many results are available, much remains to be done; there is not yet, I would say, a systematic picture. For the case of the Core and using a weak measure of distance, a rate of convergence of $1/n$ seems typical. Here n stands for the size of the economy and distance measures are per capita. To appreciate this rate I may observe that for the Shapley value, another solution concept of game theoretic origin with some connections to No-Surplus Theory, convergence to price-taking equilibria has been proved but no typical rate better than $1/n^{1/3}$ has been obtained (Mas-Colell [1977]). The contrast is great. To guarantee the same level of approximation you get with 10 agents for the Core, you would need 1000 for the Shapley value. Note that I say "guarantee"; the "average" rate may be better. Let me end my lecture by saying the rate-of-convergence work on the Cournot solution is also going on. Not long ago I heard a splendid paper by Gresik and Satterthwaite [1984] bearing on this. And it had imperfect information, to boot.

References

Aumann, R. [1964] "Markets with a Continuum of Traders," *Econometrica* 32, 39–50.
Clark, J.B. [1899] *The Distribution of Wealth: a Theory of Wages, Distribution and Profits*, New York: Macmillan.
Cournot, A. [1838] *Recherches sur les principles mathématiques de la théorie des richesses.* Paris: M. Rivière.
Debreu, G., and H. Scarf [1963] A Limit Theorem on the Core of an Economy, *International Economic Review* 4, 235–46.
Dubey, P., A. Mas-Colell, and M. Shubik [1980] Efficiency properties of Strategic Market Games: an Axiomatic Approach, *Journal of Economic Theory*, 22, 225–48.
Edgeworth, E.Y. [1881] *Mathematical Psychics*, London: Kegan Paul.
Green, E. [1980] Noncooperative Price Taking in Large Dynamic Markets, *Journal of Economic Theory*, 22, 37–64.
Gresik, T.A., and M.A. Satterthwaite [1984] "The Number of Traders Required

to Make a Market Competitive: The Beginnings of a Theory," manuscript, Managerial Economics and Decision Sciences, Kellogg School of Management, Northwestern University.

Gretsky, N., and J. Ostroy [1985] *Advances in Equilibrium Theory*, eds. Aliprantis, Burkinshaw and Rothman, Springer-Verlag 22, New York.

Grossman, S. [1981] "Nash Equilibrium and the Industrial Organization of Markets with Large Fixed Costs," *Econometrica* 49, 1149–72.

Hart, O. [1979] "Monopolistic Competition in a Large Economy with Differentiated Commodities," *Review of Economic Studies* 46, 1–30.

Hart, O. [1982] "Imperfect Competition in General Equilibrium: An Overview of Recent Work," London School of Economics Discussion Paper.

Mas-Colell, A. [1977] "Competitive and Value Allocations of Large Exchange Economies," *Journal of Economic Theory* 14, 419–38.

Novshek, W., and H. Sonnenschein [1978] "Cournot and Walras Equilibrium," *Journal of Economic Theory* 19, 223–66.

Ostroy, J. [1980] "The No-Surplus Condition as a Characterization of Perfectly Competitive Equilibrium," *Journal of Economic Theory* 22, 65–91.

Roberts, J. [1976] "Incentives for Correct Revelation of Preferences and the Number of Consumers," *Journal of Public Economics* 6, 359–74.

Roberts, K. [1980] "The Limit Points of Monopolistic Competition," *Journal of Economic Theory* 22, 141–65.

Roberts, K. [1983] "Self-Agreed Cartel Rules," IMSSS Working Paper, Department of Economics, Stanford University.

Shubik, M. [1973] "Commodity Money, Oligopoly, Credit and Bankruptcy in a General Equilibrium Model," *Western Economic Journal* 11, 24–28.

Stigler, G. [1964] "A Theory of Oligopoly," *Journal of Political Economics* 72, 44–61.

Stigler, G. [1965] "Perfect Competition Historically Contemplated," in *Essays in the History of Economics*, Chapter 8, Chicago: University of Chicago Press.

Townsend, R. [1983] "Theories of Intermediated Structures," *Carnegie-Rochester Conference Series on Public Policy* 18, eds. K. Brumner and A. Meltzer, 221–72.

1985

MENAHEM E. YAARI

On the Role of "Dutch Books" in the Theory of Choice Under Risk

I am honored to have been asked to deliver this lecture in memory of Nancy Schwartz. We who knew her as friend and colleague share a sadness that these lectures should take place in her memory rather than in her presence. Because Nancy Schwartz was professor of decision sciences at this University, it was felt that a memorial lecture devoted to the foundations of decision science – the theory of choice under risk – would be appropriate. My task is to be both general and specific at the same time. Generality alone (attempting to survey the field as a whole) would not have been feasible, and specificity alone (attempting to analyze a specific research problem) would not have been proper. My approach will consist, therefore, of trying to be general in scope but specific in point of view.

The foundations of the theory of choice under risk have now been explored systematically for more than half a century. The pioneers of this exploration were Knight, Ramsey, de Finetti, A. G. Hart, Von Neumann and Morgenstern; after them came many, many others. Yet, despite all this work, the foundations of choice under risk do not seem, even today, to have settled into a unified paradigm. Expected Utility theory, which comes closest to being a universally accepted paradigm, is an embattled position, subject to almost daily attack from various quarters. This is in sharp contrast to what we see in deterministic choice theory, where the Hicks-Allen paradigm – also formulated about 50 years ago – seems to rest unperturbed and unchallenged on its laurels.

The Expected Utility paradigm, beleaguered as it is at the foundations level, is nevertheless being used unquestioningly in applications. When analyzing such diverse phenomena as insurance markets, portfolio behavior, inventory holding, and consumption functions, economists adopt Expected Utility without even pausing to offer a justification. Here, in the realm of applications, Expected Utility shows admirable robustness. Most economists are not particularly disturbed by this apparent divergence between the precariousness at the foundations and the robustness in applications of Expected Utility theory. Using the type of arbitrage argument that economists love and cherish, they would set out to show that violations of Expected Utility behavior must necessarily be insignificant from an economic point of view. The argument runs as follows: An agent who violates Expected Utility theory is vulnerable to a so-called Dutch Book. What this means is that there exists a sequence of contracts – resulting in a sure loss of money – that this agent will accept. And since we do not observe friendly kiosks springing up at every corner and offering Dutch Books, we are entitled to conclude that non-Expected Utility behavior is a phenomenon that cannot have serious economic significance.

For the orthodox economist, considerations of immunity against a Dutch Book are a proper substitute for the theoretical foundations of the theory of choice under risk. Indeed, the fact that someone can design an experiment in which subjects systematically violate the axioms of Expected Utility theory is, for this economist, quite beside the point. Such deviant behavior, important as it may be in a psychological study of the perception of risk, is doomed to be weeded out by the market and is therefore outside the scope of economic observation. It is to this arbitrage argument – I shall refer to it as "the Dutch Book argument" – that I wish to devote today's lecture.

If the Dutch Book argument is to provide an alternative foundation for Expected Utility theory, it must consist of the following two, mutually converse, assertions: First, an agent who does *not* use Expected Utility to evaluate risky prospects is necessarily vulnerable to a Dutch Book. Second and conversely, an agent who *does* use Expected Utility to evaluate risky prospects is necessarily immune against a Dutch Book. The first assertion has been part of our folklore for many years. The converse assertion, on the other hand, has scarcely ever been discussed. In this lecture I shall review both sides of the argument, starting, naturally, with the first of the two assertions.

Consider an agent who must choose an action. The problem this agent faces is one of *choice under risk* if contemplated actions do not have unique consequences. The standard way of describing an action in this case is to write down a list of states-of-nature and to specify what the consequence of the action would be in each state. Thus, an action is a rule that associates a unique consequence with every state-of-nature. It is from among objects of this type that the agent is called upon to choose. Four conditions are required to hold if the agent's choice among actions is to accord with Expected Utility theory.

1) The agent is capable of ordering all actions, using some preference relation.
2) Judgments concerning the likelihood of states-of-nature, to the extent that such judgments are implicit in the agent's preferences among actions, must conform to the laws of probability theory.
3) Preference between two actions depends only on their consequences in states-of-nature where these consequences differ.
4) Strict preference between two actions remains undisturbed when their consequences are changed ever so slightly.

Of these four conditions, the first three can, at least in principle, be submitted to an empirical test for support or falsification. The fourth condition, however, is a metatheoretic device, designed to obtain coherence between an infinite theoretical model and a necessarily finite body of empirical observations. Thus, it seems appropriate to restrict our attention to the first three conditions and to check the extent to which they are supported by arguments of immunity against a Dutch Book.

The first condition says simply that agents have preferences and that these preferences are orderings. Will an agent who violates this condition be vulnerable to a Dutch Book? The existence of preferences, in itself, is almost definitional: An agent who must choose among actions will perforce exhibit a preference. (Note that inaction is itself an action, albeit a trivial one.) Perpetual indecision, as in the case of Buridan's ass, is not a serious issue to contend with. Whether one can assume that choices can reveal a *complete* set of preferences – every action being comparable to every other action – is a debatable matter. In any case, however, such completeness is not necessary for Expected Utility theory (Aumann [1962]). Thus, it is the second part of the condition – preferences constituting an ordering – that requires justification. Since the agent's choices among actions are observable, the question of whether the preferences gleaned from these choices form an ordering is one that can be submitted to empirical test. Here, *transitivity* is the crucial issue. (The other property needed for a weak order, reflexivity, is empirically trivial.) When making choices in risky situations, how likely are agents to exhibit intransitive preference? This was precisely the question posed by Tversky [1969]. In Tversky's experiments, subjects were asked to choose among actions of the form "receive $x if 'black,' receive $0 if 'white.'" The two states-of-nature, "black" and "white," were presented graphically to the subjects, using appropriately designed cards. Subjects were found to exhibit cyclical choices, which implies (assuming completeness) that their preferences failed to be transitive. Transitivity (or, more generally, a-cyclicity) thus fails to be confirmed empirically and, if we take this evidence seriously, we must abandon Expected Utility theory (and many other theories as well). Well, *should* we take this evidence seriously? The orthodox economist would say that we should not because such evidence can never be revealed in market behavior. To show this, the economist would offer the following argument, also discussed in Tversky's article:

Dutch Book no. 1 ("The Money Pump"). Consider an agent whose preferences among three actions, a, b, and c, are given by $a > b > c > a$, in violation of transitivity. (Here, $>$ denotes strict preference.) Let the agent choose among these three actions and assume, without loss of generality, that the agent's choice is a. (Inaction, if allowed, is itself one of the three alternatives.) We now approach the agent with the following sequence of offers:

1) For a small positive fee, we will allow you to change your mind and switch from a to c. (Offer accepted, by $c > a$.)
2) For a small positive fee, we will allow you – when holding c – to switch from c to b. (Offer accepted, by $b > c$.)
3) For a small positive fee, we will allow you – when holding b – to switch from b to a. (Offer accepted, by $a > b$.)

We find the agent being maneuvered in a cycle, merely to return to his or her initial position, while having lost a positive amount of money along the way. In a world full of hungry hyenas, such an agent would simply be wiped clean. Intransitivity cannot, therefore, be an economically viable phenomenon.

(Note that an implicit assumption has been hidden in the foregoing argument. It is the assumption that the preference pattern $a > b > c > a$ continues to hold, regardless of the agent's position in the progression from the initial position and back to that same position. If the agent's preferences change as his or her position changes, then the argument cannot be made.)

Having reached the conclusion that intransitivity cannot be an economically viable phenomenon, we now turn our attention to the second condition of Expected Utility theory, namely that the agent's judgment concerning the likelihood of various states-of-nature (or of more complicated events) must conform to the laws of probability theory. Several well-known authors had rejected this maxim (Shackle [1949], Fellner

[1961], Schmeidler [1984]); it was Ellsberg [1961] who was the first to offer empirical findings where subjects had systemically violated it. In particular, this evidence suggests that agents can regard two mutually exclusive and exhaustive events as equally likely but judge the sum of their "probabilities" to be less than unity. However, de Finetti [1937], who preceded Ellsberg by a generation, had offered an argument to the effect that observations of this type cannot enjoy economic viability. To get the simplest version of de Finetti's argument, let us consider two (mutually exclusive and exhaustive) states-of-nature, A and B. Let the symbol C stand for "certainty" ($C = A \cup B$). The actions considered by de Finetti were of the following type: An action is a triple of the form $(x_A, x_B, -x_C)$, with the interpretation that an agent who takes this action will have to *pay* an amount x_C with certainty before knowing which state-of-nature occurs, and in return the agent is to *receive* an amount x_A if A should occur and an amount x_B if B should occur (negative values are allowed). Let the agent have a preference order over these actions. Furthermore, we can take the action $(0,0,0)$ as the agent's initial position. Given this, let us write S_A for the agent's marginal rate of substitution between payment in A and payment with certainty (i.e., payment in C). Similarly, we let S_B be the agent's marginal rate of substitution between payment in B and payment in C. (Both marginal rates are evaluated at the agent's initial position.) Clearly, these marginal rates of substitution express the agent's judgments on the likelihoods of A and B. The laws of probability theory would therefore require that $S_A + S_B = 1$. What de Finetti showed was that if this equality fails (i.e., if $S_A + S_B \neq 1$), then the agent is vulnerable to a Dutch Book. The argument proceeds as follows:

Dutch Book no. 2. Assume differentiability and suppose that $S_A + S_B \neq 1$. By the definition of marginal rates of substitution, $S_A x_A + S_B x_B = x_C$ is the equation of the plane tangent to the agent's indifference surface at $(0,0,0)$. The action $(1,1,-1)$ – i.e., $(x_A, x_B, -x_C)$ with $x_A = x_B = x_C = 1$ – does *not* lie in this tangent plane. Therefore, there exists a λ, with $\lambda \neq 0$, such that $\lambda(1,1,-1)$ lies above the relevant indifference surface. In other words, there exists a λ such that $(\lambda, \lambda, -\lambda) > (0,0,0)$, with $>$ being strict preference. We now approach the agent with the following sequence:

1) Start at $(0,0,0)$.
2) For a small positive fee, we will allow you to switch to $(\lambda, \lambda, -\lambda)$. (Since $(\lambda, \lambda, -\lambda) > (0,0,0)$, this offer will be accepted.)
3) You must agree that $(\lambda, \lambda, -\lambda)$ is, in fact, the *same* action as $(0,0,0)$

because paying λ with certainty and receiving λ, whether A or B occur, is equivalent to having done nothing. (If the agent does not agree with this, another trivial Dutch Book will immediately be thrown at him or her.)

4) Observe that you are once again at $(0,0,0)$.

We find that the agent has been maneuvered in a cycle, ending at the initial position, except for a positive loss along the way. Survival in the jungles of the market would therefore force agents to comply with the additivity axiom of probability theory, i.e., to satisfy $S_A + S_B = 1$. Now de Finetti goes on to show that agents must also evaluate conditional probabilities in accordance with Bayes's rule or else be vulnerable to a similar Dutch Book. (More recently, Freedman and Purves [1969] have extended de Finetti's argument, showing that an agent who processes incoming information in a manner other than Bayesian updating of prior probabilities is also vulnerable to a Dutch Book.)

We come now to the crux of Expected Utility theory, the Independence Axiom (the third condition). To set the stage, let me define the notion of a simple action. An action will be called *simple* if there exist two numbers, x and p, with $x \geqq 0$ and $0 \leqq p \leqq 1$, such that taking the action would lead to the receipt of $\$x$ with probability p and $\$0$ with probability $1 - p$. The symbol $[x,p]$ will be used for this action. Simple actions have only two consequences, both being sums of money and one of them being 0. Moreover, probabilities take the place of explicit reference to states-of-nature. It turns out that, even when facing a choice among simple actions only, an agent who violates the Independence Axiom is necessarily vulnerable to a Dutch Book.

What is the Independence Axiom for simple actions? It is simply this: Let $[x,p]$ and $[y,q]$ be simple actions and consider the two lotteries (1) "get $[x,p]$ or get nothing, each with probability $1/2$" and (2) "get $[y,q]$ or get nothing, each with probability $1/2$." Then the agent's preference between (1) and (2) must conform to his or her preference between $[x,p]$ and $[y,q]$. Now the two lotteries, (1) and (2), are themselves simple actions. To see this, let us rewrite (1) as shown in the accompanying figure. Using Bayes's rule, we see that (1) is, in fact, equivalent to the simple action $[x,^p/_2]$. Similarly, (2) comes out to be equivalent to $[y,^q/_2]$. By de Finetti's argument, we know that the agent *must* use Bayes's rule when evaluating conditional probabilities or else be vulnerable to a Dutch Book. Hence, the agent must regard (1) as being the same as $[x,^p/_2]$ and (2) as being the same as $[y,^q/_2]$. The statement of the Independence Axiom therefore reduces to

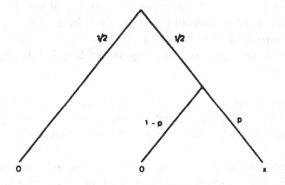

$$\left[x,p\right] \gtrsim \left[y,q\right] \quad \text{if and only if} \quad \left[x,\frac{p}{2}\right] \gtrsim \left[y,\frac{q}{2}\right]$$

where $\gtrsim$ stands for preference-or-indifference.

In recent years, a great deal of evidence has been gathered to the effect that subjects systemically violate this version of the Independence Axiom. (Such systematic behavior, in violation of the Axiom, has come to be known as "the common ratio effect.") Kahneman and Tversky [1979], for example, found that subjects tend to prefer [3000,1] over [4000,0.8], while tending to prefer [4000,0.2] over [3000,0.25], in violation of the Axiom. Should the economist be perturbed by this evidence? For an answer, we turn once again to a Dutch Book argument.

Dutch Book no. 3. Let [x,p] and [y,q] be simple actions and suppose that an agent has been found for whom the statements

$$\left[x,p\right] \gtrsim \left[y,q\right] \quad \text{and} \quad \left[y,\frac{q}{2}\right] > \left[x,\frac{p}{2}\right]$$

are true, in violation of the Independence Axiom (> indicates strict preference). The agent may now be approached with the following sequence:

1) We offer you $[x,^p/_2]$, free of charge. (Offer accepted, if $x \geqq 0$.)
2) For a small positive fee, we will allow you to switch to $[y,^q/_2]$. (Offer accepted, since $[y,^q/_2] > [x,^p/_2]$.)
3) What will actually happen is this: A fair coin will be tossed. Should tails turn up, you would collect $0 and go home. Should heads turn up, you would get [y,q]. You must agree that this is the same as holding $[y,^q/_2]$. (Agent must agree, for fear of de Finetti.)

4) For a small positive fee, we will allow you, if you should ever find yourself in possession of $[y,q]$, to switch from $[y,q]$ to $[x,p]$. (Offer accepted, by $[x,p] > [y,q]$.)
5) Please agree that you are once again holding $[x,^p/_2]$. (Agent agrees, as above.)

We find the agent being maneuvered in a cycle, starting at $[x,^p/_2]$ and ending at $[x,^p/_2]$, while having lost a positive amount of money along the way. Thus, violations of Independence cannot be an economically viable phenomenon.

The foregoing appears, in some discussions, as a *dynamic consistency* argument rather than as a Dutch Book argument. Dynamic consistency requires that the choice between two contingent actions be in conformity with what the choice would be after the relevant contingency materializes. Obviously, our Dutch Book capitalizes precisely on the absence of such dynamic consistency. Note also that the argument contains an implicit assumption, namely that the agent's preferences remain as they had been, as he or she proceeds along the cycle.

Success at last! We have established that, as economists, we need not be overly concerned about violations of Expected Utility behavior because such violations cannot be economically viable. The story does not end here, however. We have shown that violators of Expected Utility are necessarily vulnerable to a Dutch Book, but we have not shown that *adherents* of Expected Utility are necessarily immune against a Dutch Book. And, on examination, we find that this converse assertion is not true in general.

Once again, I will work with a preference order $\gtrsim$ defined over simple actions of the form $[x,p]$. As in the case of the Independence Axiom of Expected Utility theory, I will consider *mixtures* of simple actions, except that these mixtures will be formed in a different way. How shall we define a 50–50 mixture of $[x,p]$ and nothing? When Expected Utility is our goal, we define such a mixture as a *lottery* yielding $[x,p]$ and nothing, each with probability $^\pm/_2$. We then say that preference for $[x,p]$ over $[y,q]$ holds if and only if preference holds also for a 50–50 mixture of $[x,p]$ and nothing, over a 50–50 mixture of $[y,q]$ and nothing. But there is at least one other way of understanding the mixing of actions. Specifically, we can identify a 50–50 mixture of $[x,p]$ and nothing with a state in which the agent holds half a share in $[x,p]$ and half a share in "nothing." (Indeed, the phrase "half the action" is often used in precisely this sense in colloquial gambling language.) Now the mixture of half a share in $[x,p]$ and half a share in "nothing" is simply a 50 percent share in $[x,p]$ and nothing else. An Independence Axiom for this mixing operation is given, therefore, by the following: A preference for $[x,p]$ over $[y,q]$ holds if and only if preference holds also for a 50 percent share in $[x,p]$ over a 50 percent share in $[y,q]$. But a 50 percent share in $[x,p]$ is simply the action $[{}^x/_2,p]$, i.e., the action which produces half the payments produced by $[x,p]$. From this, one obtains a new axiom, which may be referred to as the *Dual Independence Axiom*:

$$[x,p] \succeq [y,q] \quad \text{if and only if} \quad \left[\frac{x}{2},p\right] \succeq \left[\frac{y}{2},q\right],$$

where $\succeq$ denotes preference-or-indifference.

It is not my intention in this lecture to examine the a priori plausibility or implausibility of this new axiom. (A detailed discussion may be found in Yaari [1985].) Suffice it to say that agents who behave according to Expected Utility theory do not, in general, satisfy this axiom. More precisely, the situation is this: An Expected Utility agent who satisfies the Dual Independence Axiom for simple actions only must have constant relative risk aversion (in the sense of Arrow and Pratt). An Expected Utility agent who satisfies the Dual Independence Axiom also for more general actions must be risk-neutral. The Dual Independence Axiom rules out general Expected Utility behavior. Yet, lo and behold, we find that failure to satisfy the Dual Independence Axiom immediately exposes the agent to a Dutch Book.

Dutch Book no. 4. Let $[x,p]$ and $[y,q]$ be simple actions and suppose that an agent has been found for whom the statements

$$[x,p] > [y,q] \quad \text{and} \quad \left[\frac{y}{2},q\right] > \left[\frac{x}{2},p\right]$$

are true, in violation of the Dual Independence Axiom ($>$ stands for strict preference). The agent may now be approached with the following sequence:

1) We offer you both $[{}^x/_2,p]$ and $[{}^y/_2,q]$, free of charge. (Offer accepted.)
2) For a small but positive fee, we will allow you to trade $[{}^x/_2,p]$ for another $[{}^y/_2,q]$. (Offer accepted, since $[{}^y/_2,q] > [{}^x/_2,p]$.)
3) You now possess two pieces of the action $[{}^y/_2,q]$, i.e., two halves of $[y,q]$. Please agree that you are in fact holding $[y,q]$. (Agent agrees, for fear of another – trivial – Dutch Book.)
4) For a small but positive fee, we will allow you to trade your $[y,q]$ for $[x,p]$. (Offer accepted, since $[x,p] > [y,q]$.)

5) You must agree that holding $[x,p]$ is the same thing as holding $[^x/_2,p]$ twice. (Agreed.)

6) For a small but positive fee, we will allow you to trade one of two $[^x/_2,p]$ actions for $[^y/_2,q]$. (Offer accepted, since $[^y/_2,q]$ > $[^x/_2,p]$.

The agent is found to have been maneuvered in a cycle, starting and ending at the same position (i.e., at the position of holding $[^x/_2,p]$ and $[^y/_2,q]$), while having lost a positive amount of money along the way. Violation of the Dual Independence Axiom cannot be economically viable. The foregoing argument depends, like previous Dutch Book arguments, on the assumption that the preference patterns $[x,p] > [y,q]$ and $[^y/_2,q] > [^x/_2,p]$ remain in force at all stages. This assumption appears to be quite strong when *hedging* is involved. However, the actions $[x,p]$ and $[y,q]$ can always be constructed in such a way that hedging is not a relevant consideration. To see this, let P be the set of states-of-nature where $[x,p]$ yields the amount x, and let Q be the set of states-of-nature where $[y,q]$ yields the amount y. If one of these two sets, P and Q, is a subset of the other – and this can always be arranged – then $[x,p]$ and $[y,q]$ cannot be used to hedge against each other.

Here the story ends. For me, its moral is that, as economists, we face the following dilemma: We must either take the extreme position that all agents are risk-neutral or else agree that agents would, in general, be vulnerable to a Dutch Book. If nonrisk-neutral behavior is economically viable, then vulnerability to a Dutch Book must also be economically viable, whether the Prophets of Arbitrage like it or not.

ADDENDUM (JULY 1985)

Friends have persuaded me that I would do well to try and clarify some points left unclear in my lecture on Dutch Books. I shall retain the notation that I had used in the lecture itself, without repeating any of the definitions. The abbreviation DB will be used for Dutch Book, with DB1 standing for Dutch Book no. 1, etc.

Consider an agent with a preference relation $\gtrsim$ and suppose that there exist nonnegative real numbers x, y, p, q, with $p \leqq 1$ and $q \leqq 1$, such that the preference statements

$$\left[x,p\right] > \left[y,q\right] \quad \text{and} \quad \left[y,\frac{q}{2}\right] > \left[x,\frac{p}{2}\right] \tag{1}$$

are true for this particular agent. We have here a violation of Independence, leading us to consider the following sequence:

$$\left[x, \frac{p}{2}\right] < \left[y, \frac{q}{2}\right]$$

$$\equiv \begin{Bmatrix} [y,q] & \text{if heads} \\ 0 & \text{if tails} \end{Bmatrix}$$

$$< \begin{Bmatrix} [x,p] & \text{if heads} \\ 0 & \text{if tails} \end{Bmatrix}$$

$$\equiv \left[x, \frac{p}{2}\right] \tag{2}$$

where $A \equiv B$ is the assertion that possessing A is equivalent to possessing B, by Bayes's Rule. By a Dutch Book argument like DB2, we must have $(A \equiv B) \Rightarrow (A \sim B)$. Hence, (2) leads to

$$\left[x, \frac{p}{2}\right] < \left[y, \frac{q}{2}\right]$$

$$\sim \begin{Bmatrix} [y,q] & \text{if heads} \\ 0 & \text{if tails} \end{Bmatrix}$$

$$< \begin{Bmatrix} [x,p] & \text{if heads} \\ 0 & \text{if tails} \end{Bmatrix}$$

$$\sim \left[x, \frac{p}{2}\right] \tag{3}$$

which describes a sequence exactly as in DB3: The agent is being led along a cycle, starting and ending at $[x, ^p/_2]$, while enjoying a positive improvement in preference along the way. This immediately brings up the following three comments:

a) If $\gtrsim$ is a reflexive and transitive relation, then (3) is false.
b) Since (1) is consistent with reflexivity and transitivity, (3) cannot be deduced from (1).
c) Indeed, the third link in (3), viz.

$$\begin{Bmatrix} [y,q] & \text{if heads} \\ 0 & \text{if tails} \end{Bmatrix} < \begin{Bmatrix} [x,p] & \text{if heads} \\ 0 & \text{if tails} \end{Bmatrix} \tag{4}$$

cannot be deduced from (1), because (4) follows from $[x,p] > [y,q]$ only under Independence, when in fact it is assumed that $\gtrsim$ does *not* satisfy Independence.

These are sound comments. (a) and (b) amount to the assertion that Independence cannot be reduced to reflexivity and transitivity. Then (c) proceeds to locate the logical flaw in an argument which, if valid, would have achieved the impossible, i.e., reduced Independence to reflexivity and transitivity.

Well, then, what about DB3? What is its message? Consider an agent with stable preferences who makes the following two undertakings:

i) At my present asset position, if I should ever be faced with a choice between $[x,p]$ and $[y,q]$, I would pick $[x,p]$.

ii) At my present asset position, if I should ever be faced with a choice between $[x,{}^p/_2]$ and $[y,{}^q/_2]$, I would pick $[y,{}^q/_2]$.

(The reference to asset position is necessary because, for an agent with stable preferences, a change asset position can account for choice reversal.) DB3 says that (i) and (ii) are inconsistent with rational choice, if the term "should ever be faced . . ." is deemed to include facing the choice after a certain coin has been tossed. Equivalently, DB3 says that, for (i) and (ii) to be consistent with rational choice, it is necessary to include within the agent's "asset position" such information as whether choices are to be made before or after the toss of a certain coin has been observed.

More formally, let c be the agent's choice function at some initial position and let c_H be the agent's choice function after being informed that a certain coin has turned up heads. The agent's two undertakings, (i) and (ii), can be written as follows:

i) $c(\{[x,p],[y,q]\}) = \{[x,p]\}$
ii) $c(\{[x,{}^p/_2],[y,{}^q/_2]\}) = \{[y,{}^q/_2]\}$.

To these, let me now add three further conditions:

iii) The choice function c is Bayes-respecting.[1]
iv) On the domain of c_H, the functions c and c_H coincide.
v) The function c is rationalizable.

What DB3 says is that the conditions (i)–(v) are incompatible. (In the lecture, condition (iv) appears somewhat obscurely, in the form of a statement concerning the agent's preferences remaining unchanged along the cycle. I should have placed more emphasis on this point.)

A similar state of affairs exists with regard to DB4. Let an agent satisfy

---

[1] Let S be a set of gambles (or actions) and define $B(S)$ to be the set of one-stage lotteries obtained from elements of S by Bayes's Rule. Then, c is said to be *Bayes-respecting* if, for all S, we have $c(B(S)) = B(c(S))$, i.e., if B and c commute.

$$[x,p] > [y,q] \quad \text{and} \quad \left[\tfrac{y}{2},q\right] > \left[\tfrac{x}{2},p\right] \tag{5}$$

and consider the sequence:

$$\left(\left[\tfrac{x}{2},p\right] \,\&\, \left[\tfrac{y}{2},q\right]\right) < \left(\left[\tfrac{y}{2},q\right] \,\&\, \left[\tfrac{y}{2},q\right]\right)$$
$$\equiv [y,q]$$
$$< [x,p]$$
$$\equiv \left(\left[\tfrac{x}{2},p\right] \,\&\, \left[\tfrac{x}{2},p\right]\right)$$
$$< \left(\left[\tfrac{x}{2},p\right] \,\&\, \left[\tfrac{y}{2},q\right]\right) \tag{6}$$

with $(A\&B)$ being the state of possessing both A and B, $(A\&A)$ being the state of possessing two copies of A, and $A \equiv B$ being the assertion that possessing A is physically equivalent to possessing B. In (6), the first and third $<$ signs supposedly follow from $[^y/_2,q] > [^x/_2,p]$, while the second $<$ sign is from $[x,p] > [y,q]$. Once again, we must have $(A \equiv B) \Rightarrow (A \sim B)$, so (6) reduces to

$$\left(\left[\tfrac{x}{2},p\right] \,\&\, \left[\tfrac{y}{2},q\right]\right) < \left(\left[\tfrac{y}{2},q\right] \,\&\, \left[\tfrac{y}{2},q\right]\right)$$
$$\sim [y,q]$$
$$< [x,p]$$
$$\sim \left(\left[\tfrac{x}{2},p\right] \,\&\, \left[\tfrac{x}{2},p\right]\right)$$
$$< \left(\left[\tfrac{x}{2},p\right] \,\&\, \left[\tfrac{y}{2},q\right]\right) \tag{7}$$

This is impossible if the agent's preference relation is reflexive and transitive. Since (5) is consistent with reflexivity and transitivity, we conclude that (7) cannot be deduced from (5). In other words, Dual Independence cannot be deduced from reflexivity and transitivity. This is obvious. If in my lecture, DB4 can be construed as claiming to deduce Dual Independence from reflexivity and transitivity, then I am guilty of misleading the reader (and the listener), and clarification is called for. Once again, it is best to look at the agent's choice function, with changes in asset position explicitly recognized. Let c be the agent's choice function at some initial asset position, and let c_A be his/her choice function at a new asset position, A. Now consider the following five statements:

i) $c(\{[x,p],[y,q]\}) = \{[x,p]\}$

ii) $c(\{[^x/_2,p],[^y/_2,q]\}) = \{[^y/_2,q]\}$

iii) $c_{[x/_2,p]}(\{[^x/_2,p],[^y/_2,q]\}) = c(\{[^x/_2,p],[^y/_2,q]\})$

iv) $c_{[y/_2,q]}(\{[^x/_2,p],[^y/_2,q]\}) = c(\{[^x/_2,p],[^y/_2,q]\})$

v) c is rationalizable.

DB4 says that, if it is agreed that possessing two copies of half the action is equivalent to possessing the action itself, then the conditions (i)–(iv) are incompatible. In order to judge the significance of this assertion, we must ask ourselves whether conditions (iii) and (iv) are a priori reasonable or not. My own feeling is that (iii) and (iv) are reasonable conditions, a priori, if the joint distribution of $[x,p]$ and $[y,q]$ is such that neither of them is a hedge against the other. Note that (iii) and (iv) are very similar in spirit to condition (iv) in the earlier discussion of DB3.

References

Aumann, R.J. [1962] "Utility Theory Without the Completeness Axiom," *Econometrica*, 30, 445–62.

de Finetti, B. [1937] "La Prévision: ses lois logiques, ses sources subjectives," *Annales de l'Institut Henri Poincaré*, 7, 1–68.

Ellsberg, D. [1961] "Risk, Ambiguity, and the Savage Axioms," *Quarterly Journal of Economics*, 75, 643–69.

Fellner, W. [1961] "Distortion of Subjective Probabilities as a Reaction to Uncertainty," *Quarterly Journal of Economics*, 75, 670–89.

Freedman, D.A., and R.A. Purves [1969] "Bayes' Method for Bookies," *Annals of Mathematical Statistics*, 40, 1177–86.

Kahneman, D., and A. Tversky [1979] "Prospect Theory: An Analysis of Decision under Risk," *Econometrica*, 47, 263–91.

Schmeidler, D. [1984] "Subjective Probability and Expected Utility Without Additivity," IMA Preprint Series #84, the University of Minnesota.

Shackle, G.L.S. [1949] "A Non-Additive Measure of Uncertainty," *Review of Economic Studies*, 17, 70–74.

Tversky, A. [1969] "Intransitivity of Preferences," *Psychological Review*, 76, 31–48.

Yaari, M.E. [1985] "Risk Aversion Without Diminishing Marginal Utility and the Dual Theory of Choice Under Risk," R.M. 65, Center for Research in Mathematical Economics, the Hebrew University.

1986

ROBERT J. AUMANN
Rationality and Bounded Rationality

I am honored to present this lecture in tribute to Nancy L. Schwartz. I did not know Professor Schwartz well, yet I am aware of her important professional contributions. First and foremost are the direct advances to the profession made through her writings. But also her indirect contributions, as a teacher and an intellectual leader, are very important. Some of the ideas and applications discussed in this lecture were developed in the excellent department she helped build.

INTRODUCTION

Economists have for long expressed dissatisfaction with the complex models of strict rationality that are so pervasive in economic theory. There are several objections to such models. First, casual empiricism or even just simple introspection leads to the conclusion that even in quite simple decision problems, most economic agents are not in fact maximizers, in the sense that they do not scan the choice set and consciously pick a maximal element from it. Second, such maximizations are often

Research for this lecture was supported by the National Science Foundation under Grant IRI-8814953. Subsequent versions of the lecture were presented at a workshop on bounded rationality at the Institute for Mathematical Studies in the Social Sciences (Economics), Stanford University, July 1989; at the Fourth Conference on Theoretical Aspects of Reasoning about Knowledge, Monterey, March 1992; and at the NATO Advanced Study Institute on Game Theoretic Approaches to Cooperation, Stony Brook, July 1994. Reprinted from *Games and Economic Behavior*, 21, no. 1/2 (1997), 2–14, with permission from Academic Press.

quite difficult, and even if they wanted to, most people (including economists and even computer scientists) would be unable to carry them out in practice. Third, polls and laboratory experiments indicate that people often fail to conform to some of the basic assumptions of rational decision theory. Fourth, laboratory experiments indicate that the conclusions of rational analysis (as distinguished from the assumptions) sometimes fail to conform to "reality." And finally, the conclusions of rational analysis sometimes seem unreasonable even on the basis of simple introspection.

From my point of view, the last two of the above objections are more compelling than the first three. In science, it is more important that the conclusions be right than that the assumptions sound reasonable. The assumption of a gravitational force seems totally unreasonable on the face of it, yet leads to correct conclusions. "By their fruits ye shall know them" (Matthew 7, 16).

In the sequel, though, we shall not hew strictly to this line; we shall examine various models that, between them, address all the above issues.

To my knowledge, this area was first extensively investigated by Herbert Simon (1955, 1972). Much of Simon's work was conceptual rather than formal. For many years after this initial work, it was recognized that the area was of great importance, but the lack of a formal approach impeded its progress. Particular components of Simon's ideas, such as satisficing, were formalized by several workers, but never led to an extensive theory, and indeed did not appear to have significant implications that went beyond the formulations themselves.

There is no unified theory of bounded rationality, and probably never will be. Here we examine several different but related approaches to the problem, which have evolved over the last ten or fifteen years. We will not survey the area, but discuss some of the underlying ideas. For clarity, we may sometimes stake out a position in a fashion that is more one-sided and extreme than we really feel; we have the highest respect and admiration for all the scientists whose work we cite, and beg them not to take offense.

From the point of view of the volume of research, the field has "taken off" in the last half-dozen years. An important factor in making this possible was the development of computer science, complexity theory, and so on, areas of inquiry that created an intellectual climate conducive to the development of the theory of bounded rationality. A significant catalyst was the experimental work of Robert Axelrod (1984) in the late seventies and early eighties, in which experts were asked to prepare computer programs for playing the repeated prisoner's dilemma. The idea of a computer program for playing repeated games presaged some of the central ideas of the later work; and the winner of Axelrod's tournament – *tit for tat* – was, because of its simplicity, nicely illustrative of the bounded rationality idea. Also, repeated games became the context of much of the subsequent work.

The remainder of this lecture is divided into five parts. First we discuss the evolutionary approach to optimization – and specifically to game theory – and some of its implications for the idea of bounded rationality, such as the development of truly dynamic theories of games, and the idea of "rule rationality" (as opposed to "act rationality"). Next comes the area of "trembles," including equilibrium refinements, "crazy" perturbations, failure of common knowledge of rationality, the limiting average payoff in infinitely repeated games as an expression of bounded rationality, ε-equilibria, and related topics. Part 3 deals with players who are modeled as computers (finite state automata, Turing machines), which has now become perhaps the most active area in the field. In Part 4 we discuss the work on the foundations of decision theory that deals with various paradoxes (such as Allais (1953) and Ellsberg (1961)) and with results of laboratory experiments by relaxing various of the postulates and so coming up with a weaker theory. Part 5 is devoted to an open problem.

Most of this lecture is set in the framework of noncooperative game theory, because most of the work has been in that framework. Game theory is indeed particularly appropriate for discussing fundamental ideas in this area, because it is relatively free from special institutional features. The basic ideas are probably applicable to economic contexts that are not game-theoretic (if there are any).

1. EVOLUTION

Nash Equilibria as Population Equilibria

One of the simplest, yet most fundamental ideas in bounded rationality – indeed in game theory as a whole – is that no rationality at all is required to arrive at a Nash equilibrium; insects and even flowers can and do arrive at Nash equilibria, perhaps more reliably than human beings. The Nash equilibria of a strategic (normal) form game correspond precisely to population equilibria of populations that interact in accordance with the rules – and payoffs – of the game.

A version of this idea – the evolutionarily stable strategy – was first developed by John Maynard Smith (1982) in the early seventies and applied by him to many biological contexts (most of them animal conflicts within a species). But the idea applies also to Nash equilibria –

not only to interaction within a species, but also to interactions between different species. It is worthwhile to give a more precise statement of this correspondence.

Consider, then, two populations – let us first think of them as different species – whose members interact in some way. It might be predator and prey, or cleaner and host fish, or bees and flowers, or whatever. Each interaction between an individual of population A and one of population B results in an increment (or decrement) in the fitness of each; recall that the fitness of an individual is defined as the expected number of its offspring (I use "its" on purpose, since strictly speaking, reproduction must be asexual for this to work). This increment is the payoff to each of the individuals for the encounter in question. The payoff is determined by the genetic endowment of each of the interacting individuals (more or less aggressive or watchful or keen-sighted or cooperative, etc.). Thus one may write a bimatrix in which the rows and columns represent the various possible genetic endowments of the two respective species (or rather those different genetic endowments that are relevant to the kind of interaction being examined), and the entries represent the single encounter payoffs that we just described. If one views this bimatrix as a game, then the Nash equilibria of this game correspond precisely to population equilibria; that is, under asexual reproduction, the proportions of the various genetic endowments within each population remain constant from generation to generation if and only if these proportions constitute a Nash equilibrium.

This is subject to the following qualification: in each generation, there must be at least a very small proportion of each kind of genetic endowment; that is, each row and column must be represented by at least some individuals. This minimal presence, whose biological interpretation is that it represents possible mutations, is to be thought of as infinitesimal; specifically, an encounter between two such mutants (in the two populations) is considered impossible.

A similar story can be told for games with more than two players, and for evolutionary processes other than biological ones; e.g., economic evolution, like the development of the QWERTY typewriter keyboard, studied by the economic historian Paul David (1986). It also applies to learning processes that are perhaps not strictly analogous to asexual reproduction. And though it does not apply to sexual reproduction, still one may hope that roughly speaking, similar ideas may apply.

One may ask who are the "players" in this "game"? The answer is that the two "players" are the two populations (i.e., the two species). The individuals are definitely *not* the "players"; if anything, each individual corresponds to the pure strategy representing its genetic endowment (note that there is no sense in which an individual can "choose" its own genetic endowment). More accurately, though, the pure strategies represent kinds of genetic endowment, and not individuals. Individuals indeed play no explicit role in the mathematical model; they are swallowed up in the proportions of the various pure strategies.

Some biologists object to this interpretation, because they see it as implying group or species selection rather than individual selection. The player is not the species, they argue; the individual "acts for its own good," not the good of the group, or of the population, or of the species. Some even argue that it is the gene (or rather the allele) that "acts for its own good," not the individual. The point, though, is that nothing at all in this model really "acts for its own good"; nobody "chooses" anything. It is the process as a whole that selects the traits. The most we can do is ask what it is that corresponds to the player in the mathematical model, and this is undoubtedly the population.

A question that at first seems puzzling is what happens in the case of interactions within a species, like animal conflicts for females, etc. Who are the players in this game? If the players are the populations, then this must be a one-person game, since there is only one population. But that doesn't look right, either, and it certainly doesn't correspond to the biological models of animal conflicts.

The answer is that it is a two-person symmetric game, in which both players correspond to the same population. In this case we look not for just any Nash equilibria, but for symmetric ones only.

Evolutionary Dynamics

The question of developing a "truly" dynamic theory of games has long intrigued game theorists and economic theorists. (If I am not mistaken, it is one of the conceptual problems listed by Kuhn and Tucker (1953) in the introduction to Volume II of *Contributions to the Theory of Games* – perhaps the last one in that remarkably prophetic list to be successfully solved.) The difficulty is that ordinary rational players have foresight, so they can contemplate all of time from the beginning of play. Thus the situation can be seen as a one-shot game each play of which is actually a long sequence of "stage games," and then one has lost the dynamic character of the situation.

The evolutionary approach outlined above "solves" this conceptual difficulty by eliminating the foresight. Since the process is mechanical, there is indeed no foresight; no strategies for playing the repeated game are available to the "players."

And indeed, a fascinating dynamic theory does emerge. Contributions to this theory have been made by Young (1993), Foster and Young (1990), and Kandori, Mailath, and Rob (1993). A book on the subject has been written by Hofbauer and Sigmund (1988) and there is an excellent chapter on evolutionary dynamics in the book by van Damme (1987) on refinements of Nash equilibrium. Many others have also contributed to the subject.

It turns out that Nash equilibria are often unstable, and one gets various kinds of cycling effects. Sometimes the cycles are "around" the equilibrium, like in "matching pennies," but at other times one gets more complicated behavior. For example, the game

	0	5	4
0	4	5	
	4	0	5
5	0	4	
	5	4	0
4	5	0	

has $((1/3, 1/3, 1/3), (1/3, 1/3, 1/3))$ as its only Nash equilibrium; the evolutionary dynamic does not cycle "around" this point, but rather confines itself (more or less) to the strategy pairs in which the payoff is 4 or 5. This suggests a possible connection with correlated equilibria; this possibility has recently been investigated by Foster and Vohra (1997).

Thus evolutionary dynamics emerges as a form of rationality that is bounded, in that foresight is eliminated.

"Rule Rationality" vs. "Act Rationality"

In a famous experiment conducted by Güth et al. (1982) and later repeated, with important variations, by Binmore et al. (1985), two players were asked to divide a considerable sum of money (ranging as high as DM 100). The procedure was that P1 made an offer, which could be either accepted or rejected by P2; if it was rejected, nobody got anything. The players did not know each other and never saw each other; communication was a one-time affair via computer.

"Rational" play would predict a 99-1 split, or 95-5 at the outside. Yet in by far the most trials, the offered split was between 50-50 and 65-35. This is surprising enough in itself. But even more surprising is that in most (all?) cases in which P2 was offered less than 30 percent, he actually refused. Thus, he preferred to walk away from as much as DM 25 or 30. How can this be reconciled with ordinary notions of utility maximization, not to speak of game theory?

It is tempting to answer that a player who is offered five or ten percent is "insulted." Therefore, his utilities change; he gets positive probability from "punishing" the other player.

That's all right as far as it goes, but it doesn't go very far; it doesn't explain very much. The "insult" is treated as exogenous. But obviously the "insult" arose from the situation. Shouldn't we treat the "insult" itself endogenously, somehow explain it game-theoretically?

I think that a better way of explaining the phenomenon is as follows: Ordinary people do not behave in a consciously rational way in their day-to-day activities. Rather, they evolve "rules of thumb" that work in general, by an evolutionary process like that discussed above (pp. 49–52), or a learning process with similar properties. Such "rules of thumb" are like genes (or rather, alleles). If they work well, they are fruitful and multiply; if they work poorly, they become rare and eventually extinct.

One such rule of thumb is "Don't be a sucker; don't let people walk all over you." In general, the rule works well, so it becomes widely adopted. As it happens, the rule doesn't apply to Güth's game, because in that particular situation, a player who refuses DM 30 does not build up his reputation by the refusal (because of the built-in anonymity). But the rule has not been consciously chosen, and will not be consciously abandoned.

So we see that the evolutionary paradigm yields a third form of bounded rationality: rather than consciously maximizing in each decision situation, players use rules of thumb that work well "on the whole."

2. PERTURBATIONS OF RATIONALITY

Equilibrium Refinements

Equilibrium refinements – Selten (1975), Myerson (1978), Kreps and Wilson (1982), Kalai and Samet (1984), Kohlberg and Mertens (1986), Basu and Weibull (1991), van Damme (1984), Reny (1992), Cho and Kreps (1987), and many others – don't really sound like bounded rationality. They sound more like superrationality, since they go beyond the basic utility maximization that is inherent in Nash equilibrium. In addition to Nash equilibrium, which demands rationality on the equilibrium path, they demand rationality also off the equilibrium path. Yet all are based in one way or another on "trembles" – small departures from rationality.

The paradox is resolved by noting that in game situations, one player's irrationality requires another one's superrationality. You must be superrational in order to deal with my irrationalities. Since this applies to all players, taking account of possible irrationalities leads to a kind of superrationality for all. To be superrational, one must leave the equilibrium path. Thus, a more refined concept of rationality cannot feed on itself only; it can only be defined in the context of irrationality.

Crazy Perturbations

An idea related to the trembling hand is the theory of irrational or "crazy" types, as propounded first by the "Gang of Four" (Kreps, Milgrom, Roberts, and Wilson (1982)), and then taken up by Fudenberg and Maskin (1986), Aumann and Sorin (1989), Fudenberg and Levine (1989), and no doubt others. In this work there is some kind of repeated or other dynamic game set-up; it is assumed that with high probability the players are "rational" in the sense of being utility maximizers, but that with a small probability, one or both play some one strategy, or one of a specified set of strategies, that are "crazy" – have no a priori relationship to rationality. An interesting aspect of this work, which differentiates it from the "refinement" literature, and makes it particularly relevant to the theory of bounded rationality, is that it is usually the crazy type, or a crazy type, that wins out – takes over the game, so to speak. Thus, in the original work of the Gang of Four on the prisoner's dilemma, there is only one crazy type, who always plays tit-for-tat, no matter what the other player does; and it turns out that the rational type must imitate the crazy type, he must also play tit-for-tat, or something quite close to it. Also, the "crazy" types, while irrational in the sense that they do not maximize utility, are usually by no means random or arbitrary (as they are in refinement theory). For example, we have already noted that tit-for-tat is computationally a very simple object, far from random. In the work of Aumann and Sorin, the crazy types are identified with bounded recall strategies; and in the work of Fudenberg and Levine, the crazy types form a denumerable set, suggesting that they might be generated in some systematic manner, e.g., by Turing machines. There must be method to the madness; this is associated with computational simplicity, which is another one of the underlying ideas of bounded rationality.

Epsilon-equilibria

Rather than playing irrationally with a small probability (as in pp. 53–54), one may deviate slightly from rationality by playing so as almost, but not quite, to maximize utility; i.e., by playing to obtain a payoff that is within ε of the optimum payoff. This idea was introduced by Radner (1980) in the context of repeated games, in particular of the repeated prisoner's dilemma; he showed that in a long but finitely repeated prisoner's dilemma, there are ε-equilibria with small ε in which the players "cooperate" until close to the end (though, as is well-known, all exact equilibria lead to a constant stream of "defections").

Infinitely Repeated Games with Limit-of-the-Average Payoff

There is an interesting connection between ε-equilibria in finitely repeated games, and infinitely repeated games with limit of the average payoff ("undiscounted"). The limit of the average payoff has been criticized as not representing any economic reality; many workers prefer to use either the finitely repeated game or limits of payoffs in discounted games with small discounts. Radner, Myerson, and Maskin (1986), Forges, Mertens, and Neyman (1986), and perhaps others, have demonstrated that the results of these two kinds of analysis can indeed be quite different.

Actually, though, the infinitely repeated undiscounted game is in some ways a simpler and more natural object than the discounted or finite game. In calculating equilibria of a finite or discounted game, one must usually specify the number n of repetitions or the discount rate δ; the equilibria themselves depend crucially on these parameters. But one may want to think of such a game simply as "long," without specifying *how* long. Equilibria in the undiscounted game may be thought of as "rules of thumb," which tell a player how to play in a "long repetition," independently of how long the repetition is. Whereas limits of finite or discounted equilibrium payoffs tell the player approximately how much *payoff* to expect in a long repetition, analysis of the undiscounted game tells him approximately how to *play*.

Thus, the undiscounted game is a framework for formulating the idea of a duration-independent strategy in a repeated game. Indeed, it may be shown that an equilibrium in the undiscounted game is an approximate equilibrium simultaneously in all the n-stage truncations, the approximation getting better and better as n grows. Formally, a strategy profile ("tuple") is an equilibrium in the undiscounted game if and only if for some sequence of ε_n tending to zero, each of its n-stage truncations is an ε_n-equilibrium (in the sense of Radner described above) in the n-stage truncation of the game.

Failure of Common Knowledge of Rationality

In their paper on the repeated prisoner's dilemma, the Gang of Four pointed out that the effect they were demonstrating holds not only when one of the players believes that with some small probability, the other is a tit-for-tat automaton, but also if one of them only believes (with small probability) that the other believes this about him (with small probability). More generally, it can be shown that many of the perturbation effects we have been discussing do not require an actual departure from rationality on the part of the players, but only a lack of common knowledge of rationality (Aumann 1992).

3.   AUTOMATA, COMPUTERS, AND TURING MACHINES

We come now to what is probably the mainstream of the newer work in bounded rationality, namely, the theoretical work that has been done in the last four or five years on automata and Turing machines playing repeated games. The work was pioneered by A. Neyman (1985) and A. Rubinstein (1986), working independently and in very different directions. Subsequently, the theme was taken up by Ben-Porath (1993), Kalai and Stanford (1988), Zemel (1989), Abreu and Rubinstein (1988), Ben-Porath and Peleg (1987), Lehrer (1988), Papadimitriou (1992), Stearns (1989), and many others, each of whom made significant new contributions to the subject in various different directions. Different branches of this work have been started by Lewis (1985) and Binmore (1987, 1988), who have also had their following.

It is impossible to do justice to all this work in a reasonable amount of time, and we content ourselves with brief descriptions of some of the major strands. In one strand, pioneered by Neyman, the players of a repeated game are limited to using mixtures of pure strategies, each of which can be programmed on a finite automaton with an exogenously fixed number of states. This is reminiscent of the work of Axelrod, who required the entrants in his experiment to write the strategies in a Fortran program not exceeding a stated limit in length. In another strand, pioneered by Rubinstein, the size of the automaton is endogenous; computer capacity, so to speak, is considered costly, and any capacity that is not actually used in equilibrium play is discarded. The two approaches lead to very different results. The reason is that Rubinstein's approach precludes the use of "punishment" or "trigger" strategies, which swing into action only when a player departs from equilibrium, and whose sole function is precisely to prevent such departures. In the evolutionary interpretation of repeated games, Rubinstein's approach may be more appropriate when the stages of the repeated game represent successive generations, whereas Neyman's may be more appropriate when each generation plays the entire repeated game (which would lead to the evolution of traits having to do with reputation, like "Don't be a sucker").

The complexity of computing an optimal strategy in a repeated game, or even just a best response to a given strategy, has been the subject of works by several authors, including Gilboa (1988), Ben-Porath (1990), and Papadimitriou (1992). Related work has been done by Lewis (1992), though in the framework of recursive function theory (which is related to infinite Turing machines) rather than complexity theory (which has to do with finite computing devices). Roughly speaking, the results are qualitatively similar: finding maxima is hard. Needless to say, in the evolutionary approach to games, nobody has to find the maxima; they are picked out by evolution. Thus, the results of complexity theory again underscore the importance of the evolutionary approach.

Binmore (1987, 1988) and his followers have modeled games as pairs (or n-tuples) of Turing machines in which each machine carries in it some kind of idea of what the other "player" (machine) might look like.

Other important strands include work by computer scientists who have made the connection between distributed computing and games ("computers as players," rather than "players as computers"). For a survey, see Linial (1994).

4. RELAXATION OF RATIONALITY POSTULATES

A not uncommon activity of decision, game, and economic theorists since the fifties has been to call attention to the strength of various postulates of rationality, and to investigate the consequences of relaxing them. Many workers in the field – including the writer of these lines – have at one time or another done this kind of thing. People have constructed theories of choice without transitivity, without completeness, violating the sure-thing principle, and so on. Even general equilibrium theorists have engaged in this activity, which may be considered a form of limited rationality (on the part of the agents in the model). This kind of work is most interesting when it leads to outcomes that are qualitatively different – not just weaker – from those obtained with the stronger assumptions; but I don't recall many such cases. It can also be very interesting and worthwhile when one gets roughly similar results with significantly weaker assumptions.

5.   AN OPEN PROBLEM

We content ourselves with one open problem, which is perhaps the most challenging conceptual problem in the area today: to develop a meaningful formal definition of rationality in a situation in which calculation and analysis themselves are costly and/or limited. In the models we have discussed up to now, the problem has always been well defined, in the sense that an absolute maximum is chosen from among the set of feasible alternatives, no matter how complex a process that maximization may be. The alternatives themselves involve bounded rationality, but the process of choosing them does not.

Here, too, an evolutionary approach may eventually turn out to be the key to a general solution.

References

Abreu, D. and A. Rubinstein (1988), "The Structure of Nash Equilibrium in Repeated Games with Finite Automata," *Econometrica*, 56, 1259–1281.

Allais, M. (1953), "Le Comportement de l'Homme Rationnel devant le Risque: Critiques des Postulats et Axioms de l'Ecole Americaine," *Econometrica*, 21, 503–546.

Aumann, R. J. (1992), "Irrationality in Game Theory," in *Economic Analysis of Markets and Games: Essays in Honor of Frank Hahn*, edited by P. Dasgupta, D. Gale, O. Hart, and E. Maskin, Cambridge and London: MIT Press, 214–227.

Aumann, R. J. and M. Maschler (1995), *Repeated Games with Incomplete Information*, Cambridge and London: MIT Press.

Aumann, R. J. and S. Sorin (1989), "Cooperation and Bounded Recall," *Games and Economic Behavior*, 1, 5–39.

Axelrod, R. (1984), *The Evolution of Cooperation*, New York: Basic Books.

Basu, K. and J. W. Weibull (1991), "Strategy Subsets Closed under Rational Behavior," *Economics Letters*, 36, 141–146.

Ben-Porath, E. (1990), "The Complexity of Computing Best Response Automata in Repeated Games with Mixed Strategies," *Games and Economic Behavior*, 2, 1–12.

―― (1993), "Repeated Games with Finite Automata," *Journal of Economic Theory*, 59, 17–32.

Ben-Porath, E. and B. Peleg (1987), "On the Folk Theorem and Finite Automata," Center for Research in Mathematical Economics and Game Theory, The Hebrew University of Jerusalem, Res. Mem. 77.

Binmore, K. G. (1987), "Modelling Rational Players I," *Economics and Philosophy*, 3, 179–214.

―― (1988), "Modelling Rational Players II," *Economics and Philosophy*, 4, 9–55.

Binmore, K., A. Shaked and J. Sutton (1985), "Testing Noncooperative Bargaining Theory: A Preliminary Study," *Amer. Econ. Rev.*, 75, 1178–1180.

Cho, I.-K. and D. Kreps (1987), "Signaling Games and Stable Equilibria," *Quarterly Journal of Economics*, 102, 179–221.

David, P. A. (1986), "Understanding the Economics of QWERTY: The Necessity of History," Chapter 4, *Economic History and the Modern Economist*, edited by W. N. Parker, New York: Basil Blackwell.

Ellsberg, D. (1961), "Risk, Ambiguity and the Savage Axioms," *Quarterly Journal of Economics*, 75, 643–669.

Forges, F., J.-F. Mertens and A. Neyman (1986), "A Counter Example to the Folk Theorem with Discounting," *Economics Letters*, 20, 7.

Foster, D. and R. Vohra (1997), "Calibrated Learning and Correlated Equilibrium," *Games and Economic Behaviov*, 21, 40–55.

Foster, D. and H. P. Young (1990), "Stochastic Evolutionary Game Dynamics," *Theoretical Population Biology*, 38, 219–232.

Fudenberg, D. and D. K. Levine (1989), "Reputation and Equilibrium Selection in Games with a Patient Player," *Econometrica*, 57, 759–779.

Fudenberg, D. and E. Maskin (1986), "The Folk Theorem in Repeated Games with Discounting and Incomplete Information," *Econometrica*, 54, 533–554.

Gilboa, I. (1988), "The Complexity of Computing Best Response Automata in Repeated Games," *Journal of Economic Theory*, 45, 342–352.

Güth, W., R. Schmittberger and B. Schwarze (1982), "An Experimental Analysis of Ultimatum Bargaining," *J. Econ. Behavior and Organization*, 3, 367–388.

Hofbauer, J. and K. Sigmund (1988), *Theory of Evolution and Dynamical Systems*, Cambridge: Cambridge University Press.

Kalai, E. and D. Samet (1984), "Persistent Equilibria," *International Journal of Game Theory*, 13, 129–144.

Kalai, E. and W. Stanford (1988), "Finite Rationality and Interpersonal Complexity in Repeated Games," *Econometrica*, 56, 397–410.

Kandori, M., G. Mailath and R. Rob (1993), "Learning, Mutation, and Long-Run Equilibria in Games," *Econometrica*, 61, 29–56.

Kohlberg, E. and J.-F. Mertens (1986), "On the Strategic Stability of Equilibria," *Econometrica*, 54, 1003–1037.

Kreps, D., P. Milgrom, J. Roberts and R. Wilson (1982), "Rational Cooperation in the Finitely Repeated Prisoners' Dilemma," *Journal of Economic Theory*, 27, 245–252.

Kreps, D. and R. Wilson (1982), "Sequential Equilibria," *Econometrica*, 50, 863–894.

Kuhn, H. W. and A. W. Tucker (eds.) (1953), *Contributions to the Theory of Games, Vol. II, Annals of Mathematics Studies*, 28, Princeton: Princeton University Press.

Lehrer, E. (1988), "Repeated Games with Stationary Bounded Recall Strategies," *Journal of Economic Theory*, 46, 130–144.

Lewis, A. (1985), "On Effectively Computable Realizations of Choice Functions," *Mathematical Social Sciences*, 10, 43–80.

——— (1992), "Some Aspects of Effectively Constructive Mathematics That Are

60   **Robert J. Aumann**

Relevant to the Foundations of Neoclassical Mathematical Economics and the Theory of Games," *Mathematical Social Sciences*, 24, 209–236.

Linial, N. (1994), "Game Theoretic Aspects of Computing," Chapter 38, *Handbook of Game Theory with Economic Applications*, Vol. 2, edited by R. J. Aumann and S. Hart, Amsterdam: North Holland.

Maynard Smith, J. (1982), *Evolution and the Theory of Games*, Cambridge: Cambridge University Press.

Myerson, R. B. (1978), "Refinements of the Nash Equilibrium Concept," *International Journal of Game Theory*, 7, 73–80.

Neyman, A. (1985), "Bounded Complexity Justifies Cooperation in the Finitely Repeated Prisoners' Dilemma," *Economics Letters*, 19, 227–229.

Papadimitriou, C. H. (1992), "On Players with a Bounded Number of States," *Games and Economic Behavior*, 4, 122–131.

Radner, R. (1980), "Collusive Behavior in Noncooperative Epsilon-Equilibria of Oligopolies with Long but Finite Lives," *Journal of Economic Theory*, 22, 136–154.

Radner, R., R. Myerson and E. Maskin (1986), "An Example of a Repeated Partnership Game with Discounting and with Uniformly Inefficient Equilibria," *Review of Economic Studies*, 53, 59–69.

Reny, P. J. (1992), "Backwards Induction, Normal Form Perfection and Explicable Equilibria," *Econometrica*, 60, 627–649.

Rubinstein, A. (1986), "Finite Automata Play the Repeated Prisoners' Dilemma," *Journal of Economic Theory*, 39, 83–96.

Selten, R. (1975), "Reexamination of the Perfectness Concept for Equilibrium Points in Extensive Games," *International Journal of Game Theory*, 4, 25–55.

Simon, H. (1955), "A Behavioral Model of Rational Choice," *Quarterly Journal of Economics*, 64, 99–118.

——— (1972), "Theories of Bounded Rationality," in *Decision and Organization*, edited by C. McGuire and R. Radner, Amsterdam: North Holland.

Stearns, R. E. (1989), "Memory-Bounded Game Playing Computing Devices," Technical Report No. 547, IMSSS, Stanford Univeristy.

van Damme, E. (1984), "A Relation between Perfect Equilibria in Extensive Form Games and Proper Equilibria in Normal Form Games," *International Journal of Game Theory*, 13, 1–13.

——— (1987), *Stability and Perfection of Nash Equilibria*, Berlin: Springer-Verlag.

Young, H. P. (1993), "The Evolution of Conventions," *Econometrica*, 61, 57–84.

Zemel, E. (1989), "Small Talk and Cooperation: A Note on Bounded Rationality," *Journal of Economic Theory*, 49, 1–9.

1987

ROBERT E. LUCAS, JR.

On the Mechanics of Economic Development

I am honored to be included in this distinguished series. I am also pleased to be included as an old friend of Nancy Schwartz. Nancy, Morton Kamien, and I were colleagues at Carnegie Tech, some twenty years ago – all three of us engaged in learning and applying the mathematics of optimal-control theory to economic dynamics. Younger faculty at Northwestern knew Nancy as a coauthor of the leading advanced text in the economic applications of control theory and (with Mort) as the foremost proponent of applying these methods to problems of industrial organization. You probably thought she was born knowing this material. But I can tell you that when we came to Carnegie none of us knew an Euler equation from a transversality condition, and everything we did was an exercise in learning by doing. Those years were a great learning experience for me, and it was incredibly lucky for me to have a colleague as smart, as serious, and as helpful as Nancy always was. It is good to have an occasion to express my debt to her publicly, and I thank you for this opportunity.

INTRODUCTION

This lecture will be concerned with the theory of economic development. The topic is a difficult one, because I don't have such a theory – and I

This lecture was based on one of Professor Lucas's papers, "On the Mechanics of Economic Development," written in 1985 and later published in the *Journal of Monetary Economics*. Readers are referred to that paper for analytical details, references, and acknowledgements. Reprinted from *Journal of Monetary Economics*, 22, Robert E. Lucas, Jr., On the mechanics of economic development, pp. 3–42, Copyright 1988, with kind permission from Elsevier Science – NL, Sara Burgerhartstraat 25, 1055 KV Amsterdam, The Netherlands.

don't believe anyone else does, either. This fact puts rather severe limitations on what you can hope to get out of this lecture. On the other hand, I hope that those of you who are at all theoretically inclined will find this situation stimulating – even stimulating enough to do something about it. Economic development is a great problem, badly in need of new ideas. In my view, the most useful ideas right now take the form of new theoretical models – new "mechanics" for thinking about economic growth.

Given this opinion, I will not spend much time conveying factual material about the world economy or about poor countries in particular. This is not my field of expertise, and I expect many people in this room are much better informed about these matters than I am. Instead, I will try to identify some theoretical questions that need to be resolved if we are to be able to think about economic development in a useful way.

I will begin at the beginning with the question: Why do we need a *theory* to think about development? Why not simply get the facts and examine them? Not surprisingly, I suppose, I will come down on the side of theory, and so will go on to ask: Given that we need a theoretical framework, what kinds of models are potentially useful? To work toward an answer to this question, I will begin by reviewing the theory of growth developed by Robert Solow, Edward Denison, and many others in the 1960s as a framework for thinking about U.S. economic growth. Third, I will consider why it is that this theory is not adequate as a theory of economic development. Fourth – last, and in a very much more open-ended spirit – I ask what alternative models can possibly do better.

WHY A THEORY?

Economic development is concerned with the levels and rates of growth in living standards in rich and poor countries and with the nature of the economic relations between rich and poor countries. By a *rich* country, I mean one with a per capita product of $8000 1975 U.S. – the United States in 1980. By *poor*, I mean *very* poor, say, $500 1975 U.S. – the per capita product in such countries as India, China, Tanzania, or Haiti. This factor-of-16 difference measures the range of income inequality in the world today. At some point, centuries ago, this range must have been much narrower, for once no country in the world was as well off as India is today, and living standards very much lower than modern India's are not consistent with subsistence. A few centuries ago, some of us moved into a phase of sustained economic growth while others did not, and out of this ill-understood process emerged the unequal world we know today.

By economic growth, I mean just the annual percentage rate of change in per capita production. (More exactly, I mean *long-term* growth rates: I will not be concerned with year-to-year fluctuations.) In these figures, too, we observe enormous variety from country to country. In recent years, a large figure is 6 or 7 percent – the 1960-80 average growth rates for South Korea, Singapore, Taiwan, Japan, Saudi Arabia, Zambia, or Jordan. The lowest growth rate for this 20-year period is Angola's: – 2.3 percent. The average for the poorest countries in the world is 1 percent. The average for the richest countries is 3.5 percent. To get an idea of what a 7 percent growth rate means, divide 7 into 69 (the log of 2) to get 10, the number of years it takes for income to double in a country where income is growing at 7 percent annually. With a 3.6 percent growth rate, the income-doubling period is 69 divided by 3.6, or 19 years. One percent growth implies a 69-year doubling time. Angola's 2.3 percent decay rate would, if continued, imply that income will halve every 20 years!

At the close of World War II, South Korea was less than twice as well off as India, with an income of $560 U.S. as compared to India's $330. By 1980, Korea's income was four times higher than India's. If present trends continue, by the year 2000 Korea's per capita income will be over 10 times India's. India will still be among the poorest countries in the world; living standards in Korea will be comparable to those in the U.S. and Western Europe today.

With such a range of experience to draw on, why do we need theoretical models? Why not simply use success stories – like Korea – as models? Why can't India send a fact-finding delegation to Korea, find out how they do it, and then go home and get Indians to do the same?

This sounds easy enough, but it is not really operational. Economists who like free markets visit Korea, observe (correctly) that the economy is largely organized on capitalist, free-trade lines, and conclude that free markets are the key to success. Economists who are predisposed toward central planning go to Korea, observe (correctly) that the Korean government intervenes actively in the economy, imposing many restrictions on trade, and conclude that wise central planning is the key to rapid growth. An economy is just too complex an entity – there are just too many things going on at once – for getting all the facts to be either possible or useful.

Faced with so much data, an observer who is unequipped with a theory sees what he wants to see, or what his hosts want to show him. One needs some principles for deciding which facts are central and which are peripheral. This is exactly the purpose of an economic theory: to isolate some very limited aspects of a situation and focus on them to the exclusion of all others.

What if your theory isolates the *wrong* aspects of the situation? Then you have a bad theory! Certainly there is no guarantee that simply writing down any internally consistent model is helpful or that all theories are equally useful or correct. The point is just that we cannot proceed with *no* theory. We need to make some hard choices about what to emphasize and what to leave out before we can think in an organized way at all.

THE THEORY OF GROWTH

The rapid growth of the Soviet Union in the 1950s (or at least what our experts *thought* was rapid growth) stimulated a wave of theoretical interest in the process of economic growth. (Remember Krushchev's boast – "We will bury you" – and Kennedy's promise to "get this country moving again"?) It is obvious now that the Soviet Union is just another backward economy and will stay that way for a long time to come, but the legacy of growth theory that was stimulated by what we saw as the Soviet challenge is still useful as a starting point in thinking about economic growth today.

What do we mean by an economic theory? In a market economy, economic growth – and resource allocation in general – is determined by millions of individual *choices*. To affect growth, a policy must alter the choices people make, so to assess growth policies we need a theory that can predict *how* these choices will differ in different circumstances. But it is not remotely possible for us to think of all choices at once. We need to focus on one or a very small number that seem to be central and pretend that these few choices are the *only* ones people have to think about. An economic model is just a simplified, fictional world in which human decision making is reduced to a few critical choices.

What are the right choices to focus on in thinking about economic growth? The theorists of the fifties and sixties focused on the savings decision: What determines the way an economy's productive capacity is divided between the production of consumption goods and the production of investment or capital goods? In a tradition dating back at least to Marx, the focus of early growth theory was on *capital accumulation*. This emphasis is surely plausible: Increased savings means more capital goods in the future, which means more production in the future, which means still more savings, and so on. Let me use a simple but graphic example to illustrate these dynamics and also the way in which they run into theoretical difficulties.

Imagine a society of primitive farmers who plant their crops by scratching in the dirt with their hands to make holes for seeds. This society survives, barely, with this technology, doing exactly the same things year after year. It does not enjoy economic growth. Now imagine that one of these farmers stops scratching for a day (thus reducing food production) and instead spends his time searching for a flat rock with sharp edges. Suppose he finds such a rock, and from tomorrow on he digs with this rock instead of with his fingers, thus increasing food production. Here is an episode of capital accumulation and growth in production, in which someone chooses to forgo current consumption in return for increased productivity in the future.

Presumably other farmers will observe the success of this innovator and follow suit, so that over time more good rocks will be found and applied to production, and the level of production will continue to expand. But as time passes, *diminishing returns* will set in. Eventually, all farmers will have switched from the old hand technology to the new rock technology. There will be only a few of them who can use two rocks simultaneously, and no one has *any* use for three rocks. The activity of searching for new rocks – the investment activity of this society – will thus eventually be limited to replacing worn-out and broken old rocks. If nothing else is involved, this society's economic growth will cease. Its citizens will enjoy a higher *level* of production than they had before the innovation occurred, but their living standard will not continue to grow indefinitely.

The moral of this story – which holds in a very wide variety of theoretical contexts – is simply that because of the Law of Diminishing Returns, capital accumulation alone is not sufficient to generate sustained per capita income growth. As a theorist, Marx was right: A falling rate of profit will bring growth arising from capital accumulation alone to a halt. As a prophet, of course, Marx was wrong: The falling rate of profit he predicted never set in! To account for the last two centuries of capitalism, we need to postulate some other force – some other "engine of growth" – in addition to the accumulation of capital.

For this purpose. Solow proposed technological change, a steady flow of new ideas. To return to my primitive example, suppose some other farmer notices that the rock technology can be improved by attaching the rock blade to a wooden handle, so that one can dig without bending over. Now the searching for good wooden handles and the fashioning of these newly designed shovels are new investment activities. Still later, someone discovers the advantages of making shovel blades of metal rather than rock, and resources are devoted to the implementation of this idea, and so on. As long as such new ideas keep coming – offsetting the Law of Diminishing Returns – economic growth can continue forever. Where do these ideas come from? This was not analyzed in the growth models of the 1960s, but simply taken as a *given* feature of the modern (post–Industrial Revolution) world.

Theoretical models based on ideas scarcely more complicated than my little example – incorporating both capital accumulation and technological change – turned out to give a pretty good account of the last century of growth in the United States and other advanced economies. These models were operational and capable of quantifying the effects of many proposed economic policies. These are important virtues, virtues that I think any useful theory of economic development must share. But they are not, I think, sufficient to permit these theories – which were devised to help understand growth in the advanced economies – to serve as a unified framework for thinking about rich and poor economies alike. I will turn to this issue next.

GROWTH THEORY AS A THEORY OF DEVELOPMENT

It is natural to ask: Can a theory that successfully fits U.S. growth be adapted to serve as a theory of economic development? That is to say, can this theory account for observed *differences* – across countries and across time – in living standards and also account for the nature of the economic relations between the very rich and the very poor? This is not what the theory was designed for, but perhaps it can serve this purpose anyway.

The answer to this question is, unfortunately, no. Standard growth theory is *not* a theory of economic development. The reason has to do, once again, with the Law of Diminishing Returns. In a nutshell: The standard model is too egalitarian to fit the observed world.

To explain what I mean by this, I will return to my example of a society of diggers and planters. This time, consider two such societies, originally developing in isolation with no contact between them. Now imagine that at some date contact is made, and each has the opportunity to observe the other. Assume for the moment that there is no trade in goods. What will happen?

Certainly at the time of initial contact, there is no reason to expect equality of living standards in this world. The level of production in each country depends on two things: the level of ideas, or technology, and the amount of capital (state-of-the-art shovels) per worker. There is no reason to expect either to be equal. But once contact is made, ideas become common property: If society A knew about wooden handles and society B did not, well, now B does.

Yet even if the transfer of ideas is immediate, incomes in the two societies will initially be unequal because capital is unequally distributed. Society B now knows it is possible and useful to equip shovels with handles, but it will take work and reduced consumption to implement this idea. With a common technology, though, the Law of Diminishing Returns implies that the return on new capital is highest in the low-capital country. Shovel handles are much more valuable in country B, which has none of them, than in A, where every worker already has one. As a result, the return to new investment is higher in B than in A, and capital will accumulate faster there. This will continue to be the case until returns in the two countries are equalized, which will occur only when capital per worker and income per worker are also equalized across countries. Thus, a central implication of diminishing returns is that inequality must diminish over time.

This is the situation in the absence of trade (except in ideas) between A and B. Now consider what happens if trade is possible, if either labor or capital or both are free to move across national boundaries. It is clear that this possibility will *accentuate* the egalitarian forces I have already described. Workers in B will want to migrate to A, where, due to the higher level of capital, per worker wage rates are higher. Capitalists in A will want to invest their high-technology shovels in B, where the return is highest. In general, labor will gravitate to capital-rich environments and capital to capital-poor environments, both operating to equalize capital-labor ratios.

The most striking feature of the modern world (at least to me) is that one cannot see these egalitarian forces at work much more strongly than we do. Certainly they were highly visible in the eighteenth and nineteenth centuries, when workers flowed (voluntarily or as slaves) from relatively land-poor Europe and West Africa to the land-rich Americas, Australia, and South and East Africa. In that case, one factor of production (land) was not mobile, so the other factor (labor) had to do all of the moving. But move it did, as many millions of people relocated their lives in exactly the way predicted by the Law of Diminishing Returns.

In the present century, labor flows have been largely shut off (to humanity's great loss, in my view). Even so, one would expect to see mobile capital flowing to capital-poor countries. But one does not see such a flow, or at least anything like as much of it as theory predicts. Nor can one see *any* trend to equality across countries in the world today (except among the subset of the very wealthy countries). For every Korea that is gaining there is an India or a Haiti that is falling ever further behind. Of course, we do not expect simple models to fit the facts exactly, but to be serviceable they need to be consistent with the main overall features of the world we are trying to understand. As a theory of economic development, the neoclassical model is not consistent with our world. I see no kinder verdict.

PROSPECTS FOR BETTER THEORIES

What lessons can we draw from the failure of the neoclassical model? I think there are two. First, the villain is the Law of Diminishing Returns. It is this feature that makes it hard to get sustained growth in a model of a single economy and that predicts too much equality (relative to what we see, not relative to what we might wish for) across economies in a model of international trade. We have to find a way to repeal this law, theoretically. Second, the neoclassical model focuses on the capital accumulation decision, but it is growth in *ideas* – not merely in capital – that drives the system. This observation suggests a shift of focus from decisions on capital accumulation to decisions that determine rate of production of ideas.

In the terminology of T. W. Schultz and Gary Becker, it suggests a shift of emphasis from *physical* to *human* capital accumulation, a focus on decisions – such as the allocation of time among activities – that affect the rate of learning, the rate of accumulation of skills and ideas. Thus, in my primitive example, the process of capital accumulation was initiated when someone took time away from current production to think about better ways to produce. The theory of human capital is designed precisely to study the tradeoffs involved between using time to increase current production and earnings and using time to increase productivity in the future – going to school, say, or learning a new, unfamiliar task on the job. This theory is very highly developed and widely tested in microeconomic applications. Surprisingly, it has not yet been very widely applied in explicit models of economic development.

Is such an application worth a try? Not if we just change the labels on the variables in the neoclassical theory, for then we will run up against the Law of Diminishing Returns in the same way we did in a theory focusing on physical capital. But there is an encouraging possibility that the law may not apply to human capital in the same way that it applies to physical capital, that the return to new skills and new ideas may not fall as more of these are accumulated. In 1965, Hirofumi Uzawa showed that a growth model based on human capital accumulation, *without* diminishing returns, can produce sustained growth without the *deus ex machina* of exogenous technological change. His paper did not attract much notice at the time – which is too bad, because his model has the interesting feature that the returns to capital can be equalized across countries with very different income levels. His model has *no* predicted tendency to equality, so it provides a much better first approximation to the facts than does the standard neoclassical setup.

Is the technology Uzawa postulated for the accumulation of human capital, free of diminishing returns, consistent with the available evidence? I do not know the answer to this, but Sherwin Rosen showed in 1976 that it fits data on *individual* earnings over a working career, which reflect human capital growth. Perhaps it can do as well applied to entire societies. A large step, to be sure, but I find this line promising.

But there are many, many unresolved issues. A key question is this: To what extent do we want to view human capital as private property (like George Brett's knowledge of the way to hit a fast ball) and to what extent should it be viewed as common property (like Kamien and Schwartz's knowledge of how the calculus of variations can be applied to economic problems)? It seems clear that most human capital involves both elements, that the accumulation of human capital confers *external* benefits on the productivity of others as well as enhancing the productivity of the one who accumulates it. If so, this implies that a market economy produces too little human capital and raises interesting possibilities for economic policy.

CONCLUSIONS

What lessons can be drawn from such a half-developed theory of economic development? Caution is obviously advisable, but two lessons come to mind. First, surely it is right to put *ideas* at the center of the story, not *things*. The reason that we are better off economically than ancient peoples is that we *think* better. The Arabs were sitting on more oil in the days of the Prophet than they are today, but no one then had any interesting ideas about what to *do* with it. Is it self-serving to assign so important a role to intellectuals, broadly defined? (My friend Larry Weiss, on reading an earlier version of this material, remarked that if we were in the aluminum-siding business we would no doubt advance arguments about the external benefits of aluminum siding!) Well, I suppose it is self-serving, but I believe it is accurate nonetheless.

Second, if Uzawa-like models of development, based on the accumulation of human capital, are at all accurate, then income equality is *not* going to come about simply in the natural course of events. The term "developing economy" suggests that societal poverty is, like childhood, a condition that is simply outgrown as time passes. If the application of Uzawa's model that I have sketched is a useful framework for thinking about development, it will take more than time and patience to bring about greater equality in this world. Equality will have to be in some sense or other consciously *engineered*. I do not claim to know either whether or how this ought to be done, but I find it hard to think of an economic question that better merits our scientific attention.

1988

TRUMAN F. BEWLEY
Knightian Uncertainty

It is truly a great honor to speak on this occasion. In her work, Nancy Schwartz maintained the highest standards of integrity and of the imaginative and skillful use of mathematics. I cannot pretend that the material I will present achieves the same level of elegance. Rather, I will describe a point of view that, when developed and applied, may lead to new economic insights and even to interesting calculations. But this point of view is still very much at a speculative and experimental stage.

My starting point is the distinction made by Frank Knight (1921) between risk and uncertainty. He defined risk as randomness with a known probability distribution and uncertainty as randomness with an unknown distribution. He argued that uncertainty was uninsurable and that the role of entrepreneurs was to undertake investment involving such uninsurable chances of loss. It is not clear from Knight's work what he thought was special about uncertainty – whether it was market failure due to moral hazard and adverse selection or whether it was differences in behavior in the face of risk and uncertainty. In a recent paper, LeRoy and Singell (1987) argue that Knight had in mind moral hazard and adverse selection. I do not wish to discuss what Knight intended, but I rather wish to propose that, in fact, there is a distinction in people's reactions to risk and uncertainty.

This assertion conflicts with Bayesian decision theory, since a Bayesian decision maker treats risk and uncertainty in the same way. He acts so as to maximize the expected value of his gain, the expected value being calculated using a subjective probability distribution. The only distinction between behavior toward risk and uncertainty is that, in the case of risk, the subjective probabilities should equal those known objectively.

Bayesian decision theory derives the subjective probabilities from a complete preference ordering over lotteries. The ordering is complete in that any two lotteries are comparable.

What I do is to drop the assumption of completeness from the list of assumptions made in Bayesian decision theory. I also add a postulate, which I call the inertia assumption. One may refer to a theorem of Aumann's (1962) to find that dropping the completeness assumption has the effect of replacing the single subjective probability distribution with a convex set of probability distributions. One lottery is preferred to another if, and only if, it has higher expected value according to all the subjective distributions. I also make an assumption that guarantees that if the probability of an event is known objectively, then the subjective probabilities of the event all equal the objective one. Thus, the von Neumann–Morgenstern theory of choice under risk is not contradicted. Incompleteness of preferences is what distinguishes behavior toward uncertainty from behavior toward risk.

The inertia assumption is that when there is such a thing as the *status quo*, it is abandoned in favor of an alternative only if the alternative is preferred to the *status quo*. The *status quo* should be thought of as previous plans. The alternative should be thought of as a new choice that had not been anticipated when the plans were made. The theory resulting from incomplete preferences and the inertia assumption I call Knightian decision theory. (The theory is elaborated in Bewley [1986].)

An immediate consequence of the theory is that a Knightian decision maker acts just like a Bayesian one, except when choosing between the *status quo* and a new alternative. He chooses decisions that are optimal according to one of his subjective distributions. In a complicated intertemporal problem with new information arriving continually, he would use Bayes rule to update one fixed distribution and use the updated distribution to evaluate alternatives, just as a Bayesian decision maker would do.

In order to make this point more formally, one must first observe that one cannot define optimality with respect to an incomplete ordering. But one can speak of maximal decisions, a decision being maximal or undominated if there is no other decision preferred to it. Think of the payoffs as measured in units of von Neumann–Morgenstern utility. Then, if one allows random choices, one can think of the set of possible choices as a convex subset of the set of functions from the underlying state space to payoffs. A maximal choice is one such that the set of points preferred to it does not intersect the choice set. By separating the preferred points from the choice set, one finds that the maximal choice is in fact optimal with respect to a linear functional that is the expected value with respect to one of the subjective distributions.

The multiplicity of subjective distributions together with the inertia assumption imply what may be called uncertainty aversion. The larger the set of subjective distributions, the less likely is the decision maker to abandon the *status quo*. A Bayesian decision maker is a Knightian one who is uncertainty neutral in that he has only one subjective distribution.

The novel aspects of Knightian decision theory, then, are uncertainty aversion, inertia, and ambiguity as to choice of the subjective distribution used in decision making. I note that Gilboa and Schmeidler (1989) also have developed a theory of decision with multiple subjective distributions but using a complete preference ordering. Their decision makers act so as to maximize the minimum of the expected returns, when the minimum is taken over the subjective distributions.

The Knightian theory I have outlined seems to me somewhat plausible. For me, it has the virtue of being able to explain absence of betting and insurance without appeal to asymmetric information. It was this application that led me to think of it. I will return briefly to insurance later, but only in support of my main objective, which is to paint a general picture of the world from the Knightian point of view. We evaluate or estimate risk by using statistical methods, and we tend to view economic life as a whole within the framework of general equilibrium theory. So I would like to examine with Knightian eyes econometrics, general equilibrium, and in particular, rational expectations equilibrium.

Econometrics seems to present a view of the world according to which all change is governed by definite stochastic processes, which it is the task of the researcher to discover. He may use as a tool of analysis a single prior distribution over distributional hypotheses. How can one reconcile this view of the world with the multiplicity of subjective distributions assumed in Knightian decision theory?

First of all, the confidence regions and significance tests of classical statistics can be interpreted as systematic ways of measuring the Knightian uncertainty associated with inference. One imagines that this uncertainty would tend to disappear as data accumulated. Since economic time series will be observed indefinitely, one wonders how significant Knightian uncertainty could exist or persist. In response to this query, I question whether economic time series are generated by stochastic processes that could ever be discovered from the data they generate. To support this point, I will outline a rigorous definition of a discoverable stochastic law. It may be shown that not all sequences are generated by such laws. (This material is elaborated in Bewley [1988].)

Turning first of all to confidence regions, I define a standardized notion of uncertainty aversion. Suppose a decision maker is presented with an event about whose likelihoods of occurrence and nonoccurrence he is equally and totally ignorant. If he were Bayesian, then by the principle of insufficient reason he would assign a probability of one-half to the event. A Knightian would assign an interval of probabilities symmetric about 1/2. The ratio of the largest to the smallest of these probabilities minus one is a measure of inherent uncertainty aversion, call it a. Consider now a measure λ on some state space with the property that if A and B are disjoint events of equal positive and finite λ measure, then the decision maker is equally and totally ignorant of the relative likelihoods of occurrence of A and B. If the decision maker has uncertainty aversion of degree a, he should assign to the probability of A conditional on A $\cup$ B, the same interval about 1/2 that was used to define a. There may be many sets of measures on the state space satisfying this condition for all A and B. But there is a unique largest set of measures. If λ is atomless, this set is the set of indefinite integrals with respect to λ of measurable functions of the state such that the supremum of f is no more than $(1 + a)$ times the infinium of f. If λ is chosen in some standardized way, then this set is a standardized set of measures reflecting uncertainty aversion of index a.

Now consider a normal linear regression model, and suppose that nothing is known about the parameters, these being the vector of regression parameters, β, and the variance of the error term, σ^2. This ignorance may also be interpreted as a stance of scientific detachment. One would like to choose a prior distribution, λ, over β and σ^2 that expresses ignorance or detachment. There is no fixed rule for doing so, but one can fix a distribution by requiring that any conclusions not depend on the units chosen for measuring the variables. This and one other invariance condition fixes the prior distribution, λ, to be the one with density σ^{-k-2}, where K is the number of independent variables. With λ so defined, the set of priors defined previously from λ and a becomes a standardized set of priors expressing detachment as well as conservatism of degree a.

The prior distributions in this set are all improper in that they integrate to infinity. Nevertheless, for given data the corresponding posterior distributions over the parameters are all proper and so may be normalized to probability laws. Consider the set of means of the regression parameter vectors corresponding to this set of posterior laws. It may be proved that this set has exactly the same form as a classical confidence region, and is a confidence region for some level of confidence. These Knightian confidence regions are indexed by the degree of uncertainty aversion rather than the confidence level.

The Knightian confidence regions have a decision theoretic interpretation. Imagine a decision problem in which the payoffs depend linearly on future values of the dependent variable of the linear regression. Imagine also that the independent variables may be forecast or predetermined. Then, by the theorem mentioned earlier, a decision would be maximal if and only if it were optimal with respect to some one of the decision maker's subjective distributions. Since the payoff depends linearly on future observations of the dependent variable, only the expected values of these future observations matter. But these expected values can be derived from the expected values of the regression coefficients. Now suppose the decision maker has the standardized set of priors mentioned earlier. Then the regression parameter posterior means he would use would be precisely those in the confidence region defined earlier. In conclusion, the confidence region is precisely the set of means it would be rational for the decision maker to use to evaluate his alternative decisions.

Similarly, the classical test of a point null hypothesis on the regression parameters has a decision theoretic interpretation. The classical test that β takes on the value $\bar{\beta}$ is to accept if $\bar{\beta}$ lies in the confidence region. In Knightian terms, acceptance means that in the above decision problem it is rational to act as if $\bar{\beta}$ were the true value. This interpretation seems to correspond roughly both to practice and the usual explanations of the meaning of the test.

Similar interpretations may be given of all the classical tests of linear hypotheses on regression coefficients.

I now turn to the question of the discoverability of stochastic laws. Recall that the question to be answered is how can a significant amount of Knightian uncertainty still exist after a process has been observed for a long time. One answer might be that the probability laws governing the series are always changing. But then would not those changes themselves exhibit some pattern? The answer seems to be that not all stochastic processes have laws that may be learned. In a trivial sense, any sequence of data has a discoverable law. The sequence is generated by the distribution assigning probability one to that sequence, and this distribution is learned as the sequence unfolds. But such learning is not useful for prediction. What one seeks is regularities. I will say that a sequence has a discoverable law if it has such regularities and if they may be learned from observation.

I attempt a more rigorous definition. For simplicity, think of a sequence of integers, which might be thought of as finite decimal expansions of numbers. Suppose for the moment the sequence is bounded. I will say that a sequence has a pattern if one can define the conditional probability that the next member will be a certain value, conditional on the fact that the previous M values have been a certain sequence. These probabilities could be estimated from relative frequencies, since for a bounded sequence, there will be blocks of M values that will occur infinitely often. The sequence is said to have a discoverable law if these relative frequencies converge as the number of observations goes to infinity for all blocks of length M, for M sufficiently large. This definition includes bounded (or essentially bounded) stationary processes and also bounded solutions of finite order difference equations.

Now consider sequences that wander off to infinity. The previous definition is of no help since every block of values of finite length may occur only finitely often. There are a number of ways one could imagine discovering a distribution for such a sequence. One way would be to transform the data via a sequence of functions $f(N, x_1, \ldots, x_N)$ into a bounded or essentially bounded sequence, $d_N = f(N, x_1, \ldots, x_N)$, $N = 1$, $2, \ldots$, this new sequence having a law discoverable in the previous sense. An example of a function f would be $x_N - x_{N-1}$. Also, in order to recover the distribution of the x_N from that of the d_N, each function $f(N, \ldots,)$ should depend in a one-to-one way on x_N. Finally, in order to be able to calculate the function f, it should be computable. Computability is defined in mathematical logic as general recursiveness. There are only countably many such functions, which makes it possible to learn the function f from the data. Roughly speaking, one tries out each of the candidate f's in turn until arriving at one that works.

This definition of discoverability probably does not include all sequences with laws that may be discovered in the loose sense, but I believe it includes all sequences likely to arise in economics.

One can easily show that there exist sequences with no law discoverable in the sense defined. Thus, it is a legitimate hypothesis to assume that the data have no discoverable law.

This being the case, it is natural to ask how one could test for discoverability. The essence of nondiscoverability is instability of structure. Thus, any subjective distribution on the data reflecting nondiscoverability should make all structure unstable. A test for discoverability would compare such a subjective distribution with distributions implying stable structure. The distribution giving the highest likelihood to the data would be favored. Thus, failure of any classical tests for structural stability of a specific structure probably means that the Bayesian test just outlined would tend to favor the hypothesis of no structure over the specific structure. Thus, if a linear regression model is under consideration, failure of a Chow test for stability of the regression parameters or any evidence of heteroskedasticity of the error terms should probably be interpreted as favoring the hypothesis of no structure as well as an encouragement to search for alternative structure.

In economics, there are obvious relations among some time series, but it is not clear that the common motions of the time series have any discoverable law. There seems to be no theoretical reason that they should. In fact, one often hears and reads that time series behavior may be represented by vector autoregressive (or VAR) models with coefficients that themselves change from time to time. The instability of typical VAR coefficients is perhaps evidence that there may be no useful structure behind the data. To say that coefficients move arbitrarily is nearly indistinguishable from saying that there is no discoverable law. It may be possible to fit any data with a VAR with time varying parameters, even if the parameters move only rarely. One must question the predictive value of such fluctuating models. If one allows coefficient variability, one has a discoverable structure only if the coefficient changes themselves obey some discoverable law. But for such models to have passed a real test, one must have enough data so that one can test the structural stability of the process governing the evolution of the coefficients. Ultimately, one should have finitely many stable parameters. Until one does, one cannot say that Knightian uncertainty has been eliminated.

Of course, to say that a body of data has no discoverable law does not mean that one can say nothing about the distribution generating the data. One could estimate bounds on the distribution or assert that it has a temporary structure that changes slowly, though otherwise unpredictably. However, such assertions allow Knightian uncertainty to persist indefinitely.

In conclusion, it seems plausible that Knightian uncertainty has a place in economic reality. Supposing that people react to it not as Bayesians but in the way I have called Knightian. I wish to discuss what happens to intertemporal general equilibrium theory and to rational expectations in an uncertain world. First of all, it is necessary to clarify the precise meaning of rational expectations.

In general equilibrium models with rational expectations, it is usually assumed that there is some underlying random variable, call it θ_t, and all agents' characteristics as well as prices and allocations can be written as functions of this random variable. Each individual in the economy observes certain functions of the θ_t, such as prices and his own characteristics, and has a probability distribution over what he observes. The rational expectations assumption is that the distributions of all individuals are derived from a common distribution over the θ_t, this common distribution being the true one. In general equilibrium, the prices should clear all markets at every realization of the θ_t. In proving the existence of equilibrium, the common distribution over the θ_t is taken as given and the equilibrium price and allocation functions of the θ_t are shown to exist.

A first question is, what should be the state space for the θ_t? One might be tempted to let it be the space of all possible sequences of prices and of agents' characteristics and to have the function defining the characteristics and prices in each period be the natural projections. But this approach makes it impossible to prove the existence of equilibrium by varying the function relating prices to states, since this function is fixed to be the projection. One would have to vary the distribution over the θ_t, which would be awkward. One could avoid this technical difficulty by letting the state space be the set of all possible sequences of agents' characteristics, that is, by not including prices in the description of the state.

But this approach meets a conceptual difficulty, as the following example indicates. Consider an economy with finitely many immortal consumers who in each period receive endowments of various goods and exchange them every period. Then, an individual's characteristics are his endowment and preference ordering in every period. Suppose that these characteristics fluctuate but that each consumer knows with certainty in the first period what his own characteristics will be in every future period, without knowing anything about the characteristics of others. Suppose also that there is no trading in futures or forward contracts, only trading in each period for current delivery. Thus, forward trading does not pin down what future prices will be.

If we let the state space be the set of all possible sequences of agents' characteristics, then the true distribution on this space gives probability one to the unique sequence that will occur. Hence, in a rational expectations equilibrium, there would be perfect foresight and no uncertainty about future prices. But this seems ridiculous. The example is artificial, but reality may be more like it than we imagine. It might well be that much of the uncertainty in economic life would disappear if all the information we all have separately could be collected and used fully.

One might try to fix up the example by imagining that each individual's entire stream of characteristics is drawn randomly from the set of all such possible streams. The "true" distribution on the state space would then describe these random draws. But this approach in turn meets the difficulty that one can create any possible set of expectations by manipulating the distribution of the random draw. In fact, different individuals need not have the same distribution on future prices.

The way out of this perplexity seems to be to appeal to the notion of discoverable law mentioned earlier. If prices obey a discoverable law and consumers have had a long time to observe them, then that law should be known nearly perfectly, so that we may assume that consumers know it. In order to capture this picture, we could define the state space of θ_t to be the set of all possible sequences of prices and the measure on that space would represent the known law. Of course, only one sequence of possible prices would be realized, but this is true of any stochastic process. Also, the probability distribution on prices would be subjective, but it would be consistent with the subjective distribution.

In this model of rational expectations, prices are themselves the state space, so that in order to prove the existence of a rational expectations equilibrium, we must vary the distribution on the state space rather than vary the function carrying states to prices. This seems impossible, but one can avoid the difficulty if the given sequence of agents' characteristics has a discoverable law. One can then place the given sequence of agents' characteristics in the space of all such sequences and give that artificial state space the law that may be discovered from the given sequences. One may prove the existence of a conventional rational expectations equilibrium in the conventional way, defining equilibrium prices to be functions of the artificial state space. The equilibrium price function together with the distribution on the artificial state space together induce a distribution on the sequence of possible prices, which will have a discoverable law if the price function is stationary. This latter distribution is that of the desired rational expectations equilibrium. I have passed over some technical and even conceptual difficulties, but have arrived at what I believe is the appropriate setting, for rational expectations equilibrium, at least in the context of the example.

With this definition of equilibrium, we see that forward markets play a double role. Not only do they make it possible for people to buy and sell insurance and to save and dissave, but also they can reduce risk by revealing information about what the future holds in store. In the example, there would be no randomness at all if markets were complete. The revelation of future states could be very important for economic welfare if one introduced intertemporal production into the model. It may be that in reality the loss we suffer from absence of futures markets has more to do with lost information than the lack of opportunities for mutual insurance and borrowing and lending.

Now I wish to discuss what happens in the example if the stream of agents' characteristics has no discoverable law. Proceeding with an artificial state space as was just done, one may produce an equilibrium in which each individual maximizes according to a subjective distribution but in which the sequence of prices may admit many possible laws, including the various distributions used by consumers. If the consumers are Knightian decision makers and if the distribution used by each individual is one of his subjective distributions, then the result may be termed a Knightian rational expectations equilibrium. Note that in such an equilibrium the probability distributions on prices used by individuals may not be uniquely defined and may differ among individuals.

The uncertainty experienced in such a Knightian equilibrium can itself be the cause of the absence of forward markets. Thinking in terms of the example discussed before, suppose we start in a Knightian rational expectations equilibrium with no forward markets and that an entrepreneur opens markets in one period forward contracts. If everyone trades in these markets, the equilibrium forward prices could reduce uncertainty. However, if we treat no forward trading as the *status quo* and the possibility of forward trading as an innovation, then according to the inertia assumption people would trade forward only if doing so would be preferred to not trading. What would be unknown to the agents would be the probability distribution of current and forward prices in future periods. If the uncertainty about these were sufficiently great, there might be no forward prices in the current period that would clear the one period ahead futures markets, except prices yielding no transactions. There might not be enough trade to support the markets.

The situation may be visualized easily in an Edgeworth box, which, of course, cannot reflect the complexity of the intertemporal example. Imagine that there are two states of the world and that trade is in contracts contingent on these two states. If the consumers are uncertainty averse and uncertain about the probabilities of the states, then the set of points preferred by one consumer to a single point will be a convex set with a corner at the given point. The corner reflects the multiplicity of subjective probabilities. Suppose that the initial endowment point is also the *status quo* of the inertia assumption. Then, the sets of points preferred to the initial point by each consumer might easily not intersect, so that there could be no mutually advantageous trade. This lack of trade would not lead to a Pareto loss in the Edgeworth box example, but it could do so in the intertemporal example if no trade meant no market and hence no information revealing prices.

Thus, uncertainty aversion gives one more reason for market failure in addition to moral hazard (pointed out by Roy Radner [1968]), adverse selection and transactions costs.

One might imagine that if one opened all N period forward markets for $N \leq M$ and M large, then uncertainty about future prices would be so reduced that forward trade would occur. But this argument fails, for there could still be a great deal of uncertainty about current prices M periods later, and this uncertainty could inhibit trade in the M period forward markets. Thus, the equilibrium could unravel from the last period.

In summary, the Knightian picture of the world is one where agents operate in an environment where much of the risk is unevaluatable and therefore uninsurable. Uncertainty aversion inhibits the development of futures markets, which could themselves help reduce the uncertainty in the environment.

References

Aumann, Robert J. (1962), "Utility Theory without the Completeness Axiom," *Econometrica*, 30, 445–462.

Bewley, Truman (1986), "Knightian Decision Theory: Part I," Cowles Foundation Discussion Paper #807, Yale University.

——— (1988), "Knightian Decision Theory and Econometric Inference," Cowles Foundation Discussion Paper #868, Yale University.

Gilboa, Itzhak and David Schmeidler (1989), "Maximin Expected Utility with a Non-Unique Prior," *Journal of Mathematical Economics*, 18, 141–153

Knight, Frank H. (1921), *Risk, Uncertainty and Profit.* Boston and New York: Houghton Mifflin.

LeRoy, Stephen F. and Larry D. Singell, Jr. (1987), "Knight on Risk and Uncertainty," *Journal of Political Economy*, 5 (April), 394–406.

Radner, Roy (1968), "Competitive Equilibrium Under Uncertainty," *Econometrica*, 36 (January), 31–58.

REINHARD SELTEN

Evolution, Learning, and Economic Behavior

It is doubtful whether I shall be able to meet the high standards set by previous speakers. I shall not prove deep theorems. I shall not present astonishing new results. Instead, I shall try to catch your attention with a fictitious dialogue. I shall employ the help of imaginary discussants like the "Bayesian" or the "experimentalist." A "chairman" will determine who speaks next, but he shall also make his own remarks.

Chairman: I open the discussion with a question: What do we know about the structure of human economic behavior?

The Bayesian has signaled his willingness to answer this question. I give the floor to the Bayesian.

Bayesian: As far as economic activities are concerned, it is justified to assume that man is a rational being. Since Savage (1954) simultaneously axiomatized utility and subjective probability, we know what rational economic behavior is. It is the maximization of subjectively expected utility.

Chairman: Among us is an economist. I would like to ask him if this is the agreed upon opinion in economic theory?

Economist: Yes, to a large extent, this is the agreed upon opinion. Most of microeconomics takes Bayesianism for granted. However, there are exceptions. Some theorists have different views.

As an example let me mention Allais. Since 1953 he has insisted that in the evaluation of risky decisions not only the expectation, but also the

Reprinted from *Games and Economic Behavior*, 3, no. 1 (1991), 3–24, with permission from Academic Press.

variance of utility must be taken into account. He has shown that his theory is in better agreement with observed behavior than Bayesianism is.

Chairman: One of our discussants is an experimentalist. His background is in experimental economics. I would like to ask him for his opinion of Allais and Bayesian decision theory and its agreement with observed behavior.

Experimentalist: If I understand the opening question correctly, we are here to discuss *human* economic behavior, not the behavior of a mythical hero called "rational man" – a mythical hero whose powers of computation and cogitation are unlimited. For this mythical hero it is easy to form consistent probability and preference judgments, but not for ordinary people like you and me.

People are not consistent. I will mention just one of many experimental results that show this. In a paper published by Tyszka (1983), he describes an experiment in which the subjects had to make choices from triples, say {A,B,C} or {A,B,D}. Tyszka succeeded in constructing triples such that 95 percent of the subjects chose A from

$$\{A, B, C\},$$

and 95 percent of the subjects chose B from

$$\{A, B, D\}$$

The choice between A and B is influenced by the irrelevant alternatives C and D. This should not be the case if consistent preference judgments are formed.

Allais's theory is in better agreement with behavior than Bayesianism is, but the agreement is only slightly better. The violations of ideal rationality observed in experiments are much more basic than the theory of Allais suggests. Rejecting Bayesianism in favor of Allais's theory is like going to the top of a skyscraper in order to be nearer to the moon!

Chairman: I agree with the experimentalist. One must make a distinction between normative and descriptive theory. My opening question was meant descriptively. Decision theory and game theory have made tremendous progress on the clarification of the concept of ideal rationality. In this discussion we are not concerned with ideal rationality, but with actual human decision behavior.

However, we should not be too quick to reject the optimization approach as nondescriptive. Evolutionary game theory, started by Maynard Smith and Price (1973), is successful in biology – and biology is thoroughly descriptive. The book by Maynard Smith (1982), *Evolution and the Theory of Games*, provides many examples. Game theory has been created as a theory of rational behavior, but it is now applied to animals and plants.

Among us is a biologist who we call the "adaptationist" because he strongly believes in adaptation in the biological sense. The adaptationist thinks that the principle of fitness maximization is applicable to human behavior. I would like him to explain his views.

Adaptationist: Let me explain what adaptation means in biology. Adaptation means fitness maximization. Fitness is reproductive success – roughly speaking, the expected number of offspring in the next generation. Natural selection drives organisms toward fitness maximization. Fitness maximization also is a powerful explanatory principle for human behavior.

However, as far as human decisions are concerned (the same holds for animal decisions), we must be aware that near to the optimum selective pressures are weak. Therefore, we often observe nearly optimal rules of thumb instead of truly optimal behavior.

The experimentalist has told us about deviations from rationality in experiments. I think that these deviations cannot be of great practical importance; otherwise natural selection would have eliminated them long ago.

Chairman: Now several discussants want to say something. The next speaker is the Bayesian.

Bayesian: I find the remarks of the adaptationist very interesting. The principle of fitness maximization permits us to construct new kinds of theories in economics. Preferences can now be explained as a result of evolution. People like what is good for their fitness.

Let me make an additional remark on rules of thumb. What seems to be only nearly optimal may be truly optimal, if decision costs are taken into account. When decision costs are taken into account, many rules of thumb may be truly optimal upon closer inspection.

Chairman: I would like to ask the experimentalist for his opinion on rules of thumb and decision costs.

Experimentalist: As many people have pointed out, decision problems tend to become more difficult when decision costs are taken into account. If one tries to save decision costs by taking them into account, one may easily end up with higher decision costs.

Adaptationist (interrupting): No! I must interrupt here. Remember that I think of rules of thumb as inherited. They are not made up on the spot. Evolution has already solved the optimization problem. The decision maker does not have to solve it any more.

Experimentalist: I concede this point. However, I wonder whether all rules of thumb that people use in everyday life are inherited. Sometimes rules of thumb have to be made up on the spot.

I would like to point out that nearly optimal rules of thumb can be far from truly optimal policies. This may not matter very much to the decision maker, but it may be important to other people. The following is an example in which the structure of experimentally observed behavior is dramatically different from that of the optimal policy.

Claus Berg (1973, 1974) published the results of an investment experiment. The subjects could invest in cash or in a risky asset. In every period they had to divide total assets into cash and the risky asset. The end was decided by a stopping probability of 1 percent.

The risky asset yielded a positive interest, say 25 percent, or a negative interest, say -25 percent. The percentage was the same in both cases. It was fixed and known to the subject. There was a fixed probability p for the positive interest. This probability was not known to the subject. Profits and losses changed total assets from period to period.

Bayesian decision theory yields the following prediction about changes of the proportion of the risky asset in total assets:

After a positive interest the risky asset proportion is increased.

After a negative interest the risky asset proportion is decreased.

This is due to an increase of the posterior probability for a positive interest after a positive interest and to a decrease of this posterior probability after a negative interest. However, in 75 percent of all cases the subjects changed the risky asset proportion in the direction opposite to the Bayesian prediction!

A closer look at the data revealed the reason for this phenomenon. The subjects tend to form an aspiration level for the total assets they want to obtain at the end of the period. Often this aspiration level is the total assets at the beginning of the last period. This has the following consequences: After a loss, as much is risked as is necessary to recuperate the loss. This requires an increase of the risky asset proportion. After a gain, no more is risked than has been won. This requires a decrease of the risky asset proportion.

Berg ran computer simulations with an idealized description of the aspiration-guided behavior observed in the experiments. He compared the results with those for Bayesian optimal policies starting from beta-distributed priors with expected values near to the true probability. Strangely enough, the results for the behavioral theory were often better than those for the optimal policies, particularly in the parameter range of the experiments. Maybe the priors were not appropriate. The success of a Bayesian policy may depend crucially on the prior. Only asymptotically the prior does not matter. But how should we choose the prior?

In any case, Berg's theory performs very well. However, its structure of aspiration-guided behavior is very different from that of the optimal Bayesian policy. The Bayesian prediction of the change of the risky asset proportion goes in the wrong direction!

Chairman: I permit the Bayesian to make a short comment.

Bayesian: I only want to say that aspiration-guided behavior may be truly optimal, if decision costs are taken into account.

Chairman: Well, this is a possibility, but a remote one. I would like to come back to the statement of the adaptationist:

Natural selection drives organisms toward fitness maximization.

Among us is a population geneticist. I would like to ask him what can be said about this statement from the point of view of population genetics.

Population Geneticist: Fitness maximization is thought of as the result of a dynamic process of natural selection. We need a justification of this idea within explicit dynamic models. Such models are the subject matter of population genetics.

Ronald Fisher, the great population geneticist and econometrician, proved a "fundamental theorem," which under certain conditions shows that natural selection increases fitness until a maximum is reached. Unfortunately, Fisher's conditions are rarely satisfied in genetic systems.

In the following I shall rely heavily on a very illuminating paper by Ilan Eshel (1988), which has been made available as a preprint. Maynard Smith and Price (1973) have introduced the concept of an evolutionarily stable strategy as an attempt to give a static description of a dynamically stable result of natural selection in game situations. We may say that evolutionary stability is the generalization of fitness maximization to game situations. Eshel's paper is concerned with the dynamic foundations of evolutionary stability.

We must distinguish two mechanisms of natural selection:

1. Adaptation of genotype frequencies without mutation
2. Gene substitution by mutation

Mendelian inheritance and selective pressures combine to change the frequencies with which genotypes are represented in the population. This is the process called "adaptation of genotype frequencies without mutation."

Moran (1964) has shown that under realistic conditions adaptation of genotype frequencies without mutation does not necessarily maximize fitness; it may even decrease fitness until a local minimum is reached. This result holds even without any game interaction. The explanation lies in the combined effects of Mendelian inheritance and linkage. Linkage is the phenomenon that genes near to each other on the same chromosome are likely to be inherited together.

After Moran's result, the idea of fitness maximization fell into disrepute among population geneticists. Only recently a new picture emerged, first in a paper by Eshel and Feldman (1984). They showed that for two-locus systems gene substitution by mutation works in the direction of evolutionary stability. This result has been generalized to an arbitrary number of gene loci by Liberman (1988).

This is very good news for those who work on evolutionary game theory. It now has a more solid dynamic foundation.

However, successful mutants are very rare. Gene substitution by mutation is very slow. Therefore, fitness maximization or evolutionary stability can be expected only as a long-run equilibrium phenomenon. It is doubtful whether any mutations have changed human economic behavior in the relatively short time since the beginning of the dispersion of agriculture about 10,000 years ago. Biologically, man may still be a hunter and gatherer not very well adapted to the necessity of long-run planning. This may be the reason why some PhD dissertations take much longer than planned. In any case, it would be silly to expect that man is genetically adapted to modern industrial society.

Chairman: The remarks of the population geneticist throw doubt on the near optimality of human economic behavior. At least we can say that natural selection did not necessarily produce this result. Among us is a naturalist, a man who knows animals and plants. He wants to comment.

Naturalist: We rely heavily on the principle of fitness maximization in the explanation of field phenomena. This principle has tremendous explanatory power. However, it must be used with care. Fitness maximization does not work absolutely, but only under structural constraints. Let me give you an example to clarify what I mean by structural constraints.

As you all know, the giraffe has a very long neck, but only seven neck bones like every other mammal. This is very inconvenient for the giraffe. It has difficulties lying down to sleep and standing up quickly when in danger. It actually sleeps very little. Why did evolution fail to increase the number of neck bones? The answer is simple: *evolution cannot change many things at once.* A change of the number of neck bones alone would be disastrous. Muscles, nerves, and other things would have to be adjusted. This would require many simultaneous mutations. Therefore, the number of neck bones acts as a *structural constraint* on the evolution of the giraffe.

A related problem is the correct strategy space in biological game models. Hammerstein and Riechert (1988) have modeled the fighting behavior of *agelonopsis aperta* (a spider). In this model the spiders ignore some useful information like the number of days passed in the season. From the point of view of fitness maximization, the spiders' strategy should depend on this information. Hammerstein and Riechert do not permit this in their model. I have no objection! The data justify the restriction of the strategy space. Structural constraints on the spiders' behavior must be working here.

I am convinced of the principle of fitness maximization, but under structural constraints. Fitness maximization alone is not sufficient to explain natural phenomena. A thorough knowledge of nature cannot be replaced by abstract principles.

Chairman: We have heard three reasons against the biological deduction of human economic behavior:

1. The slowness of gene substitution by mutation
2. The fact that genotype frequency adaptation without mutation does not necessarily optimize fitness
3. Structural constraints

We have to gain empirical knowledge. We cannot derive human economic behavior from biological principles. I would like to ask the Bayesian what he thinks about this.

Bayesian: Well, maybe the discussion has overemphasized natural selection. Rationality needs training. Small children are not yet rational. Untrained grownups still make many mistakes. Maybe none of us is sufficiently trained yet. We have to change this. Bayesian methods should be taught to future executives much more than they are now. These methods would thus become more and more widespread in business and government. Haphazard natural decision behavior would be replaced by superior Bayesian methods. This process of cultural evolution would establish descriptive relevance of Bayesian decision theory at least where it matters: in business and government.

Chairman: Thank you for mentioning cultural evolution. Up to now this topic has been neglected in our discussion. Two population geneticists, Cavalli-Sforza and Feldman (1981), have created a fascinating mathematical theory of cultural evolution. Another useful systematic exposition can be found in the book by Boyd and Richerson (1985). I would like to ask the population geneticist, who is familiar with this literature, to describe the basic ideas underlying the mathematical theory of cultural evolution.

Population Geneticist: This is a difficult task. I shall give a highly simplified picture. The theory of cultural evolution focuses on cultural traits. A cultural trait is something like the use of a dialect or the adherence to a religion. We think of cultural traits as acquired in the formative years of childhood and adolescence and not changed later in life. Of course, this is a simplification.

One can model a cultural trait as absent or present, but it is often more adequate to think of a cultural trait as a quantifiable variable measured on a scale. Somebody may more or less adhere to a religion. He may go to church every Sunday or only occasionally. In the following I shall restrict my attention to the case of a quantifiable cultural trait.

Models of cultural evolution with quantifiable cultural traits are similar to models of quantitative inheritance. The theory of quantitative inheritance had been initiated by Galton (1889) long before the beginnings of population genetics. Quantitative inheritance theory does not make use of Mendelian genetics. Nevertheless, models of quantitative inheritance continue to be useful in animal and plant breeding.

Consider a trait like "height." Quantitative inheritance of height is as follows. Three components determine the height of an individual:

1. The parents' average height
2. The population mean
3. A random component

First, a weighted average with fixed coefficients is formed by the first two components; then the random component is added.

Models of cultural evolution are similar. However, there may be many cultural parents, who may or may not include the biological parents. The cultural parents exert their influence by teaching or setting an example. They transmit an average in which different cultural parents may have different weights reflecting differences in importance.

I shall now sketch a possible model that is meant to illustrate and should not be taken too seriously. We shall look at the cultural trait "conformance to work ethics." We have to make an assumption on who becomes a cultural parent of whom. We make the simplest possible assumption: the cultural parents of an individual are a random sample of fixed size taken from the previous generation. In the transmitted average, the cultural parents have weights that increase with prestige. Economic success has a positive influence on prestige, and conformance to work ethics has a positive influence on economic success. We can see how in such a model a high level of conformance to work ethics can evolve in the population, even if this level is very low in the beginning.

I am now at the end of my short exposition. Of course, much more could be said about the theory of cultural evolution.

Chairman: I can see that models of this type may be useful to explain economic development. Cultural traits like values, ambitions, and life-styles influence economic behavior and thereby economic conditions. Economic conditions exert selective pressure on the cultural traits. In this way we obtain a feedback loop. Obviously, the application of cultural evolution theory to economics offers some interesting possibilities.

However, we should not forget evolutionary theories whose origins are within economics. Schumpeter (1934) created an evolutionary theory of innovation and imitation. Nelson and Winter (1982) present formal models in their book on "an evolutionary theory of economic change." The economist is familiar with this work, and I would like him to explain the approach of Nelson and Winter.

Economist: Nelson and Winter focus on firms rather than individuals. In their models firms do not maximize profits. Instead, they adapt to success and failure in a trial and error fashion. The best way to explain the approach of Nelson and Winter is with a short sketch of a particular model described by Sidney Winter (1971).

I shall sketch a slightly simplified version of the model. A finite number of goods is produced by many firms. Production methods connect inputs and outputs by fixed proportions. Inputs and outputs differ from method to method. An output of one firm may be an input of another.

The market as a whole ends up with a surplus of some commodities and with a deficit of others. We may think of surpluses as sold to consumers and of deficits as imported. The surpluses and deficits determine the prices by a relationship technically named "inverse demand function."

I now come to the behavioral assumptions. After a profit, a firm expands by one unit. After a loss, a firm contracts by one unit and also starts a search for a new production method, which is found and adopted with a positive probability. A firm whose production method yields zero profits does not change anything. Essentially, the same rules apply to potential firms that do not produce anything. These firms also have production methods that are considered in case of profitability. They search for new production methods if the present ones are not profitable at current prices.

Sidney Winter has shown that, under appropriate assumptions on the inverse demand function, the stochastic process defined by the model converges to an absorbing state with the properties of a competitive equilibrium. In this way he provided a new foundation to the theory of competitive equilibrium without profit maximization assumptions.

I admire the work of Nelson and Winter and, in particular, the model that I just described. However, I cannot see a close analogy to biological and cultural evolution. Firms do not reproduce and do not die. There is no cultural transmission from firm to firm – at least not in this model. I have no objection! Nelson and Winter have created an evolutionary theory in its own right, much better adapted to economics than any literal translation from biology could be.

Chairman: Maybe there is a closer analogy than one thinks at first glance. It is necessary to change the perspective. The production methods, not the firms, are the animals under selective pressure. The behavior of the firms is the environment of the production methods. Production methods are born and may die.

In equilibrium all active production methods have zero profitability. This is analogous to biological models with asexual reproduction, where in equilibrium all surviving genotypes have fitness 1. Obviously, profitability in one case has the same role as fitness in the other case. I would like to know whether a similar analogy can be established between cultural and biological evolution. Is it possible to define a cultural fitness? Maybe the population geneticist can answer this question.

Population Geneticist: The idea of cultural fitness sometimes appears in the literature, for example, in the book by Cavalli-Sforza and Feldman (1981), but I cannot remember seeing a precise definition. Nevertheless, it seems easy to give a meaning to the term. Cultural fitness could be defined as measure of the expected influence exerted as a cultural parent on the next generation. However, it is unclear whether a cultural fitness concept could be useful.

In the models I described, cultural inheritance is similar to quantitative inheritance in biology. It is unclear whether the biological fitness concept is useful in models of quantitative inheritance, unless very special assumptions are made. Two parents of optimal height usually have children of nonoptimal height, due to the random component and maybe the influence of the population mean. In equilibrium not everybody will be of optimal height. The equilibrium height distribution has a positive variance. Generally, there will not be even a monotonic relationship between fitness and representation in the equilibrium population. We obtain such a monotonic relationship only under very special assumptions on the way in which fitness depends on height. This indicates that a cultural fitness concept is not very useful in models of cultural evolution like those I have described. This may be different for other types of models.

92   **Reinhard Selten**

Chairman: The adaptationist wants to make a remark.

Adaptationist: I want to say that cultural evolution tends to the maximization of biological fitness. We do not need a concept of cultural fitness. Mechanisms of cultural evolution are shaped by biological evolution. There must be fitness advantages for transmitters and receivers. Consider the following example:

> *Parents teach their children which fruits are edible and which are poisonous.*

It is advantageous for the children to accept the transmission, and it is advantageous for the parents to transmit – after all, the children are their fitness.

The Shakers provide another example. The Shakers have the cultural trait of not having children. Therefore, they are dying out. In the long run a cultural trait that reduces biological fitness cannot persist.

Chairman: Is this really true? I would like to hear the opinion of the population geneticist.

Population Geneticist: My exposition of cultural evolution was highly simplified. I did not talk about the interaction of cultural and biological evolution. Actually, this interaction is emphasized in the literature. Cavalli-Sforza and Feldman (1981) present a model in which family size is the cultural trait under consideration. In spite of the interaction with biological evolution, in this model cultural evolution stabilizes a small family size.

Adaptationist (interrupting): No! I must interrupt here. The assumptions of the model must be wrong. In the long run natural selection would favor a tendency not to accept the cultural transmission of a small family size. If a bigger family size offers a fitness advantage, a small family size cannot persist.

Population Geneticist: Maybe in the very long run this is true, but not on the time scale of cultural evolution processes in recorded history. In the explanation of such processes we can safely ignore the interaction with biological evolution, at least if one avoids extreme examples like the Shakers.

In my simplified exposition of cultural evolution I also omitted another kind of interaction: the interaction of cultural evolution with individual learning. It seems to me that the interaction with individual learning is much more important than the interaction with natural selection. Actually, the interaction with individual learning is also emphasized in the literature. Boyd and Richerson (1985) describe the psychological learning model by Bush and Mosteller (1955), and they also explain Bayesian updating. However, they do not make any explicit use of these modeling possibilities. They only model the effect of learning. The precise mechanism is left open.

Boyd and Richerson assume that learning is guided by a criterion of success, for example, income. Moreover, they assume that at any point of time there is exactly one value of the trait under consideration, which is optimal with respect to the criterion of success. The value of an individual's trait is influenced by three components:

1. A culturally inherited value
2. The optimal value
3. A random error added to the optimal value

The idea is that the optimal value is not correctly perceived. This is expressed by the random error. Learning shifts the culturally inherited value in the direction of the misperceived optimal value. The value of the trait is a weighted average with fixed coefficients for the culturally inherited value and the optimal value modified by the random error. The optimal value is endogenous rather than exogenous; it may depend on the distribution of the trait.

Chairman: This reminds me of Arrow's (1962) theory of learning by doing. In this theory, too, only the effect of learning is modeled. It is assumed that experience results in a downward shift of the cost curve, but it leaves open how the firms learn to save costs.

If we want to describe economic behavior, it is not enough to model the effects of learning. We must ask the question, what is the structure of learning?

Maybe the experimentalist can help us answer this question.

Experimentalist: It is necessary to distinguish at least three kinds of learning:

1. Rote learning
2. Imitation
3. Belief learning

In rote learning, success and failure directly influence the choice probabilities. Rote learning does not require any insight into the situation. It is based on a general trust in the stability of the environment: what was good yesterday will be good today.

Imitation of successful others is similar to rote learning with the difference that the success of others directly influences choice probabilities.

Belief learning is very different. Here experiences strengthen or weaken beliefs. Belief learning has only an indirect influence on behavior.

We do not know very much about the structure of learning, but we know more about rote learning than belief learning. Up to now we do not have a sufficient understanding of belief learning. Therefore, I shall restrict my comments to rote learning.

Psychological learning models like the one by Bush and Mosteller (1955) describe rote learning. These models have only two possible reward levels: success and failure. This is reasonable for some animal experiments: the rat either finds food in the maze or it does not find food. For the description of learning by an economic agent motivated by profits, one needs a continuum of possible reward levels. In his 1983 book, John Cross generalized the model of Bush and Mosteller to a continuum of reward levels. As far as I know, the generalized model has not been confronted with data.

I would like to tell you about an experimental investigation by Malawski described in his unpublished PhD dissertation (1989). He looked at game situations in which subjects were given minimal information. The subjects did not even know that they were playing games. They only knew that they had to choose one of several alternatives, say A, B, or C. After each choice they were informed about their own payoff (sometimes they obtained additional information, which will not be described here). They experienced the same decision situation about 70 times.

Malawski developed a theory of "learning through aspiration," which agrees with his data.

His theory assumes that aspiration levels on payoffs are formed in the beginning of the session (the first 12 decisions). After this initial phase, only two responses to the previous experience are possible:

1. The same choice as last time, or
2. A randomly picked different alternative

Depending on the situation, one of these responses is "normal" and one is "exceptional." The normal response is given more often.

Under the condition that the aspiration level has been reached or surpassed the last time, the normal response is the same choice as the last time. Under the condition that the aspiration level has not been reached, the normal response is a randomly picked different alternative.

The normal response is taken with a probability $p > 1/2$ and the exceptional response is taken with probability $1 - p$. The probability p is a parameter that varies from subject to subject.

Once more, the good fit of this theory shows the importance of aspiration levels in economic behavior. Of course, Malawski's theory is not yet firmly established. More experiments have to be made, but his results look very promising.

Chairman: I would like to hear the opinion of the economist on the structure of learning.

Economist: I am surprised by the experimentalist's remark that we cannot say very much about belief learning. After all, Bayesian updating is a plausible model of belief learning. Bayesian updating can be descriptively right, even if subjectively expected utility maximization is descriptively wrong. Somebody who does not maximize utility can still adjust his subjective probabilities by Bayes's rule.

We can replace subjectively expected utility maximization by alternative theories in the literature, for example, prospect theory by Kahneman and Tversky (1984) or regret theory by Loomes and Sugden (1982), Bell (1982), and Fishburn (1982). However, I cannot see any alternative to Bayesian updating. The experimentalist did not even sketch an alternative model of belief learning.

Chairman: The experimentalist should answer this remark. Is it really true that we have no alternative to Bayesian updating as a model of belief learning?

Experimentalist: The trouble with Bayes's rule is that people do not obey it. It is, for example, well known that people overvalue the information content of small samples. In this connection, Tversky and Kahneman speak of a "law of small numbers" (1982a).

Since I have been accused of not sketching an alternative model of belief learning, I shall do this now. What I shall tell you is highly speculative, even if there is some experimental support. I refer to an oligopoly experiment described by Selten (1967).

If one wants to model belief learning, one first has to model a belief system. Bayes's rule operates on a belief system that is a probability distribution over all possible states of the world. However, belief systems of human decision makers may have a completely different structure. In my sketch of an alternative model of belief learning, beliefs are formed on causal links like

Advertising increases sales.

The belief structure has the form of a causal diagram composed of such causal links.

The term "causal diagram" has been used by Selten (1967). Later very similar structures have been called "cognitive maps" by Axelrod (1976). Axelrod has done interesting empirical research on cognitive maps of politicians expressed in speeches and writings.

A causal diagram shows chains that connect a decision variable like advertising with a goal variable like profits. Suppose that there are two causal chains in the diagram:

1. *Advertising increases sales and sales increase profits.*
2. *Advertising increases cost and cost decreases profit.*

Subjects reason qualitatively on the basis of such chains. The first chain is an argument for more advertising, and the second chain is an argument for less advertising. Such conflicts are resolved by judgments on the relative importance of causal links. Suppose that the causal link from advertising to cost is judged to be the least important one. On the basis of this judgment, the second chain is neglected, and a decision to increase advertising is based on the first chain. Of course, this determines only the direction of change. The amount of change has to be determined in some other way.

Belief learning exerts its influence on importance judgments. Experience may show that the influence of advertising on cost is more important than the influence of advertising on sales. The mechanism of belief learning can be modeled in a fashion similar to the mechanism of rote learning.

Chairman: These remarks show that belief learning is closely connected to boundedly rational reasoning. Not only belief systems must be modeled, but also their use in reasoning. We need to know more about bounded rationality. In my view the development of a theory of bounded rationality is one of the most important tasks of economics in our time. Bayesian updating has been mentioned favorably and unfavorably. I think the Bayesian should comment on Bayes's rule.

Bayesian: I would rather comment on bounded rationality. I may have no opportunity to do this later. Herbert Simon (1957) introduced the idea of satisficing. His view of bounded rationality did not exert a strong influence on economic theory. His work did inspire the book by Cyert and March (1963) on the "behavioral theory of the firm." Many people were very impressed by this book, in particular by the surprising empirical success of the model that describes the behavior of a department store manager with high predictive accuracy. However, the book did not start a revolution of economic theory. I will explain why.

A typical piece of research in the behavioral theory of the firm is a simulation study based on a complex model, sometimes with hundreds of parameters and with many behavioral ad hoc assumptions. Generally, no clear conclusion can be drawn from such simulation studies. What we see here is a *theory without theorems.* A theory without theorems cannot succeed.

In the behavioral theory of the firm and the evolutionary approach by

Nelson and Winter, behavior is described by ad hoc assumptions, which vary from model to model. This is very unsatisfactory. Economic theory needs a description of economic behavior based on a few general principles that can be applied to every conceivable decision situation. Bayesian decision theory meets this requirement. Bayesian decision theory should not be thrown away in favor of ad hoc explanations of experimental phenomena.

Experiments are often too quickly interpreted as evidence against Bayesian decision theory. I would like to mention the example of the finitely repeated prisoner's dilemma. This game has only one equilibrium outcome: noncooperation in every period. Nevertheless, one observes cooperation until shortly before the end. This seems to refute the rationality assumptions of game theory. However, a rational explanation has been given by Kreps, Milgrom, Roberts, and Wilson (1982). They introduced a small amount of incomplete information on payoffs of the other players. In the slightly modified game, the usual pattern of behavior is an equilibrium outcome.

Even the limits of computational capabilities permit a Bayesian treatment. Repeated games with limited memory or limited complexity have been analyzed by Neyman (1985), Aumann and Sorin (1989), Kalai and Stanford (1987), and others. Another approach to problems connected to bounded rationality is the relaxation of common knowledge assumptions explored by Neyman. We see here the beginnings of a Bayesian theory of bounded rationality. It is not necessary to construct a theory of bounded rationality outside the Bayesian framework. It is much more fruitful to do this within the Bayesian framework.

Chairman: I would like to ask the experimentalist what he thinks about Bayesian bounded rationality.

Experimentalist: Let me first comment on the paper by Kreps, Milgrom, Roberts, and Wilson. In terms of game theory, their work is very interesting, but behaviorally they miss the mark! Selten and Stoecker (1986) describe an experiment in which each subject plays 25 supergames of 10 periods each against anonymous opponents changing from supergame to supergame. In these experiments, the typical pattern of cooperation until shortly before the end did not emerge in the first supergame, but only after a considerable amount of learning. In the beginning behavior is chaotic. Cooperation is learned slowly and after cooperation the end effect. According to Kreps, Milgrom, Roberts, and Wilson, the typical pattern is due to thinking rather than learning and, therefore, should emerge immediately. In their theory there is no room for chaotic behavior in the beginning and for slow learning afterward.

I now want to comment on infinite supergames with restricted memory. In such games only the operating memory is restricted or, in other words, the storage space available for the execution of a strategy. The computational capabilities for the analysis of the game remain unrestricted. In fact, the analysis of the game tends to become more difficult by constraints on the operating memory. I cannot see any contribution to a theory of bounded rationality in this kind of work.

Let me now say something about common knowledge or the lack of it. Consider a chain of the following kind:

I know, that he knows, that I know, that he knows, . . .

Roughly speaking, common knowledge means that such chains can be continued indefinitely. Does it really matter in practical decision situations whether I have common knowledge or whether I have to break off such chains after stage 4? I do not think so. As far as human decision behavior is concerned, I dare say: a lack of common knowledge is not important; however, a very common lack of knowledge is important.

I appreciate the behavioral theory of the firm and the evolutionary approach by Nelson and Winter. I do not accept the criticism against the use of ad hoc assumptions. Look at human anatomy and physiology: bones, muscles, nerves, and so on. Human anatomy and physiology cannot be derived from a few general principles.

Let me say something else in defense of ad hoc assumptions. Experiments show that human behavior is ad hoc. Different principles are applied to different decision tasks. Case distinctions determine which principles are used where. Successful explanations of experimental phenomena have been built along these lines, for example, Selten's (1987) theory of equal division payoff bounds for three-person games in characteristic function. Let me conclude my comments with this remark: it is better to make many empirically supported ad hoc assumptions than to rely on a few unrealistic principles of great generality and elegance.

Chairman: I would like to ask the economist whether he thinks that economic theory should abolish the optimization approach in favor of a more realistic description of economic behavior.

Economist: Many economic theorists are uneasy with the usual exaggerated rationality assumptions – but they continue to use them. They do not see a clear alternative. In recent years the interest in experimental economics has increased tremendously. This offers hope for a new foundation of microeconomics. However, as long as this new foundation has not yet been established, we must continue to rely on exaggerated rationality assumptions. I do not think that present-day microeconomics will become completely obsolete. Market experiments by Smith, Plott, and others reviewed in the literature (Smith 1980, Plott 1982) confirm competitive equilibrium theory. What is now derived as a result of optimization may later be explained as a result of learning.

Bayesianism may be wrong descriptively, but this does not touch its great normative significance. Moreover, as was pointed out earlier in the discussion, teaching of Bayesian methods in universities will increase their use in business and government and thereby establish descriptive relevance for Bayesian decision theory.

Chairman: Yes, we have not yet sufficiently discussed the idea that future economic behavior will become more Bayesian than it is now due to the influence of teaching. I would like to ask the experimentalist what he thinks of the prospects of a cultural evolution toward a widespread use of Bayesian methods in business and government.

Experimentalist: The application of Bayesian methods makes sense in special contexts. For example, a life insurance company may adopt a utility function for its total assets; subjective probabilities may be based on actuarial tables. However, a general use of Bayesian methods meets serious difficulties. Subjective probabilities and utilities are needed as inputs. Usually, these inputs are not readily available.

The brain has no probability and utility book that it can consult like a telephone directory. Probability and preference judgments require information processing in the brain. They are outputs rather than inputs. There is no reason to suppose that information processing in the brain yields consistent probability and preference judgments. There is much experimental evidence to the contrary. Let me explain an example concerning probability judgments using the conjunction effect described by Tversky and Kahneman (1982b). They asked their subjects to rank a number of statements on some future events with respect to likelihood. One of the events was a tennis match involving Björn Borg. Among the statements were the following two:

Statement A: Borg will lose the first set.

Statement B: Borg will lose the first set, but he will win the match.

Subjects tend to judge statement B as more likely than statement A, despite the fact that statement B describes a subcase of statement A. This shows that probability judgments lack even one of the most basic consistency properties, namely monotonicity of the probability measure with respect to set inclusion.

The phenomenon is a "representativeness effect." The statement "Borg will lose the first set" is not representative of the image of Borg in the minds of the subjects. Borg was a winner, not a loser. The additional detail "but he will win the match" is representative and, therefore, improves the impression of credibility.

Preference judgments are as inconsistent and unreliable as probability judgments. Weber, Eisenführ, and von Winterfeldt (1988) have published an experimental investigation of "dimension splitting in multiattribute utility measurement." They show that the weight of an attribute is increased if it is split into several subattributes. This is important because multiattribute utility measurement is recommended as an instrument of decision aid by Bayesian decision theorists interested in practical applications. We see here that the result of the method depends heavily on the way in which the problem is presented to those who have to make the preference judgments.

We can conclude: Normative Bayesianism is dubious in view of the unreliability of its inputs. If you ask people to be consistent, you ask for too much. Imagine a normative theory of sports that commands: "Athlete, jump 100 meters high!" It cannot be done.

I do not see an unavoidable cultural evolution toward a more widespread use of Bayesian methods in business and government.

Chairman: It seems to be necessary to make a distinction between a *practical normative theory* and an *ideal normative theory*. A practical normative theory can be used to help people improve their decisions. Ideal normative theory clarifies the concept of rationality independently of the limitations of real persons. Even if Bayesianism fails as a practical normative theory, it still remains an ideal normative theory of great philosophical importance.

We now must end our discussion. I shall try to summarize the results. I opened the discussion with a question: What do we know about the structure of human economic behavior? I must admit that the answer is disappointing. We know very little.

We know that Bayesian decision theory is not a realistic description of human economic behavior. There is ample evidence for this, but we cannot be satisfied with negative knowledge – knowledge about what human behavior fails to be. We need more positive knowledge on the structure of human behavior. We need quantitative theories of bounded rationality, supported by experimental evidence, which can be used in economic modeling as an alternative to exaggerated rationality assumptions.

We have identified a hierarchy of dynamic processes that shape economic behavior. In the order of increasing speed, there processes are

1. Gene substitution by mutation
2. Adaptation of genotype frequencies without mutation
3. Cultural transmission from generation to generation
4. Learning (including imitation)

The speed differences are so great that for many purposes an adiabatic approximation seems to be justified. Adiabatic approximation means that if we look at one of the four processes, results of slower processes can be taken as fixed and quicker processes can be assumed to reach equilibrium instantly.

Learning, the quickest process, is the most important one for economics. Day-to-day price movements on the stock exchange and other competitive processes involve learning and imitation. For slower dynamic phenomena like economic development, cultural transmission from generation to generation is also important.

The two processes of biological evolution have shaped the inherited components of economic behavior. Gene substitution by mutation maximizes fitness, but slowly and under structural constraints. Adaptation of genotype frequencies without mutation is nonoptimizing.

It is interesting to speculate on the evolution of behavioral tendencies. One may, for example, construct theories on the influence of prehistoric or even prehuman environmental factors on mechanisms of cultural evolution. However, such speculations, as interesting as they may be, are no substitute for empirical research. It makes no sense to speculate on the evolution of unicorns unless unicorns have been found in nature. Biological theory cannot be used as an instrument to discover facts by armchair reasoning.

We must do empirical research if we want to gain knowledge on the structure of human economic behavior. In order to replace unrealistic rationality assumptions, we need theories of bounded rationality. As I have said already, we need quantitative theories that can replace the usual rationality assumptions in economic models.

In the near future, theories of limited range must be built that apply to restricted areas of experimental research. A number of such theories already can be found in the literature. Some of them have been mentioned in the discussion. It can be hoped that eventually many theories of limited range will grow together and evolve into a comprehensive picture of the structure of human economic behavior. Only painstaking experimental research can bring us nearer to this goal.

I close the discussion now. Whoever wants to add something must do so in private conversations.

References

Allais, Maurice. 1953. Le comportement de l'homme rationnel devant le risque critique des postulates et axiomes de l'ecole Americaine. *Econometrica* 21 (October):503–46.

Arrow, Kenneth J. 1962. The economic implications of learning by doing. *Review of Economic Studies* 29:155–73.

Aumann, Robert I., and Sylvain Sorin. 1989. Cooperation and bounded recall. *Games and Economic Behavior* 1:5–39.

Axelrod, Robert. 1976. *Structure of decision. The cognitive maps of political elites.* Princeton: Princeton University Press.

Bell, D. E. 1982. Regret in decision making under uncertainty. *Operations Research* 30:961–81.

Berg, Claus C. 1973. *Individuelle entscheidungsprozesse: laborexperimente und computersimulation.* Wiesbaden.

———— 1974. Individual decision concerning the allocation of resources for projects with uncertain consequences. *Management Science* 21:98–105.

Boyd, Robert, and Peter I. Richerson. 1985. *Culture and the evolutionary process.* Chicago and London: University of Chicago Press.

Bush, R. R., and F. Mosteller. 1995. *Stochastic models of learning.* New York: John Wiley & Sons.

Cavalli-Sforza, L. L., and M. W. Feldman. 1981. *Cultural transmission and evolution: a quantitative approach.* Princeton: Princeton University Press.

Cross, John G. 1983. *A theory of adaptive economic behavior.* Cambridge: Cambridge University Press.

Cyert, R. M., and J. G. March. 1963. *A behavioral theory of the firm.* Englewood Cliffs: Prentice Hall.

Eshel, Ilan. 1988. Game theory and population dynamics in complex genetical systems: the role of sex in short term and in long term evolution. Working Paper #24, Game theory in the behavioral sciences. ZiF, Universität Bielefeld.

Eshel, Ilan, and Marcus W. Feldman. 1984. Initial increase of new mutants and some continuity properties of ESS in two locus systems. *American Naturalist* 124(5):631–40.

Fishburn, P. C. 1982. Nontransitive measurable utility. *Journal of Mathematical Psychology* 26:31–67.

Galton, F. 1989. *Natural inheritance.* New York: Macmillan.

Hammerstein, Peter, and Susan E. Riechert. 1988. Payoffs and strategies in territorial contests of two ecotypes of spider, *Agelonopsis aperta. Evolutionary Ecology* 2:115–38.

Kahneman, Daniel, and Amos Tversky. 1984. Prospect theory: an analysis of decision under risk. *Econometrica* 47 (March):263–91.

Kalai, Ehud, and W. Stanford. 1987. Finite rationality and interpersonal complexity in finitely repeated games. *Econometrica* 56:397–410.

Kreps, D., P. Milgrom, J. Roberts, and R. Wilson. 1982. Rational cooperation in the finitely repeated prisoner's dilemma. *Journal of Economic Theory* 27:245–52.

Liberman, V. 1988. External stability and ESS: criteria for initial increase of new mutant allele. *Mathematical Biology* 26:447–85.

Loomes, Graham, and Robert Sugden. 1982. Regret theory: an alternative theory of rational choice under uncertainty. *Economic Journal* 92 (December): 805–24.

Malawski, Marcin. 1989. Some learning processes in population games. Diss. University of Bonn.

Maynard Smith, John. 1982. *Evolution and the theory of games*. Cambridge: Cambridge University Press.

Maynard Smith, John, and G. R. Price. 1973. The logic of animal conflict. *Nature* 246:15–18.

Moran, P. A. P. 1964. On the nonexistence of adaptive topographies. *American Human Geneticist* 27:343–83.

Nelson, Richard, and Sidney G. Winter. 1982. *An evolutionary theory of economic change*. Cambridge: The Belknap Press of Harvard University Press.

Neyman, A. 1985. Bounded complexity justifies cooperation in the finitely repeated prisoner's dilemma. Manuscript.

Plott, Charles R. 1982. Industrial organization theory and experimental economics. *Journal of Economic Literature* 20:1485–1527.

Savage, Leonhard I. 1954. *The foundation of statistics*. New York: John Wiley & Sons.

Selten, Reinhard. 1967. Invetitionsverhalten im oligopolexperiment. In *Beiträge zur experimentellen Wirtschaftsforschung*, ed. H. Sauermann, vol. 1, 60–102. I. C. B. Mohr (Paul Siebeck) Tübingen.

———— 1987. Equity and coalition bargaining. In *Experimentation in economics*, ed. A. Roth. Cambridge: Cambridge University Press.

Selten, Reinhard, and Rolf Stoecker. 1986. End behavior in sequences of finite prisoner's dilemma supergames. *Journal of Economic Behavior and Organization* 7:47–70.

Simon, Herbert A. 1957. *Models of man*. New York: John Wiley & Sons.

Smith, Vernon L. 1980. Microeconomic systems as a science. *American Economic Review* 5:923–55.

Schumpeter, I. A. 1934. *The theory of economic development*. Cambridge: Harvard University Press.

Tversky, Amos, and Daniel Kahneman. 1982a. Belief in the law of small numbers. In *Judgment and uncertainty, heuristics and biases*, ed. D. Kahneman, P. Slovic, and A. Tversky, 23–31. Cambridge: Cambridge University Press.

———— 1982b. Judgments of and by representativeness. In *Judgment and uncertainty, heuristics and biases*, ed. D. Kahneman, P. Slovic, and A. Tversky, 84–98. Cambridge: Cambridge University Press.

Tyszka, T. 1983. *Contextual multiattribute decision rules*. In *Decision processes and decision analysis*, ed. L. Sjöberg, T. Tyszka, and J. Wise. Doxa, Lund.

Weber, Martin, Franz Eisenführ, and Detlof von Winterfeldt. 1988. The effects of splitting attributes on weights in multiattribute utility measurement. *Management Science* 34:432–45.

Winter, Sidney G. 1971. Satisficing, selection and the innovating remnant. *Quarterly Journal of Economics* 85:237–61.

1990

VERNON L. SMITH

Experimental Economics: Behavioral Lessons for Microeconomic Theory and Policy

It is an honor on this occasion and by this means to pay tribute to the memory of Nancy Schwartz. Although Nancy's work was that of an accomplished theorist, and not of an experimentalist, she had an interest in experimentalism that was born of her natural curiosity about all economic matters. It is also a pleasure, once again, to visit my many friends at Northwestern.

Almost everyone wants to know if things work, and experimental economics asks whether and under what circumstances our models work. Over the past 30-odd years, this intellectual effort has developed a methodology for providing experimental answers to this question, integrating them with field observations and, where appropriate, for modifying our models in response to the resulting evidence. In this address I want to talk about what we have learned and the consequences of this learning for how we do theory. I will also have something to say about the potential implications of our learning for microeconomic policy.

For economic theory there is both good news and bad news. The good news is that we are on the right track, generally, in modeling the relationship among institutional rules, individual incentives, and marker performance. Institutions clearly matter. The lesson here can be said to provide a perspective on the biblical imperative (slightly reinterpreted from Romans): For rules are not a terror to good works, but to bad. That perspective is the following: Rules determine incentives, and incentives determine the performance of markets by encouraging desirable

Reprinted with permission from Vernon L. Smith, *Papers in Experimental Economics* (Cambridge University Press, 1991), 802–12.

behavior and discouraging undesirable behavior in a way that is self-regulating. As much of the non-Western world, outside China, now realizes, if you do not rely on self-regulating rules, your economic system cannot be made to work.

Furthermore, our models of noncooperative behavior are fairly good; they often are able to do a credible job of predicting observations, even in quite complex environments, although it is plain that there is room for improvement and, of course, interpretation. The bad news for theory is that we can't seem to get our interpretation of the information and environmental conditions right for these models, so that the models correctly correspond to both the conditions and the results of the experiments. We need more institution-specific theory, whose rigorous development is guided by comparably rigorous empirical learning. The good news is that, by and large, markets work the way we think they should to coordinate the dispersed actions of economic agents. The bad news is that, in the meantime, as theorists, we have been less than successful in showing how our concepts of incentive compatibility and strategy-proofness can be implemented beyond the impossibility theorems suggesting that the world can't work the way we observe it working in the laboratory. As a consequence, our scientific advance is handicapped by our failure to pursue the exciting implications of the fact that things sometimes work better than we had a right to expect from our abstract interpretations of theory.

INFORMATION AND NONCOOPERATIVE EQUILIBRIA

It is widely believed and repeated that noncooperative equilibria are attainable only under the condition of complete and common information on preferences, i.e., where each agent knows the utility values for all agents. Indeed, these presumed strong information requirements are often cited as "the weakness of the Nash (noncooperative) equilibrium concept" (Sonnenschein 1983, 16). In a parallel vein, neoclassical economists from Jevons to Samuelson have assumed that competitive equilibria also required complete information on (or "perfectly foreseen") supply and demand. These assumptions have scarce empirical support in the context of single-decision games. But in the less artificial context of repeated games, these assumptions do not just fail to be supported by decades of experimental data. Rather, the data support the opposite proposition that noncooperative and competitive equilibrium concepts are best able to predict behavior under private incomplete information; that under complete information conditions, these concepts either fail, or do less well, in predicting behavior than under private information conditions. These experimental results have come from a wide spectrum of institutions: posted-price, bilateral-bargaining games; oligopoly markets; a variety of sealed bid auctions; continuous double auctions (see McCabe, Rassenti, and Smith 1989(a) for a partial summary); and many more. This is very encouraging in that our experimental observations tell us that the well-known embarrassment of multiple equilibria in repeated games of complete information is largely a cockpit problem for the theorist, not a behavioral problem for real, motivated people.

The economics of incentives is alive and well in the laboratory; the stuck zippers are in the profession, not in our behavioral data. The theoretical change is to develop formulations showing that noncooperative equilibria are sustainable under private incomplete information; that under complete information, agents can identify more attractive states than the noncooperative outcomes and can attempt to achieve these states; that these attempts are more likely to be successful when the number of competitors is only two, but become less likely to be successful as the number increases above two.

In some very long oligopoly games under full information on own-demand, cooperation is increased, but still declines as N increases above two (Friedman and Hoggatt 1980). I should note also that the incidence of tacit cooperation where numbers are low occurs in experiments in which buyers' behavior is *simulated* to be fully demand revealing as assumed in currently tractable theory. But where oligopoly experiments have used human buyers as well as sellers, the results show that the strategic behavior of buyers is important in helping to countervail seller cooperation (Kruse 1988). To my knowledge, we have no complete oligopoly models of the behavior of both buyers and sellers. Duopoly games with simulated buyers are really just bilateral bargaining games for the division of surplus.

But why is it so natural and commonplace to suppose that complete information is necessary for noncooperative equilibria? I think it is because we cannot imagine, untutored by observation, how agents might achieve an equilibrium except by rational cognition and, as theorists and experimentalists, *we* have to have complete information to *calculate* such an equilibrium. It is important here to distinguish theory from the casual assertions of theorists. For, in fact, the condition of complete information is not a formal part of the theory of how an equilibrium is achieved, and lacking such a process theory, we have simply tacked on to the formal theory the ad hoc assertion that agents have to know what we have to know. But if noncooperative states, in truth, possess an equilibrium property, it is conceivable that agents could grope around and find it without calculation, just as a marble thrown into a bowl will find the bottom without knowledge of Newtonian mechanics.

Although I have emphasized noncooperative theory, these comments also apply to the Nash model of cooperative bargaining. Roth and Malouf (1979) summarize experimental data that support (often with very low variance) the Nash model under private information, but which strongly contradict the model under complete information.

Finally, let me report the best news of all. Theorists are increasingly becoming concerned with these long-standing discrepancies between theory and experiment. D. Easely, J. Ledyard, D. Friedman, M. Satterthwaite, S. Williams, R. Wilson (see Wilson 1990), and others have all made important contributions to the analysis of the exceptionally challenging problem of modeling double auctions; Kalai and Lehrer (1990) have an important theorem providing conditions under which incompletely informed players in a bimatrix game converge to a noncooperative equilibrium (also see Canning 1989). Selten's (1989) Schwartz lecture is a magnificent essay on the mutual dependence between theory and experiment. These are exciting scientific developments, as they portend significant methodological changes in the way that we do, and think about, economic theory. Deeper experiments are sure to follow breakthroughs in theory.

COMMON INFORMATION AND COMMON KNOWLEDGE OR EXPECTATIONS

The theoretical problem that an equilibrium of a model might be approximated without agent knowledge or understanding of the model has important implications for the concept of common knowledge that allegedly underlies contemporary game theory. I avoid using the term "common knowledge," preferring instead to use two distinct and more appropriate terms, "common information" and "common expectations." This is because all that one can achieve, operationally, in a given experimental or field situation is a state of common information. All subjects in an experiment can receive a public rendition of the instructions and payoffs for all participants; then all see the situation and all see that all see it. But it does not follow from such common information alone that "knowledge" in the sense of expectations, or knowing what others will do, will be common. I could give everyone in this room common, complete information, and yet each of you would face uncertainty concerning how others will behave, given this information.

Empirically, common expectations are achieved through shared experience. By all observing what all do, over time groups come to have common expectations. This has been the result in an immense variety of different experiments: in simple repeated games, in rich n-person markets, in fiat money experiments, and in laboratory stock markets. The assumption of common knowledge in game theory models, while enabling us to "defend" game theory solutions, also has limited severely our progress by begging the key question of the processes whereby agents come to have common knowledge. This is where the action – the dynamics – is to be found; where we discover how it is that groups learn their way from initial states to equilibrium states.

In the stock market experiments, fundamental share value is derived from dividends whose per-period probability distribution is common information. Since expected share value in any period is just expected single-period value times the number of trading (or dividend) periods remaining, fundamental value declines linearly from period one to the final period. Capital gains are necessarily zero-sum across all traders. But common information is not sufficient to induce common expectations. Inexperienced subjects produce large volume price bubbles that deviate substantially from intrinsic dividend value. When the subjects return for a second session, volume is reduced and the price bubble is less pronounced relative to dividend value. Where subjects return for a third session, volume is thinner at prices much closer to intrinsic value as the wellsprings of hope for capital gains finally run dry. Through this sequential experience subjects acquire the common expectation that exchange value is near dividend value. Having experienced it, they believe it, and we have not been successful in reinflating a bubble with twice-experienced subjects using similar environments.

What is incorrect in both the rational expectations and game theory models is the assumption that common information eliminates behavioral or strategic uncertainty. In the stock market context, this uncertainty is resolved through shared experience in a stationary environment. This expectations interpretation is supported by the observation that in finite horizon-price search experiments (Cox and Oaxaca 1989), individual subjects behave in accordance with the predictions of a rational backward-induction model. But this is a game against nature in which subjects have only to anticipate their own behavior later in the game, not the behavior of others.

The problem that common information on payoffs is not sufficient to yield common expectations is recognized by those game theorists who argue that common knowledge must include knowledge of the model itself (Aumann 1987, 473). This means that the predictions of the model apply only to those who agree as to the game being played and how to analyze it. Therefore, my conclusion was that game theory was a predictive science only to the extent that it applied to game theorists or their cognitive equivalents.

But my colleague Kevin McCabe has corrected me by noting that game theorists disagree on solution concepts and the analysis of games. Thus, the requirement that the model be common knowledge simply substitutes an unspecified process of pregame agreement for the experiential process by which agents arrive at common expectations, and the disagreement among game theorists suggests that no logical agreement process exists – at least not yet. All the important theoretical action is relegated to an unmodeled pregame process. The same considerations apply to Nash-Muth rational common expectations theory, which has found support in hundreds of double-auction experiments under incomplete information.

Concerning common "knowledge," the lesson here for economics, as in other sciences, is that theorists vitally need the assistance of data (and vice versa, as any experimentalist can tell you) and that speculative theory that goes too far beyond observation, although entertaining, incurs the hazard of becoming entangled in its own bootstraps.

But let me return to the experimental stock markets. Economists living on both coasts had trouble believing the first 30 experiments. Others felt that the results corresponded to what they expected, but their expectations came from intuition, not from formal models. The problem, I was assured by the first group, was that the subjects could not sell short, that transactions cost was virtually zero (you trade electronically by pressing buttons), or that the subjects were students, not business persons. Everybody had his (they were all males) own pet explanation of what was wrong with the first set of experiments, but none of these explanations was theory-based. Of course, each of these suggestions had merit, but the important point is that there was little consensus. When widely accepted models fail, the best and the brightest grasp for straws.

Some 50 experiments later we had answers to these questions and many others. Briefly, the bubble propensities summarized above are not eliminated when subjects have the right to sell short or buy on margin or are required to pay a transactions fee; nor do they go away when we use business persons or stock traders as subjects. On the contrary, the bubbles are somewhat worse with margin buying, which lends credence to the widespread imposition of margin limits by the brokerage industry as well as by regulators. Bubbles are also, if anything, worse with business persons, though not with stock traders.

Furthermore, the widely recommended use of limit price change rules in the wake of the October 1987 worldwide stock market crash is not found by experiment to be efficacious. Limit price rules actually intensify bubbles. We think this is because the limit on price declines in each period induces a perception of reduced downside risk, causing the boom to carry further and longer before a crash occurs.

But on the positive side, we find that the introduction of a futures contract that expires at the midpoint of the horizon does help to dampen bubbles by focusing traders' initial attention on their expectations of share value at mid-horizon. A futures market appears to reduce myopia in the spot market by giving subjects an advance reading on their expectations at mid-horizon. A reasonable interpretation is that the function served by the institution of futures markets is not so much to predict the future, but to allow the market to achieve common expectations; to resolve behavioral uncertainty – in advance of an event.

This consensus building function is also served in the context of other asset trading environments (Forsythe, Palfrey, and Plott 1982) and in simple extensive form bargaining games (Harrison and McCabe 1993). In the bargaining games, subjects acquire the common expectations needed to backward-induct properly by first playing the last two rounds of a three-round sequence before playing the full three-round sequence. Thus, each subject plays the "future" in advance, discovers what to expect of her opposite, and is then able to solve correctly the three-round game, which of course cannot be solved without compatible expectations.

PRACTICE AND INSTITUTIONS IN MARKET LEARNING

Many years of experimental research have made it plain that real people do not solve decision problems by thinking about them in the way that we do as economic theorists. Only academics learn primarily by reading and thinking. Those who run the world, and support us financially, tend to learn by watching, listening, and doing. Try learning to operate a computer by merely reading one of those horrible instructional manuals. When experiments approximate the predictions of theory, it is because subjects experience the choices of others and then choose based on what they have learned to expect. This feedback process can be realized in repeated market games, with each decision disciplined by the social interaction of people through the rules of the trading institution. Just as the computer and the piano are human tools that we learn to use almost exclusively by practice, so the set of rules of an institution, such as those of the oral double-auction, is a social tool that can guide the collective to achieve outcomes that are individually and – if the rules are right – socially optimal.

In fact, people tend to perform poorly when they must rely completely on their unaided and untutored cognitive powers in stating how they would choose in simple games against nature, e.g., in selecting among gambles. This is shown in the instructive opinion choice surveys of Kahneman and Tversky (1979), which may tell us little about the equilibrating forces whose effects we observe in experimental markets, but much about the untrained thinking processes of humans isolated from each other and from institutions. Moreover, there are many cases in which behavioral convergence to noncooperative states in repeated games does not require Cournot convergent theory designs.

By Cournot convergent, I refer to a strategy sequence that converges to a noncooperative equilibrium when each agent on round $t + 1$ chooses her best response on the assumption that all other agents will simply repeat their previous choices on round t. The robustness of empirical convergence in Cournot divergent designs was first shown by John Carlson (1967) in the context of his "Cobweb Theorem" experiments. These results have been extended by Wellford (1989). Similar findings were obtained in my Groves-Ledyard public good experiments (Smith 1979) and in countless Cournot oligopoly experiments, which appear likely to be unstable, theoretically, under the adaptive expectations hypothesis (Szidarovszky and Okuguchi 1987). These cases suggest that the structural form of expectations, not just their parameterization in a fixed form, is adaptive. Such adaptation appears to be stimulated when people find that their current myopic responses are serving them poorly.

EXPERIMENTER INDUCED FAIR OUTCOMES?

Experimenters must be alert to the possibility that their experimental procedures constitute an unintended treatment, which contaminates their interpretation of the experimental results. Experimentalists often do supplementary experiments designed to check for such artifactual elements. A long-respected scientific rule in experimentalism is that important variables likely to affect observations should either be controlled as treatments or their effects randomized to reduce systematic error bias. For example, initial endowments, agent roles, and rights to act are commonly assigned at random among individual subjects. The objective is to avoid introducing any systematic correlation between such assignments and the personal characteristics of subjects.

Like all good rules, this one should be applied with sensitivity to the possibility of exceptions. This is particularly important in experimental economics, where our methods, techniques, and subject matter often differ from those of other experimental sciences. Since we are only at the beginning, much is yet to be learned about shaping the technology of experiment in economics.

Apparently, the idea that one should randomize effects that are not controlled comes from biology, where you randomize treatments among plots of land to prevent differences in soil quality from being attributed accidentally to the treatments. But human subjects are not plots of land, and the method of assignment may not have a neutral effect on behavior. This lesson has been clearly demonstrated in the bargaining experiments of Hoffman and Spitzer (1985). Subject pairs in these experiments bargain over the division of surplus under different property right arrangements. Under one arrangement, the agent whose productive activity causes harm to the other agent has the right to inflict this harm. This is the "polluter's" rights model. Under the alternative arrangement, the harmed agent has a right to be compensated for damage. This is the "pollutee" rights model.

According to the so-called Coase (1960) theorem, the creation of social surplus, or the gain from exchange, is not altered by the property right arrangement, although certainly the distribution of the surplus between the two parties may be altered. The Hoffman-Spitzer experiments provide strong support for this proposition. All pairs bargain to the solution that maximized their combined gains from exchange. But in every case, the person designated as the "controller" who was endowed with the privileged right failed to take advantage of this right. The controller, instead of extracting her individually rational share of the gains, agreed to an equal split of the gains. This outcome is commonly reported in bargaining experiments and is interpreted to be the result of a "fairness" ethic.

In Hoffman-Spitzer, all bargaining was face-to-face and was monitored by the experimenters, who had the impressionistic suspicion that this outcome might be influenced by the fact that the assignment of the controller right was determined by flipping a coin. Thus, they replicated their experiments, but assigned the role of "controller" to the winner of a pregame contest. The instructions emphasized that the winner had *earned* the right to be the controller. The effect of this new treatment on outcomes was dramatic: two-thirds of the bargaining pairs now negotiated individually rational outcomes. This is particularly impressive under face-to-face bargaining where lack of anonymity might be thought to increase the pressure on the controller to be accommodative.

The random assignment of rights is widely perceived to be a fair method of allocation; for example, hunting rights, student basketball tickets, and tied trades on stock exchanges are allocated by lottery. Consequently, when you flip a coin to select which of two persons is to be assigned an advantageous endowment, or right, the subjects are likely to believe that you are doing this to be fair. So if you are being fair to them, why should they not be fair to each other? These results call into question the interpretation of data from the large literature in bilateral bargaining that is characterized by a first-mover, or other asymmetric advantage, randomly assigned. The point is not that fairness criteria are unimportant. I believe they are. Rather, the question is whether inducing fair behavior is the appropriate way to frame the test of a bargaining theory that assumes self-interested agents whose interests conflict, as with management and labor.

Now, if one were to replicate all the asymmetric bargaining experiments, assigning privileged rights only to those who earned them, and still observed fair outcomes, then this would call into question the relevancy of the theory. Since that has not been done, I do not believe that the current state of experimental testing is adequate to support rejection of the theory in its present form. Fairness considerations are important – too important to be slipped in artifactually as an inadvertent product of a procedure intended for a different purpose.

REWARD MOTIVATION AND DECISION COST

I first learned the full significance of reward saliency in experiments from the psychologist, Sidney Siegel (1961). The context was the very simple Bernoulli trials experiment. On each trial the subject's task was to predict which of two independent events would occur. The more frequent event occurred with probability π (say, 70%) and the less frequent event with probability $(1 - \pi)$, where π is usually not known by the subject. For two decades before Siegel's 1961 paper, psychologists had been doing these experiments, always instructing the subject to "do your best" to predict correctly on each trial. The standard observed outcome was probability matching in which the proportion of times the more frequent event is chosen is $p = \pi$. Of course if your objective is to maximize the number of correct predictions, then as soon as you have determined which is the more frequent event, you should predict it 100% of the time. Consequently, the typical conclusion from the data was that the model of rational maximizing behavior had to be rejected. Sid Siegel thought that this was a curious conclusion because subjects had no incentive to maximize the number of correct predictions other than perhaps the homegrown satisfaction of being correct.

Siegel argued that, from the subject's point of view, the task was excruciatingly boring, and hypothesized that the subject's diversification of his prediction strategy was a means of reducing this boredom. Specifically, he hypothesized that the subject's choice criterion was composed of two additive subjective utilities: the utility of a correct prediction and the

Table 1. *Prediction Results, Final Block of 20 Trials for* $\pi = 0.70$

Treatment	No payoff	Payoff	Payoff-loss
No. of subjects	12	12	12
Mean value of p	0.70	0.77	0.93
Decision error	0.069	0.062	0.058

utility of variability, where the latter was proportional to $p(1 - p)$, which is the variance of outcomes in a Bernoulli process with parameter p. This assumption has the property that the utility of variability was greatest when $p = \frac{1}{2}$; i.e., when diversification, or boredom relief, was greatest. Siegel then deduced two propositions: first, the optimal response is $p^* = \pi$ (probability matching) if the marginal utility of a correct response is equal to the marginal utility of variability, and second, the optimal response p^* would increase with an increase in the marginal utility of being correct.

An obvious way of increasing p^* was to introduce monetary rewards for a correct prediction. He conducted experiments in which subjects were run under three motivation treatments: no payoff ("do your best"); payoff (reward for each correct prediction); and payoff-loss (a reward for a correct, and a charge for an incorrect, prediction). Siegel's model predicted:

$$\pi = p \text{ (no payoff)} < p \text{ (payoff)} < p \text{ (payoff-loss)}.$$

Siegel (see Siegel, et al. 1964) reported only the mean observed values of p, but the standard error for each treatment is computed from his raw data, and reported in Table 1 as decision error. As the stakes are increased, decisions approach the monetary maximizing strategy and decision error declines. These results strongly support the Siegel hypothesis, that the phenomenon of probability matching was actually the exception that proved the utility maximizing rule. But he went further; he showed that estimating the parameters for one value of π allowed predictions of behavior to be made at another level of π, that the model worked for children as well as adults, and that the choice proportion p could also be increased by a treatment that afforded subjects a means of relieving boredom without having to vary their prediction.

Although Siegel could not have known it at the time, in retrospect we now know that he developed perhaps the first formal model of decision opportunity cost that explicity modeled the individual's subjective cost of transacting. Economists often make reference to transactions costs in post hoc explanations of observed deviations from optimality, but the topic is rarely treated at the theoretical-empirical depth illustrated by this example.

It is worth mentioning as a footnote in the history of ideas that as inspiration for his model Siegel cites Herbert Simon (1956, 271): "To predict how economic man will behave, we need to know not only that he is rational, but also how he perceives the world – what alternatives he sees and what consequences he attaches to them." Siegel interpreted Simon's argument as suggesting that the rational model is essentially correct, but more or less incomplete. To make it complete, it was necessary to examine decision problems carefully from the utilitarian point of view of the decision maker (not just from the point of view of the experimenter/theorist). Note that this interpretation differs from the "satisficing" and "bounded rationality" constructions that were later put on Simon's original idea constructions that were critical of the very foundation of rational behavior as conventionally defined. In Siegel's implementation, actions differ from the predictions of the standard model because of decision cost. Since the latter is necessarily part of the problem of realizing rational outcomes, the result is not just a better descriptive/predictive model. It is a better normative model of action as experienced by the individual. Thus, the distinction between the descriptive and the normative model of behavior becomes clouded; neither is cast in objective reality independent of experience. I believe this is the right way, although certainly not the easiest way, to approach the problem of modeling rational behavior.

Over the past three decades there have been many investigations of the effect of payoffs on outcomes in simple games and in market experiments. The most common effect of increased payoffs is to reduce decision error, but the central tendencies in the data can also shift with increased reward. Recent research in first-price auctions has varied the conversion rate of "tokens" into money among the five levels 0, 1, 5, 10, and 20 times the normal earnings in laboratory experiments. At a 20 to 1 conversion rate, subjects can easily earn \$125 per hour.

In Figure 1, we chart the marginal means that result from summing over four experience levels at each of the indicated five payoff multiples. The top chart shows decision error plotted against payoffs. Decision error is measured by the standard error of the estimated (linear) equilibrium bid function, where the auction is modeled as in incomplete information game. In the lower chart we provide a measure of risk aversion (the slope of the bid function, which increases directly with constant relative risk

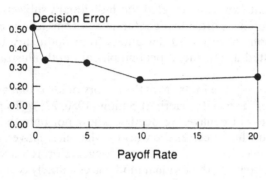

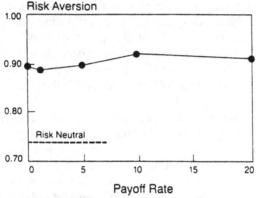

Figure 1. Effect of Payoff Level in First Price Auction Experiments

aversion) plotted against payoffs. Contrary to claims sometimes made in the literature, the predictions of the risk-neutral model are not supported as payoff (and payoff opportunity cost) increases; if anything, subjects become more risk averse at higher payoff conversion rates.

STRATEGY-PROOFNESS IN THEORY AND BEHAVIOR: AN EXAMPLE

It has long been recognized that it would be desirable if the rules of a market institution were such that the market was strategy-proof. This worthy objective has been elusive and has held theoretically only under limited conditions. Since mechanism theory informs us that almost any price-allocation institution can be strategically manipulated by a sufficiently sophisticated agent (Satterthwaite 1987), it is important to ask how motivated agents actually behave in a situation that is not theoretically strategy-proof.

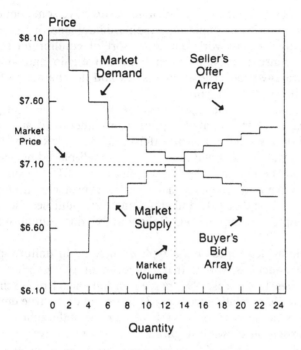

Figure 2. Example of Bid-Offer Array Crossing

Figure 2 provides an example of what happens in the competitive, or uniform price, sealed bid-offer (two-sided) auction. The induced market demand and supply schedules are depicted by the solid step functions. There are four buyers and four sellers, each with a capacity to buy (or sell) six units. All value (cost) information is private. The institution is one in which buyers submit a limit demand price for each unit they desire to buy and sellers submit a limit supply price for each unit they desire to sell. The limit buy prices are arranged from highest to lowest, while the supply prices are ordered from lowest to highest. Where the resulting arrays cross determines the market price and volume exchanged. In the example, these arrays are shown as dotted step functions. Since each buyer and seller is assigned multiple units on the market demand and supply schedules, it follows that those who are assigned induced values and costs near to the competitive market price are in position to influence the price. Thus, if all buyers (and sellers) were to bid at their respective values (costs), a buyer with a marginal demand unit can lower the market price by underbidding her value for that unit. This would raise the profits earned on that buyer's higher-valued units.

But this conventional manipulation argument poses the wrong question. The actual situation is one in which *all agents* have some opportunity to manipulate price by concealing their true demand or supply. In this situation, do subjects work out some sort of equilibrium that is efficient, in the sense of maximizing their collective gain, and which is behaviorally strategy-proof. The answer is yes, and the character of that equilibrium is illustrated in Figure 2.

Notice that most of the bids and offers are close to the market price with many ties, or near ties, at this price. Consequently, if any buyer lowers her bid or any seller raises his offer in the next period, the likely result is that the agent's unit will not trade, will be displaced by another agent's unit, and the market price will be unaffected. This unconscious group equilibrium has the property that each side is protected from price manipulation by the other side and simultaneously punishes the other side for attempted manipulation. Behaviorally, this equilibrium is strategy-proof.

This example, which represents a typical outcome in uniform-price, sealed-bid-offer auctions, shows that concealment is not inimical to efficient outcomes. In this case, 99.1 percent of the gains from exchange were realized, while revelation was only 31.9 percent of the true demand and supply. The strategy is unconscious because none of the subjects have the global information shown in Figure 2 and therefore have no awareness of the collective ends achieved by their strategies. But in repeat interaction they discover what works. Extant theory is unable to predict, or come to terms with, this kind of strategy-proof behavioral equilibrium.

EXPERIMENTAL MICROECONOMIC POLICY

Perhaps the most important new direction for experimental economics in the last decade has been defined by the demands of the deregulation and denationalization movement that pervades much of the world. Here is the challenge. Can we design self-regulating market institutions to replace the regulatory procedures traditionally employed in public utility industries such as natural gas and electric power transmission networks? Or, where command systems are likely to continue being used, as in the U.S. space station and space shuttle programs, can market mechanisms be used to improve resource allocation (Banks, Ledyard, and Porter 1989). In researching these questions, we use the experimental laboratory as a test-bed to evaluate the efficiency and price performance of proposed new institutions of exchange.

The traditional decentralized property right arrangements are problematic in gas pipeline and power transmission networks characterized by highly interdependent delivery technologies. Computerized central dispatch over large regions is essential if economies of coordination are to be fully captured and the full power of network competition is to discipline prices. My colleagues and I have proposed a "smart" computer-assisted market institution to solve this problem (McCabe, Rassenti, and Smith 1989b).

For example, in the natural gas case, wholesale buyers of gas submit location-specific bids for gas delivered to their city gates, wellhead owners submit location-specific offers of gas into the pipeline system, and pipeline owners submit leg-specific offers of transportation capacity. A computerized dispatch center applies linear programming algorithms to these decentralized bids and offers to compute prices and allocations so that the reported gains from exchange are maximized. The dispatch center itself would be a joint venture of all users governed by a cotenancy contract of the kind used for the co-ownership of pipelines, power lines, and power plants.

The objective is to combine the information advantages of decentralized ownership with the coordination advantages of central processing. Laboratory experiments show that even thin networks can achieve high efficiencies and competitive pricing. In effect we offer a solution to the Lange-Lerner-Hayek controversy of the 1930s in which Hayek argued that centralism could not be made to work by following marginal cost pricing rules; that only decentralized agents had the information and incentives needed to fuel the pricing system.

Government-specified property right systems offer the potential for providing a private market solution to the general problem of natural monopoly price regulation. Suppose a single capital facility (such as a pipeline or transmission line) is adequate to supply the needs of a community. The American model is to give legal monopoly status to a single owner of the facility, and then to regulate this monopoly with prices determined by cost plus a specified profit rate of return. As a consequence, the incentives to control cost are weak, as is made plain by the staggering cost overruns in nuclear power.

An alternative to this regulatory mechanism is the following: the government specifies that such natural monopoly facilities be governed by a competitively ruled cotenancy property right regime. Under this mechanism, the facility and its operations are held in a separate management company with multiple co-owners who compete to supply services using the common facility. Many precedents now exist using this mechanism: specialized printing facilities co-owned by morning and evening newspapers, shopping malls, power generators, and pipelines. The shopping mall is a superb example of a contractual institution providing economies of scale and scope under one roof in which firms produce competing and complementary services, while they share common parking, walkway, security, utilities, and custodial services. Power generators are typically built to exhaust scale economies; then capacity drawing rights are allocated among several co-owners in proportion to the fixed capital cost borne by each. Each user has a small condominium package of capacity, and each benefits from the low unit cost of a large facility.

But existing, naturally occurring, cotenancy contracts are not competitively ruled. For example, it is common for such contracts to specify that capacity cannot be expanded except through agreement by all the cotenants. This would be replaced by a free entry property right rule permitting any cotenant, or any outsider, to expand capacity unilaterally and to thereby obtain new capacity rights equal to the expansion.

These are only a few of the exciting current challenges to our ability to design new self-regulating institutions for solving problems of contestability, or poor performance, in product and financial markets. The proposed institutions are based on what we have learned from theory and past experiments about the economics of incentives; on field experience with component building blocks, such as the cotenancy contract; on the enormous power of the computer to construct new forms of exchange never before imagined or imaginable; and on the experimental laboratory where our incentive design errors can be corrected at low cost before the proposals are tried elsewhere.

Sid Siegel would be proud to know that the field of experimental economics that he helped to found has flourished so vigorously, but I suspect he would emphasize that we have learned little relative to that which is yet to be learned. After 30 years we are, indeed, only just getting started.

References

Aumann, Robert, 1987. Game theory. In *The new Palgrave*, vol. 2, edited by J. Eatwell, M. Milgate, and P. Neuman, 460–79. London: The Macmillan Press.

Banks, Jeffrey, John O. Ledyard, and David Porter. 1989. Allocating uncertain and unresponsive resources: an experimental approach. *Rand Journal of Economics* 20: 1–25.

Canning, David. 1989. Convergence to equilibrium in a sequence of games with learning. London School of Economics and Political Science. Discussion Paper. TE/89/190. March 1989.

Carlson, John. 1967. The stability of an experimental market with a supply-response lag. *Southern Economic Journal* 33: 305–21.

Coase, Ronald. 1960. The problem of social cost. *Journal of Law and Economics* 3: 1–44.

Cox, James C., and Ronald Oaxaca. 1989. Laboratory experiments with a finite horizon job search model. *Journal of Risk and Uncertainty* 2: 301–29.

Forsythe, Robert, Thomas R. Palfrey, and Charles R. Plott. 1982. Asset valuation in an experimental market. *Econometrica* 50: 537–67.

Friedman, James W., and Austin C. Hoggatt. 1980. *An experiment in noncooperative oligopoly.* Greenwich, Conn: JAI Press.

Harrison, Glenn W., and Kevin A. McCabe. 1993. Testing non-cooperative bargaining theory in experiments. In *Research in experimental economics*, vol. 5, edited by R. M. Isaac, 137–69. Greenwich, Conn: JAI Press.

Hoffman, Elizabeth, and Matthew L. Spitzer. 1985. Entitlements, rights, and fairness: an experimental examination of subjects' concepts of distributive justice. *Journal of Legal Studies* 14: 259–97.

Kahneman, Daniel, and Amos Tversky. 1979. Prospect theory: an analysis of decisions under risk. *Econometrica* 47: 263–91.

Kalai, Ehud, and Ehud Lehrer. 1990. Learning by rational players. Paper delivered at the Public Choice/Economic Science Association Joint Meetings, Tucson, Arizona, March 1990. Published as Rational learning leads to Nash equilibrium. *Econometrica* 61 (Sept. 1993): 1019–45.

Kruse, Jamie. 1988. Contestability in the presence of an alternative market: an experimental examination. University of Colorado. Working paper. Published as Brown-Kruse, J. L., *Rand Journal of Economics* (1991): 136–47.

McCabe, Kevin A., Stephen J. Rassenti, and Vernon L. Smith (a) 1989. Lakatos and experimental economics. Discussion Paper No. 89–24. Economics Science Laboratory, University of Arizona. Published in *Appraising economic theories*, edited by Neil de Marchi and Mark Blaug. London: Edward Elgar, 1991.

McCabe, Kevin A., Stephen J. Rassenti, and Vernon L. Smith (b) 1989. Designing "smart" computer-assisted markets: an experimental auction for gas networks. *European Journal of Political Economy* (North-Holland) 5: 259–83.

Roth, A. E., and M. K. Malouf. 1979. Game theoretic models and the role of information in bargaining *Psychological Review* 86: 574–94.

Satterthwaite, Mark A 1987. Strategy-proof allocation mechanisms. In *The new Palgrave*, vol. 4, edited by J. Eatwell, M. Milgate, and P. Newman, 518–20. London: The Macmillan Press.

Selten, Reinhard. 1989. Evolution, learning, and economic behavior. 1989 Nancy L. Schwartz Memorial lecture, J. L. Kellogg Graduate School of Management. Northwestern University.

Siegel, Sidney. 1961. Decision making and learning under varying conditions of reinforcement. *Annals of the New York Academy of Science* 89: 766–83.

Siegel, Sidney, Alberta Siegel, and Julia Andrews, 1964. *Choice, Strategy, and utility.* New York: McGraw-Hill.

Simon, Herbert. 1956. A comparison of game theory and learning theory. *Psychometrica* 21: 267–72.

Smith, Vernon L. 1979. Incentive compatible experimental processes for the provision of public goods. In *Research in experimental economics*, vol. 1, edited by V. Smith, 59–168. Greenwich, Conn: JAI Press.

Sonnenschein, Hugo. 1983. The economics of incentives: an introductory account. 1983 Nancy L. Schwartz Memorial Lecture, J. L. Kellogg Graduate School of Management, Northwestern University.

Szidarovszky, Ferenc, and Koji Okuguchi. 1987. Notes on the stability of quadratic games. *Keio Economic Studies* 24: 33–45.

Wellford, Charissa P. 1989. A laboratory analysis of price dynamics and expectations in the cobweb model. Discussion Paper No. 89–15, Department of Economics, University of Arizona.

Wilson, Robert. 1990. Strategic analysis of auctions. Stanford Business School, February 19, 1990.

GARY S. BECKER
Habits, Addictions, and Traditions

INTRODUCTION

It is a great honor and privilege to be this year's Nancy Schwartz Lecturer, given the distinguished economists who preceded me, and the person honored by the series. I did not know Nancy Schwartz well personally, but I have known and learned from her work. Economic theory and industrial organization lost an important contributor at too early an age.

The usual assumption in most discussions of behavior over time is that choices today are not directly dependent on choices in the past. The great economist J. R. Hicks expressed strong disapproval of this assumption:

> It is nonsense that successive consumptions are independent; the normal condition is that there is a strong complementarity between them. [1965, page 261]

It is ironic that this sentence comes at the end of a rather lengthy monograph on economic growth that relies throughout on the independence assumption.

The assumption of independence is not "nonsense," for it usefully

I have had helpful comments from Joseph Hotz, Kevin Murphy, Richard Posner, and Sherwin Rosen, and useful assistance from David Meltzer. I am indebted to a grant from the Lynde and Harry Bradley Foundation to the Center for the Study of the Economy and the State, to the National Institute of Child Health and Development (Grant 5 R37 HD22054), and to the National Science Foundation (Grant SES-9010748) for support. This essay is reprinted from *Kyklos* 45, no. 2 (1992): 327–46, with permission from Helbing and Lichtenhahn Verlag AG, Basel, Switzerland.

simplifies many problems that are not crucially affected by dependencies over time. But the assumption has discouraged economists from grappling with other issues of considerable significance – including addictions, work habits, preference formation, why children support their elderly parents, preference solutions to the problem of future commitments, and the evolution and stability of institutions. These are the kinds of questions I address in this lecture.

A growing literature during the past two decades has assumed instead of independence that current consumption is affected by past consumption. The most influential work has been by Boyer [1978], Houthakker and Taylor [1966], Kydland and Prescott [1982], Phlips [1974], Pollak [1970], Ryder and Heal [1973], Spinnewyn [1981], von Weizacker [1971], and various colleagues and students at Chicago: Iannoccone, Murphy, Hansen, Stigler, Constantinides, Heaton, and Hotz. I will not try to review, summarize, or reference these contributions, but will concentrate on the issues that have interested me.

HABITS

Some influences of past consumption on present behavior are obvious. If I just ate a filling dinner, I do not want to eat another dinner in the near future – not even a Persian delight cooked by my wife. Essentially all goods are substitutes if the time intervals are sufficiently close and the quantities consumed are big enough. Even lovers of potato chips or those most hooked on crack do not want any more now if they consumed large quantities during the past hour.

But for many goods, when the time periods compared are not very close, greater consumption earlier stimulates greater, not lesser, consumption later. Following common usage, I define *habitual* behavior as displaying a positive relation between past and current consumption; economists call these goods complements. Well-known examples include smoking, using heroin, eating ice cream or Kellogg's Corn Flakes, jogging, attending church, telling lies, and often intimacy with a lover.

A full discussion needs to consider both short-term substitutions in consumption and the longer-term complementarities. Murphy and I [1988] present a model of cycles or binges in the amount of eating that has both substitutions and complementarities over time in food consumption, and Heaton [1991] finds both types of relations in the time series on aggregate consumption in the United States. This lecture concentrates on the complementary relations because these are responsible for the habitual behavior I want to highlight.

Of course, there are vast differences in the degree of habituation to the same activity: most people can drink or work regularly without ever becoming alcoholics or workaholics. And the likelihood that a person becomes habituated to any activity varies with circumstances and age. Soldiers who became addicted to drugs while in Viet Nam usually stopped the habit soon after returning to civilian life, while former smokers and alcoholics often resume their habits after becoming unemployed or when their marriages break up.

Habits are *harmful* or "bad" if greater present consumption lowers future utility, as in the detrimental effects on future health of heavy smoking or drinking. Similarly, habits are *beneficial* if greater present consumption raises future utility; regular swimming or regular church attendance may be examples. It is natural that bad habits get more attention than good ones, but as we will see, rational behavior also implies that the observed strong habits are more likely to be harmful than beneficial.

If greater past consumption of a good increased the marginal utility of present consumption, myopic persons who do not consider the future consequences of their actions would increase their present consumption. But higher current utility does not guarantee that rational forward-looking persons consume more than in the past. Rational consumers also consider how greater current consumption affects the marginal utilities or disutilities in the future.

Murphy and I provide a necessary and sufficient condition for a rational forward-looking consumer to develop a habit [1988]. It is indeed necessary for greater past consumption to raise the marginal utility from present consumption – this corresponds to what is called "reinforcement" in the addiction literature. But several other parameters are also important, including the rate of discount on future utilities, and the rate of decay or depreciation in the contribution of past consumption to current utility. The larger the rate at which either the future or past is discounted, the more likely that a good with a given amount of reinforcement is habitual, and the stronger is the habit (see Appendix 1). This conclusion is intuitive, for the bigger are these discount rates, the smaller are the effects on future utility of greater present consumption. Then reinforcement has the more dominating effect.

An *addiction* is defined simply as a strong habit. Technically, a habit becomes an addiction when the effects of past consumption on present consumption are sufficiently strong to be destabilizing (see Appendix 1). Therefore, a shock to an individual, such as unemployment, may lead for a while to larger and larger increases over time in the amount consumed of addictive goods. Demand for addictive goods tends to be bifurcated: people either consume a lot, or they abstain because they anticipate that they will become "hooked" if they begin to consume. Smoking is a good example of bifurcation, for 70 percent of adults in the United States do not smoke, while persons who do smoke generally consume at least half a pack a day.

A habit may be raised into an addiction by exposure to the habit itself. Certain habits, like drug use and heavy drinking, may reduce the attention to future consequences – there is no reason to assume discount rates on the future are just given and fixed (elsewhere I have developed an analysis of endogenous discount rates [Becker, 1990]). Since an increase in the discount rate strengthens the commitment to all habits, there would be further induced increases in discount rates. The result may be an explosive expansion of certain habits into powerful addictions.

The presumption from the theory that addictions are partly caused by heavy decay rates on past consumption in a way is consistent with the medical evidence. For the damage to lungs, liver, and other organs declines rather quickly after a person stops heavy drinking or smoking, unless the point of no return had been reached.

Since people who heavily discount the future and past would place little weight on the future consequences of their behavior, they are less likely to be deterred from "harmful" activities that reduce future utility, even when these are not habitual. And they would be less attracted by "beneficial" activities that raise utility in the future, even when these are not habitual, such as limiting cholesterol intake. But since high discount rates on the future and past also foster strong habits and addiction, people with high rates would be *especially* attracted by harmful activities that are addictive, or at least highly habitual.

Therefore, we expect addictions to be associated with harmful activities. This can explain why addictions usually cause duress – declines in well-being over time. It can also explain why drug addictions and crime tend to go together, and why religious people tend to be law-abiders, even if drug use and religion do not affect the propensity to engage in crime, and even if crime and religion are not addictive.

Nothing in the analysis of forward-looking utility-maximizing behavior presumes that people know for sure whether they will become habituated or addicted to a substance or activity, although that is sometimes claimed by critics of this approach. An individual may have considerable uncertainty about whether she would become an alcoholic if she begins to drink regularly. A troubled teen-ager who begins to experiment with drugs may expect, but not be certain, that his life will begin to straighten out, perhaps because of a good job or marriage, before he becomes addicted. Since these and other choices are made under considerable uncertainty, some persons become addicted simply because events turn out to be less favorable than was reasonable to anticipate – the good job never rescued the drug user. Persons who become addicted because of bad luck may regret their addictions, but that is no more a sign of irrational behavior than is any regret voiced by big losers at a race track that they bet so heavily.

I define *traditional* behavior as habits that are sensitive to choices in the more distant past – including sometimes choices made by parents and others in the past – because the effects of the past decay slowly. Tradition-related habits are unlikely to be addictive because low depreciation rates reduce the strength of a habit. Such habits are especially important for understanding culture and institutions, as I will try to show later.

INVIDIOUS COMPARISONS

Economists usually do not consider why preferences are what they are, but it is advisable to discuss habit formation since many writers have claimed that habitual behavior is not fully rational. Although little is known about the mechanisms behind the development of habits, it is not obvious to me that they are less rational than other preferences.

Alcohol, heroin, cocaine, nicotine, and certain other drugs have well-documented biological-pharmacological effects on consumers that raise their desire for the drugs. Habit helps economize on the cost of searching for information, and of applying the information to a new situation (see Stigler and Becker [1977, pp. 81–83]). And most people get mental and physical comfort and reassurance in continuing to do what they did in the past. Thomas Jefferson was surely right when he asserted in a letter to an acquaintance that "He who permits himself to tell a lie once, finds it much easier to do it a second and third time, till at length it becomes habitual" [1785].

Another promising lead in understanding the formation of habit comes from recognizing that the utility of many goods depends on how present consumption of these goods compares with the amounts consumed in the past. For example, a given standard of living usually provides less utility to persons who had grown accustomed to a higher standard in the past. It is the decline in health, rather than simply poor health, that often makes elderly persons depressed. And what appeared to be a wonderful view from a newly occupied house may become boring and trite after living there for several years.

Goods that involve such invidious comparisons with the past are "harmful" in the sense I am using this term because greater consumption now lowers future utility by raising the future standard of comparison. What is more interesting for present purposes and less obvious is that such goods also tend to be habitual: current consumption is encouraged by greater past consumption in order to come closer to the standard set by past behavior.

Indeed, a good *must* be habitual if utility from the good depends on the difference between current consumption and a weighted sum of the amounts consumed in the past. Note that in such cases the effect of comparisons with the past is so powerful that a good must be habitual *regardless* of the discount rate on future utilities or the decay rate on past consumption. The habit is stronger when past consumption has a bigger weight, and it is an addiction when past consumption is weighted more heavily than present consumption (see Appendix 2).

If utility depends on comparisons between present and past consumption, it would be highest just after consumption rose to a permanently higher level, and it would decline over time as the person became accustomed to that level. Similarly, utility would be lowest just after consumption fell to a permanently lower level.

If the standard of living itself involved such comparisons with the past, the nouveau riche would tend to be the happiest of people, the new poor the most miserable, and the long-term rich may not be so much happier than the long-term poor. Indeed, the long-term rich are only a little happier than the long-term poor when the weight on past consumption almost equals the weight on present consumption (see Appendix 2, and Ryder and Heal [1973]). Suicides might be more closely related to declines in the living standard – perhaps due to a loss of wealth or health – than to the level itself.

Adam Smith [1976] has a few wonderful paragraphs in *The Theory of Moral Sentiments* on the transitory gains in utility from a higher standard of living:

> The poor man's son, whom heaven in its anger has visited with ambition ... pursues the idea of a certain artificial and elegant repose ... which, if in the extremity of old age he should at last attain to it, he will find to be in no respect preferable to that humble security and contentment which he has abandoned for it. [pages 299–300] (I owe this reference to George Stigler.)

Rapid economic growth raises the level of happiness partly by increasing the number of new rich and reducing the number of new poor. Indeed, a mere slowing of the growth rate could lower utility even when incomes continue to rise if the habitual component to the standard of living were sufficiently powerful.

PRICE AND WEALTH EFFECTS

It is often claimed that habitual and traditional behavior, especially addictions, do not respond much to changes in prices and wealth. The explanation sometimes offered is that habits influence behavior in ways that are independent of calculation, or that habits are locked in by the past. I will consider only the responses of rational habitual behavior since I am claiming in this lecture that habitual behavior does not imply a reluctance to "calculate."

An unexpected fall in the price of an habitual good may have only a slight impact on demand as long as past consumption has not changed much. This is probably the basis for the claim that habits get locked in by the past. But the magnitude of the response to say a permanent fall in price would grow over time as consumption continues to increase, even if it only increased slightly at first. By the definition of highly habitual goods, each increase in consumption of these goods raises future consumption by relatively large amounts. Therefore, it is not surprising that the long run price elasticity of demand between steady states is *larger, not* smaller, for the more strongly habitual goods (see Becker and Murphy [1988]). Moreover, short run changes in demand are misleading since the ratio of short run to long run elasticities is smaller for the stronger habits (see Becker, Grossman, and Murphy [1991]).

Mike Grossman, Murphy, and I [1990] recently used the rational habit model to study empirically the demand for cigarettes in the United States. We find cigarette demand to be rather strongly habitual, a not very surprising conclusion. The responses to price changes are not small: a 10 percent permanent fall in the price of a pack of cigarettes increases smoking by 4 percent one year later, and by almost 8 percent after a few years. Perhaps more surprising is the evidence that smokers are not myopic – they do consider future consequences, as measured by the effects of future prices on current consumption.

There are strong differences of opinion in the United States about whether drug use should be legalized, differences that cut across political labels of liberal or conservative. Everyone agrees that legalization would greatly reduce the retail price of drugs, but much of the disagreement comes from different views about how legalization will affect the demand for drugs. Since many drugs are strongly habitual and even addictive, the analysis of rational addiction suggests that the demand for drugs may not increase much shortly after legalization, but that it would increase by a lot in the long run – especially by the poor (see Becker-Grossman-Murphy [1991]) – unless legalization has other effects than simply lowering price.

One important other effect concerns peer pressure, which induces some teenagers to smoke, drink heavily, and experiment with drugs. Although I do not know of convincing reasons why strongly habitual and addictive behavior is *generally* more subject to pressure from peers than other behavior, it is straightforward to show that habitual behavior is more *vulnerable*, in the sense that a given level of peer pressure has an especially large effect on habitual behavior. Strong peer pressure can convert moderately habitual behavior into what appears to be a strong habit or even an addiction.

Consider a fall in price of a habitual good subject to peer pressure. Each consumer would increase his demand, partly because price is lower, and partly because other consumers have raised their demands. Habit increases demand over time, and so too does the pressure to consume more when peers also do. This synergy between peer pressure and habit implies that peer pressure has a larger effect on the elasticity of demand when the habit is stronger; similarly, a stronger habit has more of an effect on the long run elasticity where there is greater peer pressure (see Appendix 3). Consequently, it may only appear that peer pressure is stronger for habitual behavior since such pressure has greater effects on demand when habits are stronger.

The importance of peer pressure in the market for drugs generally strengthens the conclusion that legalization would greatly increase the use of drugs. One qualification would be if pressure to use drugs declined when they became legal. Another would be if the synergy between peer pressure and habits produced sections of positively sloped demand curves (see Appendix 3), and hence multiple equilibria in the drug market. Legalization might then lower both price and drug use by shifting the market to a wholly different equilibrium. As yet, however, there is no evidence that the drug market is characterized by such multiple equilibria.

Econometric studies usually find that high taxes on incomes and other taxes on work effort do not have large effects on the hours worked by men. Yet more than fifty years of weak work incentives under communist rule in Eastern Europe and elsewhere had a shattering effect on work effort in these countries. The commitment to hard work apparently has also eroded in countries like Sweden that greatly raised the effective tax on work effort during the past quarter century.

The econometric findings can be reconciled with these other observations by recognizing that work is a tradition-habit that builds up very slowly over time, perhaps partly under the influence of examples set by parents and others. As Victor Hugo said, "Nothing is more dangerous than discontinued labor – it is habit lost. A habit easy to abandon, difficult to resume" [1909, Vol. II, p. 159]. The long time it takes for high taxes and other policies to break down slowly accumulated work habits is not easily captured by econometric studies, even by studies that use a few years of panel data to discover some effects of work habits (see, e.g., Bover [1991]).

Countries can take advantage of the slow decay of good work habits by imposing heavy *temporary* taxes on effort. But the pessimistic side of the story is that Eastern Europe and the Soviet Union will have difficulty rebuilding the good work habits eroded during the many decades of mismanagement and weak incentives.

Being on welfare may create a bad habit if children and parents lose their initiative by becoming dependent on government handouts. Then many families may refuse to go on welfare, even when eligible – as is the case in the United States – because the cost of dependency exceeds the value of the payments. Although a sizable fall in welfare payments might greatly increase the number who decline to go on, it could *initially* have only a minor impact on the number of families who remain on welfare since they have become habituated to the welfare payments (see Sanders [1991]).

The permanent income model explains why total consumption often does not respond much to income shocks by assuming that many shocks have a large temporary component. Yet some critics have argued that aggregate consumption in the United States is too stable – the excess stability issue – to be explained by the permanent income story because aggregate shocks are alleged to have a small transitory component. Even if they are right about aggregate shocks, and there is considerable disagreement, the problem is not with the permanent income concept – which is surely basically correct – but with the assumption that preferences are separable over time. If current consumption depends on past consumption, even a permanent shock to income may initially have only a small effect on consumption.

The effect of habitual behavior on the consumption responses to possibly permanent shocks can explain most of the behavior commonly explained since Friedman's work by nonhabitual responses to transitory shocks. For example, Friedman showed that higher-income groups would save a larger fraction of their incomes than lower-income groups if only because these groups contain relatively many persons who received positive transitory income shocks. However, higher-income groups save a lot perhaps also because they contain relatively many persons who are *newly* rich. I believe that the effects of habits as well as the distinction between permanent and transitory income are needed for a satisfactory explanation of aggregate consumption behavior (see Heaton [1991] and Ferson and Constantinides [forthcoming]).

PREFERENCE FORMATION

Let me turn to a few more speculative but very important issues. Each person is born perhaps not as a *tabula rasa*, an empty slate, but with limited experiences that get filled in by childhood and later experiences. These experiences influence teen-age and adult desires and choices partly by creating habits, addictions, and traditions. The habits acquired as a child or young adult generally continue to influence behavior even when the environment changes radically. For example, Indian adults who migrate to the United States often eat the same type of cuisine they had in India, and continue to wear the same style of clothing. A woman who was badly sexually abused as a child may forever fear and dislike men, including those who would treat her with consideration and respect. A person may remain an alcoholic until he dies mainly because he started drinking heavily as a teen-ager.

Childhood experiences can greatly influence behavior over a person's entire life because it may not pay to try to greatly change habits when the environment changes. Childhood-acquired habits then continue, even though these would not have developed if the environment when growing up had been the same as the environment faced as an adult.

The Freudian emphasis on the crucial influence of early childhood on later behavior would be consistent with utility-maximizing forward-looking behavior if behavior were highly habitual. For then experiences while a child could have a very large effect on adult preferences and choices.

Children spend their early years under the care of parents and close relatives who determine what they eat, read, observe, and hear. The enormous influence this has on children's preferences explains the close link between parents and children in many attitudes and choices, including religious and political party affiliations, the propensities to smoke, eat breakfast, or divorce, and the taste for Chinese, Iranian, or Southern-style cuisine.

A natural way in a utility-maximizing framework to model the influence of parents on children is to assume that the preferences of children and adults evolve from early childhood and later experiences under the influence of habitual, including addictive and traditional, behavior. Indeed, some of my remarks will go well beyond habitual behavior to other recursive influences of early childhood and other past experiences on present and future preferences.

Altruistic parents maximize their own utility in part by maximizing their children's. They would try to direct the evolution of children's preferences toward raising the utility of children. For example, parents may refrain from smoking even when that gives them much pleasure because their smoking raises the likelihood that the children will smoke. Or they may take their children to church, even when not religious, because they believe exposure to religion is good for children. Indeed, many parents stop going after their children leave home.

Selfish parents do not care about the welfare of children, but they too are often concerned about the evolution of children's preferences. They may want to be taken care of when old or ill, but cannot have a contract with their children to help out. However, they can try to shape the formation of children's preferences to raise the chances their children will help voluntarily.

The preferences children get when young, in effect, can *precommit* them to helping out much later when they are adults and their parents are elderly. Parents can help make the children altruistic, or can make grown children feel "guilty" when they do not help. Propensities toward guilt may lower the lifetime utility of children – selfish parents do not care – but helping out of guilt may raise the utility of adult children, *conditional on their past experiences.*

Therefore, even selfish parents do not necessarily neglect or abuse children, for they might spend considerable time, money, and emotional resources on children to rig the evolution of preferences in their own favor. This sounds calculating and selfish. It is. Yet the opportunity to "commit" children to helping out when parents need it can induce selfish parents to treat their children much better than they would if adult preferences and behavior did not evolve from childhood experiences and treatment. It also implies that selfish parents become meaner when they need not rely on their children, perhaps because the government becomes committed to helping out the elderly in need.

Children carry along into adulthood the baggage of experiences they had only a limited role in shaping. Therefore, a rational person can meaningfully state that she does not "like" her preferences in the sense that she doesn't like the inherited baggage: the guilt, the sexual fears, the propensity to smoke or drink heavily, and so forth. She can change the stock of experiences over time, but how much a rational person wants to change depends on how long she expects to live, the strength of the influence of the past on present choices, and other factors. We all are to some extent prisoners of experiences we wish we never had.

Economists are so conditioned to identifying rational choice with separable preferences that we often call "irrational" quite rational behavior that is the result of past experiences. We have trouble understanding the people who take good care of elderly parents even when not forced by social norms or altruism – I have tried to indicate why this can be utility-maximizing behavior once the importance of guilt and other results of past experiences is recognized.

A prominent example is the literature on "endowment" effects (see Kahneman, Netsch, and Thaler [1990]). A family may refuse to sell for half-a-million dollars the house it has lived in for twenty years, even though it would be unwilling to spend anywhere near that amount for an otherwise equivalent house. Of course, the qualifier "otherwise" is crucial since twenty years in the same house presumably built up memories and attachments to *that* particular house, not to a seemingly "equivalent" house that is really not equivalent.

A more difficult example of the endowment effect concerns a person like Sherwin Rosen who stores a young bottle of wine that cost a few bucks. By luck the bottle turns out to be worth several hundred dollars after ten years. But Sherwin refuses to sell, even though he would never contemplate paying that much for an otherwise equivalent bottle. Irrational? Or like the family that refused to sell its house, a case where the experience of "consuming" a particular bottle for a long time raised the value attached to *that* bottle, not to an otherwise equivalent bottle?

Other "rational" interpretations of the refusal are possible; e.g., Sherwin may get pleasure from bragging about his shrewdness in acquiring such a bottle. And an interpretation that uses the effects of owning the bottle for ten years on present demand for it may seem forced since the bottle was not "consumed" during the decade. But such a reaction partly reflects the economist's narrow conception of "consumption." People consume paintings, and old rugs and coins simply by looking at them occasionally, and they may value such objects more over time as they grow attached to them.

COMMITMENT, INSTITUTIONS, AND CULTURE

Game theory has shown the crucial importance of commitment in the strategic interactions over time of two or more participants. The equilibria that emerge from decisions over time are often highly sensitive to whether players can commit future behavior. Yet it may be difficult to enforce commitment since people can renege on promises or slip out of contractual obligations. Still, I believe the difficulty of obtaining binding commitments has been exaggerated because of the common assumption that preferences are independent of the past, so that a person's utility-maximizing choices at any moment do not directly depend on past choices.

For habits, addictions, traditions, and other preferences that are directly contingent on past choices partly control, and hence commit, future behavior in predictable ways. Indeed, habits and the like may be very good substitutes for long-term contracts and other explicit commitment mechanisms.

Consider, for example, a firm that would charge consumers a lower price now if they agree to buy more of the good for some time into the future. Unfortunately, it is not possible to write a contract that ensures future purchases. But a contract may not be necessary if the good is habitual since habituated consumers are automatically committed to buying more in the future when they buy more now.

A firm may help finance investments in a worker's general skills if the worker will remain with the firm. A written contract that commits the worker to stay is not enforceable, but the firm may know that the worker is likely to remain after he has been there for a while since the job becomes a habit.

I have already shown how parents may be reasonably confident their children will help out when they become adults and the parents are elderly because the parents help structure the children's adult preferences by controlling childhood experiences.

Such influences of habitual and other recursive preference relations on behavior get incorporated into the optimal strategies of players in sequential games. For example, a parent may save less to support herself when elderly if her children are conditioned to help out. A boss may exploit his workers' attachments to their jobs, or society may punish crimes more severely now because that raises social support for punishments in the future.

Elsewhere, Grossman, Murphy and I [1990] consider the optimal pricing of a monopolist who sells an habitual good. We show that wealth-maximizing prices are below the prices where current marginal revenue equals marginal cost since a lower price now, in effect, "commits" consumers to increase their future consumption. Therefore, the optimal prices will be higher if consumers are prevented from raising their future consumption. This analysis can explain the rise in price-cost margins, and hence "profits," of cigarette companies during the past few years. The continuing growth in legislation that restricts smoking is a major observable obstacle to future increases in the demand for cigarettes. Producers are induced to raise cigarette prices and current "profits," even though they are obviously hurt by legislated restrictions on smoking.

These examples of the effects of preferences on commitment are rather straightforward, although some of you may be dubious. You will then be far more dubious of the following examples, which extend the analysis of habits and traditions to include institutions and culture. I was led to this line of argument by reading in the *Federalist Papers* James

Madison's criticisms of Jefferson's proposal for temporary constitutions that are rewritten by each succeeding generation. Madison did more than just claim that a constitution protects fundamental rights and helps commit the actions of future generations. He recognized that a basic problem is whether people are willing to obey a constitution: the world is strewn with wonderful constitutions that are ignored or evaded.

Madison argued in effect that a constitution is more likely to be followed out of habit and tradition the longer it has been around. The frequent changes advocated by Jefferson would deprive a constitution of – I can do no better than quote Madison's words –

> that veneration, which time bestows on everything, and without which perhaps the wisest and freest governments would not possess the requisite stability

and

> when the examples which fortify opinion are ancient as well as numerous, they are known to have a double effect. (Madison [1787])

Madison and others – he apparently was following Hume [1748] – claim that preferences are formed not simply by what a person did in the past, what his parents did, and what contemporary peers are doing, but also by the behavior of past generations of "peers." This extensive influence of the past on present beliefs and behavior helps stabilize older institutions and cultures. As Madison argued in rejecting Jefferson's suggestion for frequent change, the ultimate strength of the support for an institution depends on whether there is time to cumulate the support over several generations.

Sometimes, support for an institution or ethic, such as the belief in honesty, is called "unthinking" attachment to a culture or ethic. Wordsworth claimed that "habit rules the unreflecting herd" [1822]. But this is no more "unthinking" than other preferences that are formed by what happened in the past.

Obedience to institutions often can be utilized in social decision making. The armed forces try to instill the habit of obedience to commands during fighting by emphasizing military traditions, rigid rules, and response to peer pressure. Young people asked to contribute heavily to social security may not have to worry that the next generation will refuse to support them when they become elderly, even though it might *appear* to be in the next generation's self-interest to do so. Indeed, this generations' support of the elderly may well strengthen the tradition-habit that will induce the next generation to support the elderly.

I readily admit that I do not know how far one can push this point of view. And the stress on institutions influenced by tradition-habits and peer pressure may seem to be an ad hoc trick invented to solve intractable commitment and collective choice problems. But this approach does come out of an attention to more straightforward problems, such as heavy drinking, drug use, and brand preferences. And the evolution of preferences out of past experiences seems far more intuitive, even when extended to institutions and culture, than the opposite assumption so dominant in economics that preferences are independent of the past.

Some of you might be surprised to hear a coauthor of the "de gustibus" point of view, with its emphasis on stable preferences, waxing enthusiastically about the formation of preferences. But what de gustibus assumes is that *meta* preferences are stable. Meta preferences include past choices and choices by others as arguments in a person's current utility function. In fact, addictive behavior and social interactions were two of the major examples analyzed by Stigler and myself.

The message of that paper is not that preferences at time t for different people depend in the same way on their consumption at t. Rather, it is that common rules determine the way different variables and experiences enter the meta preferences that motivate most people at most times. And that forward-looking rational actors maximize the utility from their meta preferences, not from current preferences alone, because they recognize that choices today affect their utilities in the future.

CONCLUSION

My concluding remarks can be brief. I have tried to show that the past casts a long shadow on the present through its influence on the formation of present preferences and choices. These links between the past and the present do not simply provide a technical generalization of the independence assumption regarding preferences that permits a few more wiggles in the data to be explained.

The systematic analysis of habitual, addictive, and traditional behavior, and of other ways the past influences present preferences, have profound implications for the analysis of many kinds of economic and social phenomena. These surely include the demand for branded goods, how income shocks affect aggregate consumption, and short and long run changes in smoking due to higher taxes on a pack of cigarettes. They also include a better understanding of how legalization would change drug use, the effect of income and other taxes on effort and work habits in the long run, and why the nouveau riche and new poor are so different from the long-term rich and long-term poor.

With a still bolder vision and a lot of luck, the link between the past and present choices may also explain why and how parents influence the formation of children's preferences, how people get committed to future decisions, and the formation and support of institutions and culture.

This may be enough food for thought and controversy on one hot afternoon!

APPENDIX 1

Let the utility function at time t be

$$U(t) = U(y(t), c(t), S(t)),$$ (1.1)

where y is a non-habitual good, c is habitual, and $\dot{S}(t) = c(t) - \delta S(t)$, where δ is the depreciation rate on past consumption of c. The overall utility function at t = 0 is the discounted value of the U(t), where σ is the rate of discount. I assume that overall utility is maximized subject to a wealth constraint, where the amount of wealth is given.

A good is *habitual* if

$$[dc(s)]/[dS(t)] > 0$$ (1.2)

when the marginal utility of wealth is held constant. That is, when a "compensated" increase in past consumption raises present consumption. Since at a steady state, $c = \delta S$, it is natural to define an *addiction* as a habit strong enough that

$$[dc(t)]/[dS(t)] > \delta.$$ (1.3)

This implies that a steady state is unstable if c is addictive near this state.

Becker and Murphy show that a necessary and sufficient condition for a good to be habitual near a steady state is that

$$(\sigma + 2\delta)U_{cs} > -U_{ss},$$ (1.4)

Where $U_{cs} = (\partial^2 U)/(\partial c \partial S)$,
and $U_{ss} = (\partial^2 U)/(\partial S^2)$.

APPENDIX 2

Let utility from the habitual good c at time t be separable from the other goods (y), and expressable as

$$V(t) = V[c(t) - \alpha \delta S(t)],$$ (2.1)

where α is a constant >0. Since δ is the depreciation rate on past consumption of c, $\delta S(t) = \bar{c}(t)$, a weighted average of past consumption. Then

$$V_{cc} = V''$$

$$V_{cs} = -\alpha\delta V''$$

$$V_{ss} = (\alpha\delta)^2 V''$$

and

$$2\delta V_{cs} = -2\alpha\delta^2 V'' > -V_{ss} = -\alpha^2\delta^2 V''$$

for all $\alpha < 2$.

Therefore, for all σ and $\delta > 0$, the modified Stone-Geary utility function in equation (2.1) satisfies the condition in equation (1.4) for c to be a habit. It can be shown that the habit is stronger when α is greater, and it is an addiction when $\alpha > 1$.

Equation (2.1) implies that in a steady state where $c = \delta S = \bar{c}$,

$$U = V[\bar{c}(1 - \alpha)],$$

and (2.2)

$$V_c = V'(1 - \alpha).$$

Therefore, a rise in c between steady states has a smaller effect on utility when the habit (α) is stronger (given the value of V').

The effect on steady state consumption of a permanent change in the price of c compensated to hold the marginal utility of wealth (λ) constant is

$$(dc)\big/(dp_c) \cong \lambda\big/\left[V''(1 - \alpha)^2\right] \text{ if } \sigma \cong 0. \tag{2.3}$$

(This is a special case of Equation (18) in Becker-Murphy [1988].) Clearly, the effect on c is greater when α – the strength of the habit – is bigger.

APPENDIX 3

I now expand the utility function in equation (2.1) to include peer pressure:

$$V(t) = \left[c(t) - \alpha\delta S(t) - \gamma\bar{C}(t)\right], \tag{3.1}$$

where $\gamma > 0$ measures the strength of the pressure, and $\bar{C} = \Sigma c_j/N = c$ when all N consumers are identical. Peer pressure alters the effects of a change in the price of c on its steady state consumption to

$$(dc)/(dp_c) \cong \lambda/\left[V''(1 - \alpha)(1 - \alpha - \gamma)\right] \tag{3.2}$$

if $\sigma \cong 0$.

A proof is straightforward. The first order condition for each consumer near a steady state is

$$V_c + V_s/(\sigma + \delta) = \lambda p_c.$$

Differentiating with respect to p_c while holding λ constant, assuming $c = \delta S$, and $\bar{C} = c$, we get

$$\left[V_{cc} + V_{cs}/\delta + V_{c\bar{c}} + (V_{ss}/\delta + V_{sc}V_{s\bar{c}})/(\sigma + \delta)\right](dc)/(dp_c) = \lambda.$$

Substituting $V'' = V_{cc'} - \alpha\delta V'' = V_{cs'}$
$\alpha^2\delta^2 V'' = V_{ss'} - \gamma V'' = V_{c\bar{c}'}$ and
$\alpha\gamma\delta V'' = V_{s\bar{c}'}$ and setting $\sigma = 0$, we get

$$V''(1 - 2\alpha - \gamma + \alpha^2 + \alpha\gamma)(dc/dp_c) = \lambda$$

which is Equation (3.2).

Clearly, $[d/d(\gamma)][(dc)/(dp_c)]$ is greater in absolute value when α is greater. Moreover, the demand curve becomes unstable $((dc)/(dp_c) > 0)$ when $\alpha + \gamma > 1$.

Bibliography

Becker, Gary S. "Optimal Discounting of the Future," Department of Economics, University of Chicago, April, 1990.

Becker, Gary S., Grossman, Michael, and Murphy, Kevin M. "An Empirical Analysis of Cigarette Addiction," NBER working Paper no. 3322, April, 1990.

———. "Rational Addiction and the Effect of Price on Consumption," *American Economic Review Papers and Proceedings* 81, no. 2 (May 1991): 237–41.

Becker, Gary S., and Murphy, Kevin M. "A Theory of Rational Addiction," *Journal of Political Economy* 96, no. 4 (August 1988): 675–700.

Bover, Olympia. "Relaxing Intertemporal Separability: A Rational Habits Model of Labor Supply Estimated from Panel Data," *Journal of Labor Economics* 9, no. 1 (January 1991): 85–100.

Boyer, Marcel. "A Habit Forming Optimal Growth Model," *International Economic Review* 19 (October 1978): 585–609.

Ferson, Wayne, and Constantinides, George. "Habit Persistence and Durability in Aggregate Consumption: Empirical Tests," *Journal of Financial Economics*, forthcoming.

Heaton, John. "An Empirical Investigation of Asset Pricing with Temporally Dependent Preference Specifications," Massachusetts Institute of Technology, February, 1991.

Hicks, John R. *Capital and Growth* (Oxford: Clarendon Press, 1965).

Houthakker, H.S., and Taylor, Lester D. *Consumer Demand in the United States 1929–1970* (Cambridge, MA: Harvard University Press, 1966).

Hugo, Victor. *Les Misérablés* [1862], Saint Denis, Book II, Chapter I. Translated by Charles E. Wilbour (New York: J.M. Dent & Sons, 1909).

Hume, David. *An Enquiry Concerning Human Understanding* (1748).

Jefferson, Thomas. Letter to Peter Carr, August 19, 1785.

Kahneman, Daniel, Netsch, Jack, and Thaler, Richard. "Experimental Tests of the Endowment Effect and the Coase Theorem," *Journal of Political Economy* 98 (no. 6, December 1990): 1325–48.

Kydland, Finn E., and Prescott, Edward C. "Time To Build and Aggregate Fluctuations," *Econometrica* 50, no. 6 (November 1982): 1345–70.

Madison, James. *Federalist Papers*, no. 49, 1787.

Phlips, Louis. *Applied Consumption Analysis* (Amsterdam: North-Holland. 1974).

Pollak, Robert A. "Habit Formation and Dynamic Demand Functions," *Journal of Political Economy* 78, no. 4, pt. 1 (July/August 1970): 745–63.

Ryder, Harl E., Jr., and Heal, Geoffrey M. "Optimum Growth with Intertemporally Dependent Preferences," *Review of Economic Studies* 40 (January 1973): 1–33.

Sanders, Seth. "A Dynamic Model of Welfare Participation," Ph.D. Thesis, Department of Economics, University of Chicago, 1991.

Smith, Adam. *The Theory of Moral Sentiments* (Indianapolis, IN: Liberty Classics, 1976).

Spinnewyn, Frans. "Rational Habit Formation," *European Economic Review* 15 (1981): 91–109.

Stigler, George J., and Becker, Gary S. "De Gustibus Non Est Disputandum," *American Economic Review* 67 (March 1977): 76–90.

von Weizsacker, Carl C. "Notes on Endogenous Changes of Tastes," *Journal of Economic Theory* 3 (1971): 345–372.

Wordsworth, William. *Ecclesiastical Sonnets*, pt. II, Sonnet 28, "Reflections" (1822).

1993

PETER A. DIAMOND
Issues in Social Insurance

It is an honor to have this opportunity to pay tribute to such a widely respected scholar. Nancy Schwartz was an excellent theorist. She wrote papers that developed models of real world phenomena. Thus it is fitting that I draw on my experience in social insurance as both a theorist and a policy analyst to discuss a topic where theory has been important in informing policy discussion and policy discussions have shaped issues for theoretical analysis. I will use the provision of retirement income as the social insurance issue to be discussed.

Two analytical characteristics particularly distinguish the writings of economists. One is the primary focus on the self as motivation for behavior, with the use of utility maximizing models as the analytical device for modeling this focus. The second is the use of equilibrium constructs to determine the outcomes that follow from individual choices. Analysts of social insurance generally recognize that a critical part of the case for having social insurance is the failure of individuals to adequately look ahead and provide for their own retirements.[1] Thus social insurance analysis is one place where the rationality assumptions of economists are not given as full a reign as in most other areas of economic analysis.[2] However, the constraints imposed by equilibrium remain critical for

[1] For example, see Diamond (1977), Feldstein (1985), Valdés-Prieto (1993a). For an assessment of theories of savings behavior, see Thaler (1990).

[2] The complexity of insurance design and the difficulty in evaluating the financial health of the providers of insurance represent a "consumer protection" basis for concern about insurance that would continue even if there were no "myopia" issues. For example, of 4000 existing fire insurance companies, only 1000 survived the Great Chicago Fire of 1871 and the Boston Fire of 1872 (Meier, 1988, page 52).

social insurance analysis. In this presentation, I will focus on equilibrium analysis. That is, I will focus on who bears the risks that are shifted from workers as a result of social insurance. With this focus, it is convenient to assume that individuals satisfy economists' usual postulates of rationality, rather than considering more realistic models of individual behavior.

One of the tenets of equilibrium analysis is that the risks that confront people in the economy must be borne somewhere. That is, if an individual is to be protected, at least somewhat, against adverse outcomes in risky situations (to be provided at least partial insurance in other words), then the risk being covered by insurance is shifted elsewhere.[3] This raises two important and interesting basic issues. One is the consequences of having risks borne by different groups. The second is that different methods of shifting risks have different effects. I will proceed by discussing risk shifting in private insurance, and then consider how social insurance differs from private insurance.

1. AN IDEALIZED PRIVATE MARKET FOR ANNUITIES

Let us begin with a 65 year old (with no dependents, who has just retired and is considering using some of the money that he has accumulated to purchase an annuity. That is, rather than living on the interest earnings on his accumulated capital, plus possibly spending out of the value of his capital, our retiree is considering purchasing a sequence of fixed monthly payments that will last for as long as he lives. In the U.S. one cannot purchase an annuity where the amounts of monthly payments are indexed to the consumer price level, the way that Social Security benefits are indexed to the consumer price level. In other words, it is not possible to buy an annuity that is a guaranteed fixed real payment.[4] Since Social Security is indexed and private annuities are not, this is a major difference between them. In order to keep the focus on the nature of risk shifting, I will ignore this important difference and simply assume that, as in some other countries, such real annuities are available.[5]

---

[3] I will ignore the complications that arise in models with an infinite number of generations where, in some circumstances, it is possible to shift costs to nowhere – the infinite future.
[4] There do exist annuities that are indexed to actual rates of return in the market, and thus are affected by inflation, but then leave the rate-of-return risk on the annuitant.
[5] Let us note that the provision of Treasury debt indexed to the consumer price index would permit insurance companies to hold such debt as backing for annuities and thus would make the availability of such annuities more likely. For a discussion of the recent reappearance of private indexed debt and possible implications for pensions, see Bodie

In considering the decision to put some money into annuities, our 65 year old retiree recognizes that he does not know how long he will live. The risks associated with the uncertainty about the length of his life are the basis for seeking the insurance inherent in an annuity. We will assume that he has an accurate picture of the probabilities of dying in different years. If he does not purchase an annuity, he faces a dilemma. If, as is possible, he dies in the near term, then a considerable portion of his accumulation would be left in his estate. I will assume that, in this event, he would have preferred a higher level of consumption and a smaller estate. On the other hand, if he starts his retirement years with a higher rate of consumption, then he runs the risk of living long enough to require a significantly declining spending level as he ages and spends down his wealth. The purpose of annuities is to permit this retiree to convert his accumulation of funds into a level payment that lasts precisely as long as he lives.[6]

Let us assume that our retiree goes to purchase such an annuity from a stock (rather than mutual) insurance company, one that is owned by shareholders. The insurance company employs an actuary to evaluate the risks associated with how long our retiree will live. For now, we assume that the actuary has the same information about life expectancy as does our retiree. If our retiree purchases an annuity, the insurance company will have the purchase price to invest to finance the payments. The insurance company employs an investment manager to decide how to invest these funds and what interest rates should be used in calculating the premiums to be charged for different annuities. There are also costs associated with running an insurance company that are relevant for pricing an annuity. We note from the *1992 Life Insurance Fact Book* that approximately fourteen percent of life insurance company income goes for operating expenses plus dividends to shareholders, with roughly one-third of this going for selling costs. Let me note that the administrative costs of organizing insurance vary considerably with the type of organization. For example, despite the popularity of viewing the government as inefficient, the cost to the Social Security system of collecting payroll taxes and paying retirement benefits is less than one percent of the benefits paid.

For the purpose of focusing on risk bearing it is convenient to discuss an idealized setting, so I will ignore the administrative costs of running insurance companies. Whether the costs are high or low, there remains

---

(1988). Of course, there are a variety of complications in the choice of an index to be used for indexed annuities; but that issue would lead us astray. For a discussion of the existence (and nonexistence) of indexed debt, see Fischer (1986).

[6] I ignore the psychological reasons that lie behind the popularity of annuities that guarantee a minimum number of payments, often five or ten years' worth of payments.

the issue of bearing the risks associated with uncertain benefit payments. When our retiree pays the premium to the insurance company and the insurance company invests the money, the return to the economy is the actual return on the physical assets that are financed from this additional investment. From the viewpoint of the present, these future rates of return are uncertain, however safe the bonds that the insurance company might choose to invest in. There is a well developed theory of the allocation of the risks from the aggregate of investments in the economy by means of a well developed set of asset markets. Since I am focusing on insurance, I pass quickly over this issue, just noting that the risks are shifted by the asset markets to those most willing to bear them and we have an efficient allocation of today's distribution of the bearing of investment risks.[7] That is, the physical investments financed by the annuity premium have uncertain returns, while the bonds held by the insurance company have certain returns. These two patterns are made possible by other investors who absorb the risk (and are compensated for absorbing the risk).

To simplify my presentation, I will assume that the investment manager of our insurance company chooses to perfectly hedge these risks. That is, I will assume that the investment manager of the insurance company chooses to invest in bonds with no default risk and interest payments that, like the promised annuities, are indexed to the consumer price index. Thus the risks of the return on the investment of the accumulation of our retiree are shifted to the asset markets as a whole.

I come now to my central topic – the risk of how long our retiree will live and will, therefore, collect payments from the insurance company. This risk is shifted to the shareholders of the insurance company since the profits of the company vary with how long our retiree actually lives. If the annuitant lives a longer time, the shareholders of the insurance company will have lower returns. If he dies sooner, they will make a higher return.

However, there are many people buying annuities who have sufficiently independent mortality risks that we get a great deal of averaging of these risks. The aggregate payments year by year are highly predictable in the sense that their percentage variation is very small. This is the law of large numbers. This is referred to as pooling over the set of insurees. The insurance company, by pooling, faces considerably less risk (in percentage terms) than the sum of the individual risks of the insurees. The insurance company still faces some residual risk from the realization of mortality not being precisely equal to the calculated expected

---

[7] On the inefficiency that can come with trading over time, see Hart (1975).

value. For the shareholders of the insurance company, this risk is small enough to be of no consequence, so that the actuary could make expected value calculations (to a close enough approximation). In any event, the risk to the shareholders is being shared by many investors who hold diversified portfolios of stock. In the circumstances I have described, the mortality risks associated with providing this annuity are negligible and the economy spreads them around among many investors.[8]

2.   COMPLICATIONS IN THE PRIVATE INSURANCE MARKET

There are three widely recognized complications that move actual insurance markets away from this description of idealized insurance. These are moral hazard, adverse selection, and aggregate risk issues.[9]

Moral Hazard

The term moral hazard is used by students of insurance to refer to activities by an individual that affect the size of the risk being borne by the insurance company. In the case of annuities, there is not an important moral hazard problem. That is, the insurance company is not concerned that the insuree will do all sorts of things to live much longer than he would have lived if he had not been able to purchase an annuity. While declining income levels possibly associated with spending out of a fixed sum of money might well affect life expectancy, this is not a problem on the scale of moral hazard issues that arise elsewhere in insurance. For example, the willingness to invest to avoid fires, or to have early warning to reduce the cost of fires that do occur, is affected by the availability of fire insurance. The presence of liability insurance affects the willingness to invest to alter buildings and parking lots to avoid accidents. Similarly there are many other activities where taking care has major impacts on risks. In these cases, insurance companies give advice on reducing risks and monitor the behavior of insurees. This is not the case with annuities.

There are some new issues that arise when we consider the annuity

[8] This argument has been made precise by Malinvaud (1972).
[9] In addition, the competitive pressure from individuals seeking out the best available insurance policy is not nearly as strong as in an idealized competitive market. It is not the case that an insurance policy that is slightly less favorable than the best alternative has no takers. But I want to focus on risk-bearing, and so I will not explore the size and determinants of the deviations of competition in actual insurance markets from the competitive ideal.

purchase decision from an earlier point in time. Let us move 25 years earlier, so that our 65 year old retiree is now a 40 year old worker. Ideally, he would be thinking about his future retirement already. He might be considering the purchase of an annuity that would not begin benefit payments until he was 65. In this way, he would be addressing some risks that he would ignore if he waited to buy his annuity at age 65. One of these risks is that he might die before age 65. If he does die without having bought an annuity, his accumulation goes into his estate. If he buys an annuity with a delayed beginning, the insurance company knows that it will not have to pay him benefits if he should die before age 65. Thus the insurance company can give him a larger annuity beginning at age 65 than if he waits to buy one then. In other words, by buying annuities early, he converts money in his estate in the event he dies before 65 into higher retirement income if he lives past 65. Whenever we move our point of analysis earlier in time, we identify new risks that represent additional insurance opportunities.

The shift in time frame introduces another risk where moral hazard is important. We have assumed that our worker knows that he will want to retire precisely at age 65. More realistically, people can not predict what their future job opportunities will be, what their future health conditions will be, and other factors that affect the likelihood that they will want to work until age 65. In the vocabulary of risks, for a 40 year old, the length of his desired working life involves a risk that he would like to insure against. In part we do provide such insurance opportunities by having disability insurance and workers compensation insurance. That is, if the individual receives an easily measurable bad health or accident outcome, he will start collecting annuity payments before age 65. However, the complication is that there are many events that would make an individual prefer retiring early that are hard to measure. He might be less healthy, but not disabled. He might have limited job opportunities rather than good ones. There is a problem here that economists refer to as an asymmetric information problem. The individual may know the truth about how hard or unpleasant it is to go on working; or how few job opportunities really exist. But an outsider, an insurance company or a government, may have trouble telling the difference between someone who has great difficulty working and someone claiming to have great difficulty working. Similarly an insurance company or a government may have great difficulty distinguishing a person who can not find a suitable job from a person who isn't trying to find a suitable job, or at least not trying very hard.

This is the source of a moral hazard problem. Insurance theory tells us that when individuals have risks that can not be adequately measured, then partial insurance and only partial insurance should be offered.[10] If our worker retires at 62, he will have a smaller accumulation than if he went on working to 65. He may also have a longer (expected) retirement to finance if his life expectancy is not affected. He would like to insure against this risk – he would like to have his accumulation augmented if he retires before 65, paying for this with a smaller accumulation if he goes on working until 65. Making such an arrangement is providing him with insurance. Making such an arrangement so that his retirement benefit was the same whether he retired at 62 or 65 would be providing too much insurance since his incentive to continue working would decrease too much. Partial insurance balances the desire to provide insurance against this risk against the disincentive to work. In tax parlance, there is an implicit tax on the work of those who are eligible for retirement pensions. In insurance parlance, the increase in benefits from delaying the start of benefits is less than the amount that would be actuarially fair. This balancing of insurance and incentives is a property of the optimal provision of insurance against the risk of a short working life.[11]

Recognition of this problem leads to a natural role for government in that the government has an advantage in monitoring the earnings levels of individuals since the IRS is already monitoring earnings levels. This is similar to a proposal that has recently been made in California to finance part of automobile insurance by a tax on gasoline.[12] This would create a price for insurance that varies with miles driven, which is correlated with accident risk. However, this imperfect measuring device is available to the government but not available to private insurance companies (at a reasonable cost).[13]

The fact that with only imperfect monitoring of the true risk (poor health or poor job opportunities) we get only imperfect insurance is not, by itself, an argument for social over private insurance. If the same limitations exist on the government's monitoring of individuals, then, in theory, the government can not do better than the market in providing insurance. But, sometimes, the government can monitor more efficiently.

---

[10] See Shavell (1979).
[11] For analyses of this problem, see my three papers with Mirrlees (1978, 1986, forthcoming).
[12] See Tobias (1993).
[13] The need to consider externalities from accidents is one complication in automobile insurance that is not present with annuities. Thus, Smith and Wright (1992) find multiple equilibria where higher premiums and more uninsured drivers go together.

Adverse Selection

Returning to our 65 year old buying an annuity, so that moral hazard is not a serious issue, we turn to the second of the three issues I identified above, the adverse selection problem. The adverse selection problem is the tendency of those people who believe themselves to have long expected lives to be the ones most likely to purchase annuities. Assuming that there is some correlation between the belief in a long life and actually having a long life, the mortality table relevant for people buying annuities is different from the mortality table for the population as a whole.[14] Even if we had a law requiring everybody to purchase annuities, we would have a selection problem, although the problem would affect equilibrium differently. Insurance companies would particularly want to sell annuities to those with short life expectancies rather than long life expectancies. This problem of trying to identify a good group to insure is of high visibility in the area of health insurance. In the case of annuities the major effect is probably the adjustment made in the mortality table. It is common practice for insurance companies to use different mortality tables when doing calculations for the sale of annuities and for the sale of life insurance. This reflects the different life expectancies of the people likely to buy the two different kinds of policies. In turn, this means that those with lower life expectancy are even less likely to buy annuities because they are priced for individuals with above average life expectancy.[15]

Insofar as insurance companies can identify individuals as having different life expectancy risks, they can classify people into different groups and set different premiums for different groups (either with a single company having several classifications or with different companies specializing in different groups of the population). Risk classification is familiar to all of us from automobile insurance and health insurance. Since risk classification is not perfect, the selection issues outlined above remain relevant within any single risk classification. If our retiree does place some value on having an estate to leave to his heirs, a correct price on the conversion of wealth into an annuity is a necessary part of an efficient decision between lifetime consumption and bequests. Similarly correct pricing of auto insurance for different drivers is relevant for efficient decisions about who should own cars. Thus risk classification is

[14] Recognizing that different people have different levels of wealth that they want to invest in annuities, the wealth weighted average of life expectancies relevant for the calculations of an insurance company will depend on the relationship between the amount of annuities bought and life expectancy.

[15] This issue is analyzed by Friedman and Warshawsky (1990).

part of the market process of using prices to guide allocation decisions. However, risk classification does raise another issue.

To see this issue, let us again move earlier in time and consider our 65 year old when he was 40, thinking about the future and knowing he will buy an annuity when he reaches 65. Above we noted the relevance of the possibility of dying before age 65 for the pricing of annuities to begin at age 65. Once we recognize that there will be risk classification at age 65, there is an additional risk from the perspective of age 40. At age 40 our worker does not know how he will be classified when he is 65.[16] Thus he faces a risk as to which classification he will be placed in. While he would be very happy to learn that he had a long life expectancy, this information would also mean that annuities were expensive and his accumulation could only finance a low annual income for the rest of his life. In contrast, should he be declared a "good risk" with a low life expectancy, he will be able to buy a higher income per year with the same accumulation.[17] At age 40, he would like to arrange to have higher income if expecting a longer life at age 65, and is willing to pay for it with lower income if he is expecting a shorter life when he reaches age 65. A 40 year old who buys an annuity to start when he is 65 is covering this risk.

We see this problem much more starkly in health insurance. For someone buying an individual health insurance policy, illness this year may well mean higher insurance premiums in later years. There is no direct (unbundled) way to buy insurance against being classified a high risk in the future. This combination of wanting correct pricing for people to decide how large a bequest to leave and wanting to insure against being classified as high risk in the future suggests a need for striking a balance between these two goals, much as a balance was part of the optimal response to moral hazard, as described above. As far as I know, this is a research question that has not been addressed in the literature.

Adverse selection does create a potential case for social insurance. By requiring everyone to provide for their retirements, the terms of annuities change. Along with the efficiency gains from having annuities purchased by everyone, there is generally some redistribution as well. Interestingly, in some circumstances, everyone can be made better off by requiring everyone to buy some level of annuities.[18]

[16] For a discussion of some questions raised when considering the timing of annuity purchase, see Brugiavini (1993).
[17] I am ignoring any health or other expenditures that might be correlated with his risk classification.
[18] For a discussion of the role of social security to offset some of the problems from adverse selection, see Eckstein, Eichenbaum, and Peled (1985).

Table 1. *Variations in Mortality Rates (Annual Percentage Reduction)*

Period	Male	Female
1900–36	0.81%	0.95%
1936–54	1.60	2.54
1954–68	−0.19	0.79
1968–88	1.56	1.58
1900–88	0.99	1.39

Adapted from Table 3.4 of the *Social Security Technical Panel Report* to the 1991 Advisory Council on Social Security (Washington, DC: 1991 Advisory Council on Social Security, 1991), p. 29.

Aggregate Risk

I turn now to the third issue identified above, that of aggregate risk. I have assumed that the actuary employed by our insurance company knows the mortality risk of the population of annuity purchasers. Let us look at a more realistic picture of the task that she faces. The actuary has at her disposal data on mortality rates of men and women of different ages in different years. Let us assume that our retiree is known to be a typical member of the population from which these mortality statistics have been collected. The actuary must project mortality rates into the future. To do this, it is natural to start with the mortality rates for the most recent year for which they have been calculated and to recognize that there has been trend improvement in mortality rates. If our actuary knows perfectly well what the mortality rates will be in the future, then, she can calculate how large a monthly annuity can be supplied and still have the expected present discounted value of payments to our retiree exactly equal to the amount he spends to purchase the annuity.

Throughout this century there has been a trend of improvement in mortality rates. However, as shown in Table 1, this trend has not been at a uniform rate. There have been periods when mortality rates have improved rapidly, and periods when the improvement has been considerably smaller or, as seen in Table 1, not there at all. There is heated debate among demographers about the eventual shape of the mortality table and therefore the likely pattern for projected mortality improvements in the future. Not knowing the future course of mortality risk represents a major risk which, in this case, is again borne by the shareholders in this insurance company. The risk associated with not knowing the mortality table is a risk that must be borne by some group however we organize the provision of annuities.

What distinguishes this risk from the risk associated with the actual length of life given a known mortality table is that we do not get pooling. Improvements in the mortality table make the provision of all annuities more expensive (in expected value). Thus the risk that falls on shareholders of stock insurance companies is sizable. Moreover, in the language of uncertainty theory, there are missing markets so that these risks are bundled with other risks that affect the earnings of insurance companies and are not traded independently. Thus the typical annuity buyer pays a higher price which includes a risk premium to the shareholders for bearing the risk associated with an uncertain projection of the mortality table. The annuity contract does not directly place some of this risk on those who buy annuities from stock insurance companies. If such risks were to be shared, the level of the benefit would vary with the aggregate mortality realization. While one could imagine writing such contracts, stock insurance companies do not.

3.   MUTUAL INSURANCE COMPANIES AND PENSION PLANS

With the purchase of an annuity from a for-profit insurance company, the risks that are shifted from the annuitant are borne by the shareholders owning that insurance company. In contrast to this pattern, there are many mutual insurance companies. A mutual insurance company is "owned" by its policyholders, not its shareholders. In this case, the risks are borne by current and future purchasers of insurance. The exact pattern of the distribution of these risks across different purchasers of insurance will depend on the practices being followed by the mutual insurance company (including the accumulation of reserves), the demand behavior of future purchasers of insurance, and the constraints from competition in the insurance market. When mortality turns out to be lower than that which was projected when pricing annuities, the cost of paying annuities is greater than anticipated and the cost of providing life insurance is less than anticipated.[19] Depending on the balance of the different kinds of policies being sold by an insurance company and the rules for dividing a deviation from forecasts among the different kinds

---

[19] Some people buy annuities to shift income from the contingency that they are no longer alive at some time to the contingency that they are alive at that time. Some people buy life insurance to shift income from the contingency that they are alive at some time to the contingency that they are not alive at some time. Over their lives, people often switch from

of policies, some of this risk is borne by different purchasers of insurance, present and future.

To see how this risk might be borne by annuitants, but is not in practice, let us consider a mutual insurance company that is formed solely to sell annuities to a group of 65 year olds buying them today. Then, year by year into the future, the risks associated with deviations from forecasted mortality must be borne by the annuitants themselves. If more of them are alive, they will have fewer resources per capita. There remains a degree of choice as to how to spread the implication of what's been learned up to some particular year over that year's benefits and anticipated insurance benefits over the remaining life of the annuitants.

Group provision of pension benefits by employers or unions has some of the same character as purchases from a mutual insurance company; some of the risks are shifted to future employees rather than to future insurance purchasers as with mutual insurance.[20] The purchase of group insurance (whether pensions, life insurance or health insurance) has obvious advantages in terms of administrative costs and bargaining power with insurance providers. In addition, if the group is formed for some purpose other than the purchase of insurance per se, the use of grouping is a way of reducing the adverse selection problem. In the U.S. having employers organize pensions is a major element in our provision of retirement income. It would take me too far astray to discuss the role of pensions in the labor market.[21] I merely want to point out the parallel between pensions, where the details of pension plans can be changed over time and mutual insurance companies. This is clearest in the case of unionized firms where collective bargaining can set both the wages of current workers and the pension benefits of retirees. The ongoing health of the industry then becomes an important part of the future development of pension income.

4. SOCIAL INSURANCE

As I indicated at the start, a major reason for government intervention in the provision of retirement income is the myopia of people contem-

wanting additional income if they are not alive to wanting additional income if they are alive. Thus some people buy life insurance when young (and with dependents) and then buy annuities when older. People would not want to buy both types of policies for the same risk.

[20] It is common to suggest that workers do not bear rate-of-return risks in defined benefit private pension systems. This is only correct if neither wages nor benefit formulas nor firm viability are affected by rates of return. All of these seem problematic.

[21] For a discussion of pensions in terms of the insurance provided, see Bodie (1989).

plating a distant retirement. A second major reason is the use of the startup of social insurance to do redistributions to the current old. I want to skip these two issues and continue to focus on the pattern of risk-bearing. Of course, this depends on how the social insurance institution is legislated and how future legislation might change benefits and taxes.

Above, I identified three sources of deviation from ideal insurance in the private provision of annuities. One was the moral hazard problem. We indicated that this problem continues for social insurance, although government powers can enhance the set of tools available for improving the equilibrium. We saw how adverse selection can and does cut sharply into the equilibrium level of use of annuities. We indicated that resource allocation can sometimes be improved when the government requires people to provide for their retirement. The third issue is aggregate risk. That is the one I want to concentrate on here as part of my focus on who bears the risk.

The discussion of risk-bearing in the private insurance market has seen two types of considerations. One is the terms written into explicit insurance contracts and the second is the nature of the insurance market that will exist in the future. I turn now to social insurance where the parallel considerations are the current laws and possible future legislation. I want to contrast three different methods of providing annuities to examine the patterns of risk-bearing that go with them. The first is the privatization of social security that has been done in Chile; the second is a pure pay-as-you-go system; the third is a stylized version of what we seem to do in the U.S.

Privatized Social Security in Chile

The first method I will describe is one that was adopted in Chile in 1981, has been widely admired, and is under serious consideration for imitation in much of the world.[22] The heart of the reform is a privatized mandatory savings plan, together with an annuities market to help conversion of accumulations into retirement income streams. All covered workers must place 10% of monthly earnings in a savings account with an approved (regulated) intermediary.[23] Each intermediary manages a

[22] For descriptions of the Chilean experience, see Diamond and Valdés-Prieto (1994) and Myers (1992).
[23] In addition to the 10% payment, workers must pay a commission charge levied by the intermediaries to finance mandatory survivors and disability insurance (providing benefits according to a government defined benefit formula less the accumulation in a worker's fund) and to provide income to the intermediary to cover costs and profits.

fund, with the complete return on the fund allocated to the individual accounts. On becoming eligible to receive pension benefits a worker can choose between a sequence of phased withdrawals (with maximum size limited by formula) or the purchase of an annuity from an insurance company.[24]

Administrative costs of the new system include both those of the intermediaries that manage the mandatory accumulation and those of the insurance companies that sell annuities. These costs appear to be roughly comparable to those in private insurance markets.[25] With full privatization of social security, the private market solution for risk-bearing described above is also the description of risk-bearing under this (mandatory) social insurance system.[26]

Literal Pay as You Go

The Chilean system is fully funded. Resources are put aside today to pay for future benefits. An alternative polar extreme to a fully funded pension system, is a literal pay-as-you-go system (PAYG). As far as I know, no country has ever adopted such a system. Nevertheless it is an interesting theoretical exercise to consider what would happen if a system planned on having no fund for the provision of future benefits and was designed without the necessity of future legislation. Thus I will be contrasting two social insurance systems both of which can be on automatic pilot.[27]

Any social insurance system needs a rule for determining revenue, a rule for determining benefits, and a procedure for dealing with events if these two do not match. With a literal PAYG system, annual taxes are the only source of revenue and there must be a rule for adjusting benefits to revenues.[28] That is, the match between taxes and benefits must be legislated. For example, the tax rule might be a payroll tax at a given rate. This will generate some level of revenues each year. To match benefits

[24] The fact that Chile has a long history of using indexed debt has made it easy for the annuity market to be restricted to indexed annuities.
[25] Valdés-Prieto (1993b).
[26] In addition, in Chile, there is a sizable guaranteed minimum pension for any worker with twenty years of contributions.
[27] The fact that both systems are on automatic pilot does not make them immune to having their rules changed. Similarly, a private insurance system is always subject to possible changes in tax treatment and regulation.
[28] One could design a system with fund accumulation and rules adjusting benefits to the available tax revenues plus interest earnings less planned fund growth. Like the Chilean system, such a system could have privatized fund management, although the benefit based system can not easily have individual fund choice.

to this revenue, we could have rules based on past earnings that determine each individual's share of total revenues. The level of benefits are then set by giving each recipient a benefit equal to his or her share of actual revenues.[29] Thus, there is no necessity of future legislation to adjust to deviations between what actually happens and what was forecasted by people designing the law. In this system the risks associated with both earnings growth in the economy and mortality of benefit recipients are borne by the benefit recipients themselves.

Of course, this procedure could be reversed. Benefits could be legislated to generate some desired pattern of replacement rates and taxes could be adjusted automatically to cover these expenditures. And there are formula possibilities so that both benefits and taxes are adjusted to divide the difference between benefits at some ideal level and taxes at some ideal level. With a system like this, none of the mortality risk is being allocated by a capital market, all of the risk falls on future payroll taxpayers and benefit recipients. This is an interesting contrast with the reliance on the capital market in Chile.

The issues raised by moral hazard in this system are the same as those above. But there are interesting new aspects in the way that this system handles differences between people. A central difference between these two approaches comes with risk sharing and redistribution related to life expectancy. To see some of the issues, let us compare men and women. They differ in life expectancy. Women do not seem to have a proportionately longer (ideal) working life to finance a longer retirement. A contribution based system is less favorable to women than is a benefit based system since a benefit based system does not adjust benefits for anticipated length of life. That is, on average, women receive smaller annuities than men per dollar of accumulation in a private annuities market. With defined benefits, however, the benefit level is independent of forecasted life expectancy. Moreover since a longer life expectancy with the same earnings possibilities represents a poorer individual on a lifetime basis, the benefit based system would probably be judged to have a better income distribution. Above, we discussed the basically similar issue of the desire for insurance against an adverse risk classification when one goes to buy an annuity in the future. The Chilean system does not provide this insurance; a PAYG benefit based system does.

---

[29] It is impossible to predict revenues exactly ahead of time. A small fund could be used to cover deviations from prediction or part of benefits could be held up until revenues are determined and then paid afterward.

Social Security in the U.S.

The third system I want to talk about is that in the U.S., where benefits are controlled by one set of rules, tax revenue is controlled by another set of rules, and it is expected that there will be legislative changes as the future evolves in a way that does not adequately match these to each other. Of course, this introduces a new pattern of risk, namely that associated with what future legislatures might do. Future legislatures might tap general revenue, or raise payroll taxes, or cut benefits. Thus the U.S. system resembles a mutual insurance company, while the Chilean one resembles a stock insurance company. This raises the question of how well legislatures respond to needs that develop over time as well as how well they set up different social security systems to begin with.

In terms of the origination of systems, there is a question of income redistribution between high and low earners (who have the same life expectancy). While either benefit or contribution based systems could be used as a vehicle for redistribution,[30] the politics is probably different in the two cases. In Chile, the redistribution has been done through a minimum pension rather than through the earnings related pension system. Typically, benefit based systems redistribute through the benefit formula. One could explore how well such redistribution reflects one's ethical norms.

After startup, one needs to consider how legislatures adjust social security systems. Short term surpluses in social security (as are inevitable in the startup of a funded pension program) might lead politicians to redistribute to people who are not poor and/or to raise benefits to unsustainable levels. Short term deficits in the general budget might lead politicians to reduce benefits in order to finance expenditures elsewhere. Yet there are not matching cuts in privately financed benefits. The fact that these retirement benefits flow through the government is not a good reason for them to vary with the state of the government budget more than similar incomes that do not flow through the government. Changing the tax treatment of private pension income (or social security benefits) as part of a general budget tightening is different from cutting benefits in parallel with other government expenditure cuts. Thus, one wants to insulate social security from short run fiscal issues. This can be done by privatizing social security, as in Chile. It can also be attempted by the

---

[30] For example, contributions to an individual account need not be exactly the amount taxed, allowing redistribution on an annual basis. See, for example, Boskin, Kotlikoff, and Shoven (1988).

design of a budget process that distances social security from the rest of the budget.

Looking around the world one can recognize the significance of these legislative risks and the desirability of insulation of retirement income from political risks. In Chile, this insulation appears to be one of the benefits of a privatized system. In my hypothetical literal PAYG system, there was automatic response to the state of the economy. It is interesting to speculate if there would be further legislated variation with short run fiscal conditions. In the U.S., we have avoided the worst of the sharp changes in benefits that have occurred in some other places. But examination of the politics of social security would lead me too far afield.

I hope I have given you a sense of the use of economic theory to guide social insurance analysis, and of the use of analysis of this important policy question for identifying interesting questions for theorists.

References

American Council of Life Insurance, 1992, *1992 Life Insurance Fact Book*, Washington: American Council of Life Insurance.

Bodie, Zvi, 1988, Inflation, Index-Linked Bonds, and Asset Allocation, NBER WP 2793.

Bodie, Zvi, 1989, Pensions as Retirement Income Insurance, NBER WP 2917.

Boskin, Michael J., Laurence J. Kotlikoff, and John B. Shoven, 1988, Personal Security Accounts: A Proposal for Fundamental Social Security Reform, in Susan M. Wachter (ed.), *Social Security and Private Pensions*, Lexington, Massachusetts: Lexington Books.

Brugiavini, Agar, 1993, Uncertainty resolution and the timing of annuity purchases, *Journal of Public Economics*, 50, 1, 31–62.

Diamond, Peter, 1977, A Framework for Social Security Analysis, *Journal of Public Economics*, 8, 275–298.

Diamond, Peter, and James Mirrlees, 1978, A Model of Social Insurance with Variable Retirement, *Journal of Public Economics* 10, 295–336.

Diamond, Peter, and James Mirrlees, 1986, Payroll-Tax Financed Social Insurance with Variable Retirement, *Scandinavian Journal of Economics*, 88 (1), 25–50.

Diamond, Peter, and James Mirrlees, forthcoming, Social Insurance with Variable Retirement and Private Saving, *Journal of Public Economics*.

Diamond, Peter, and Salvador Valdés-Prieto, 1994, Social Security Reform, in Barry Bosworth, Rudiger Dornbusch, and Raul Laban (eds.), *The Chilean Economy*, Washington: The Brookings Institution.

Eckstein, Zvi, Martin Eichenbaum, and Dan Peled, 1985, Uncertain lifetimes and the welfare enhancing properties of annuity markets and social security, *Journal of Public Economics*, 26, 3, 303–326.

Feldstein, Martin, 1985, The Optimal Level of Social Security Benefits, *Quarterly Journal of Economics*, 100, 2, 303–320.

Fischer, Stanley, 1986, *Indexing, Inflation and Economic Policy*, Cambridge: MIT Press.

Friedman, Benjamin M., and Mark J. Warshawsky, 1990, The Cost of Annuities: Implications for Saving Behavior and Bequests, *Quarterly Journal of Economics*, 105, 1, 135–154.

Hart, Oliver, 1975, On the Optimality of Equilibrium When the Market Structure Is Incomplete, *Journal of Economic Theory*, 11, 418–443.

Malinvaud, Edmond, 1972, The Allocation of Individual Risks in Large Markets, *Journal of Economic Theory*, 4, 2, 312–528.

Meier, Kenneth J., 1988, *The Political Economy of Regulation – The Case of Insurance*, Albany: State University of New York Press.

Myers, Robert J., 1992, Chile's Social Security Reform, After Ten Years, *Benefits Quarterly*, 7, 41–55.

Shavell, Steven, 1979, On Moral Hazard and Insurance, *Quarterly Journal of Economics*, 93, 541–562.

Smith, Eric, and Randall Wright, 1992, Why Is Automobile in Philadelphia So Damn Expensive?, *American Economic Review*, 82, 4, 756–772.

Social Security Technical Panel, 1991, *Report to the 1991 Advisory Council on Social Security*, Washington, DC: 1991 Advisory Council on Social Security.

Thaler, Richard H., 1990, Anomalies: Saving, Fungibility, and Mental Accounts, *Journal of Economic Perspectives*, 4, 1, 193–205.

Tobias, Andrew, 1993, *Auto Insurance Alert!*, New York: Simon and Schuster.

Valdés-Prieto, Salvador, 1993a, Earnings-Related Mandatory Pensions: Concepts for Policy Design, unpublished, Washington: The World Bank.

Valdés-Prieto, Salvador, 1993b, Administrative Costs in the Chilean Pension System: Evidence from an International Comparison, unpublished, Washington: The World Bank.

1994

ROBERT B. WILSON
Negotiation with Private Information: Litigation and Strikes

NEGOTIATION WITH PRIVATE INFORMATION

I am glad to contribute this twelfth annual lecture celebrating the memory of Nancy Schwartz. Many of us remember the years in the 1970s when the most exciting developments in the theory of industrial organization were in the series of articles by the prolific team of Morton Kamien and Nancy Schwartz. Nancy's work with Mort initiated a renaissance based on explicit analysis of strategic behavior in dynamic contexts. Subsequent work on entry, limit pricing, and durable goods has continued from their seminal studies; and their results (and important survey article) on the effects of market structure on technological innovation remain classics. We were directors of doctoral programs at the same time, and I can attest too that she was an effective leader in that role. All who knew her are sad that she is not with us now.

In keeping with her interest in strategic behavior, my theme today examines negotiations where private information hinders efforts to settle disputes efficiently. I develop the hypothesis that informational differences are likely an important cause of the costly impasses that afflict litigation and wage negotiations. I think she would have welcomed the use of game theory to address this practical problem; after all, her studies of competitive battles examine a similar kind of bargaining with limited means of credible communication.

My studies of wage negotiations are conducted jointly with John Kennan of the University of Wisconsin, and of litigation, with Robert Mnookin of Harvard Law School. I have also benefited greatly from discussions with Peter Cramton of the University of Maryland. Kenneth Arrow, Ian Ayres, Lee Ross, and Amos Tversky at the Stanford Center on Conflict and Negotiation have been steady sources of inspiration. I am deeply indebted to these colleagues. The Hewlett Foundation and the National Science Foundation provided generous support for research.

I have chosen negotiation to illustrate the effects of private information in markets. Bilateral bargaining about the terms of a transaction is the simplest context for studies of price formation. We can examine the parties' strategic behavior without the complications present in multi-lateral trading. To be specific, I focus on two cases. One is litigation in which a plaintiff and a defendant negotiate the terms of a settlement to avoid trial. In the other, a union and a firm negotiate the base wage in an employment contract.

In these specific contexts, I emphasize that informational disparities impose limits on the efficiency of the outcome. In particular, some settlement negotiation are likely to fail, requiring a costly trial on the merits; and some wage negotiations are likely to entail costly strikes. My theme is that self-interested behavior based on private information runs the risk of an outcome that is inferior for both parties. This theme is part of a broad hypothesis that costly disputes reflect fundamental barriers to successful negotiation. Some barriers stem from strategic behavior; others from cognitive biases, social processes, and institutional factors. This hypothesis may seem counter to the enthusiasm for "alternative dispute resolution" procedures that encourage cooperative problems solving based on mutual understanding and goodwill. Nevertheless, understanding the root causes of failure can aid the design of better negotiation procedures.

SOME HISTORY

To introduce the issues, I first recount some key insights. For my purpose here, the main ideas are in the work of George Akerlof (1970) on adverse selection, and Michael Spence (1973, 1974) on signaling. They were among the first to demonstrate how informational disparities impair efficiency.

Akerlof's Analysis of Adverse Selection

Akerlof studied a hypothetical market for used cars. He supposed that the seller knows more than the buyer does about the quality of her car. The significant conclusion is that they may fail to trade, even if they both know they could gain from trading. This inefficiency stems from the asymmetry of information: not knowing the quality, the buyer doesn't know which prices are mutually advantageous. Any particular price will be rejected by the seller if her car's quality is correspondingly higher. The buyer anticipates, therefore, that the seller's acceptance of a deal indicates that the quality is low compared to the price – and in that case the buyer may judge the price too high. Indeed, there may be no price acceptable to both parties.

Nowadays Akerlof's analysis is conducted using the mathematical theory of incentive compatibility. To apply this theory, one writes down the necessary conditions implied by any self-interested strategic behavior in any negotiation procedure, and then shows that these conditions are violated by all strategies that might result in trade. Or when trade is incentive-compatible, these conditions prescribe limits on the efficiency attainable.

This style of analysis reveals that the crucial ingredient is a feature popularly called the winner's curse. The quality affects each party's valuation of the car, and therefore the range of prices acceptable to each. Not knowing the actual quality, the buyer infers the likely range of qualities from the prices acceptable to the seller. Trade fails when the buyer realizes that every price, if it were acceptable to the seller, implies too low a range of possible qualities for it to be acceptable to him too.

The winner's curse is an important feature in other trading contexts. It is most familiar in auctions. Often the value of the item is inherently similar for all bidders, and each bidder bases his bid on an estimate of that value. In this case, each bidder must adjust his bid downward to guard against the likelihood that he wins only when his estimate is higher than others' estimates. That is, winning reveals that his estimate is biased high – even though it is unbiased beforehand.[1]

The same feature afflicts negotiations during litigation. Both the plaintiff and defendant encounter a version of the winner's curse that discourages generous settlement offers, and thereby raises the likelihood of an impasse and recourse to a trial.

Spence's Analysis of Signaling

Spence elaborated Akerlof's analysis by adding the possibility that the seller advertises, or *signals*, her car's quality. The buyer is still unable to verify quality directly, so the seller must offer a credible signal to persuade the buyer. A typical example of a signal that credibly connotes

---

[1] The phrase *winner's curse* is used also to describe bidders' failure to adjust bids appropriately. See Holt and Sherman (1994) for experimental evidence that this is due to inadequate application of the principles of statistical inference, rather than a misplaced desire to win.

high quality is a credential, such as a mechanic's certification or a warranty, that would be more expensive if the quality were low, indeed too expensive to justify the expenditure. Thus, a credible signal is one that the seller would find unprofitable to imitate if her car's quality were any lower than it actually is.[2] The conclusion from Spence's analysis is that the seller can overcome the informational barrier to trade by providing a credible signal about its quality. Nevertheless, the outcome is inefficient if the expenditure on the signal does not improve the quality, or does not improve it enough to justify the cost.

These days, the analysis of signaling is a refined art form. Modern versions address dynamic contexts in which signaling continues throughout extended negotiations, or is invoked continually during repeated encounters. For instance, sustained signaling can be used to build and maintain a reputation. In some cases the predictions parallel Spence's analysis: credible signaling enables trade that would otherwise be thwarted by the buyer's fear of adverse selection. Akerlof's conclusions persist in other cases where credible signals are too expensive or the parties' interests are opposed. Entry deterrence provides examples of both cases: as a warning to potential entrants, an incumbent firm might use its price to signal its cost; or, it might meet entry with aggressive pricing to sustain a reputation for ferocity that deters subsequent entrants.[3]

Subsequent analyses emphasize that the buyer has options too. The buyer's *screening* strategy is dual to the seller's signaling strategy. Screening is usually implemented via price discrimination, in which the buyer offers a menu of options among which the seller can choose. A typical menu offers several prices depending on the extent of the warranty obligation accepted by the seller. Though they differ in who takes the initiative, screening and signaling can result in similar outcomes in static contexts. But dynamic scenarios imply substantially different predictions. When the seller is impatient, the buyer can screen dynamically by offering a sequence of prices increasing over time, provided there is a fixed and long interval between price increases. That is, the seller

[2] Spence's exposition actually focused on a competitive market for new employees at firms. In this context, the quality of a worker's labor is some measure of her ability, perhaps enhanced by skills acquired through education. A credential that signals high ability is an educational degree that would be too difficult or costly to obtain if her ability were low. Education might enhance the worker's productivity, but the analysis remains valid even if it does not.

[3] In technical terms these differing predictions are called separating and pooling equilibria, depending on whether (a) signaling enables a party to convey credibly its private information; or (b) imitation is sufficiently inexpensive to enable a high-cost incumbent to maintain a reputation that its cost might be low enough to remain profitable in a price war with an entrant.

prefers to accept a profitable offer immediately, rather than wait for a higher price later. This kind of price discrimination is not very profitable for the buyer if the interval is short, because the seller does not incur a significant cost of delay from waiting for a higher price. In contrast, signaling by the seller is unaffected by the length of the interval between offers; she can signal credibly by waiting longer than she could do profitably were her quality or reservation price lower than it actually is. Thus, the buyer screens by imposing a costly delay on the seller for rejecting each serious offer; whereas the seller signals by incurring a delay cost sufficient to make her claim credible, even without serious offers in the interim.

Optimal strategies for signaling and screening depend sensitively on the details of specific situations. Nevertheless, several features are true generally. Their advantage is credible communication, which allows mutually profitable trade when otherwise it might be prevented by informational disparities. Their disadvantage is wasteful expenditure on signals, or costly delays in reaching agreement on the price.

Signaling and screening are intrinsic features of other negotiations affected by informational disparities. Later we interpret costly delays in wage negotiations in these terms. Strikes, lockouts, and work slowdowns arguably fit patterns predicted by theories of signaling and screening.[4] Although inefficient, enduring curtailed production long enough signals credibly that the firm cannot afford a high wage. The screening scenario is similarly palatable to the union: it exploits its monopoly power to price discriminate by lowering its wage demand gradually. It is less important to classify strikes according to whether they reflect signaling or screening tactics than to recognize that in either case they are the predictable consequence of informational differences.

It is well to recognize, however, that this hypothesis cannot be verified conclusively. Disputes have many causes, and informational disparities are peculiarly inaccessible to outside observers. One can attempt at most to check whether aggregate data fit predicted profiles of strike incidence, duration, and wage settlements.

LITIGATION

I turn now to consideration of negotiations between a plaintiff and a defendant to settle a suit. In the event of an impasse, the default is a trial.

---

[4] Basic references on signaling models of negotiation are Admati and Perry (1987), Cho (1990, 1994), Cramton (1992), and Noldeke and van Damme (1990); and on screening. Ausubel and Deneckere (1993), Gül and Sonnenschein (1988), and Rothschild and Stiglitz (1976).

Several features distinguish litigation from wage disputes. One is that neither party can force the other to curtail production or employment; rather, the main cost of an impasse is the cost of preparing and conducting a trial. Delay costs are less important than the lump-sum cost of trial, and in any case delays are limited by the plaintiff's right to a timely trial. Another is that settlement involves only a cash transfer from the defendant to the plaintiff, whereas the consequences of an impasse are uncertain for both parties. Apart from expenses, the trial judgment is also a cash transfer in the amount of the damages awarded the plaintiff, if any. It is the likelihood and magnitude of the judgment that is most uncertain.

A model of litigation requires two ingredients to capture these features. The first is that the parties' total gain from settling the suit is the sum of their costs of a trial. The second is that each relies on an estimate of the judgment, usually in the form of a probability that the defendant will be found liable, and if so, the amount of the damages. An attorney usually provides these estimates of the trial cost and the magnitude of the judgment. The attorney provides expert assessment of these dollar amounts, as well as counsel during settlement negotiations and the preparation and conduct of a trial.

These ingredients reveal several aspects. One is that litigants "bargain in the shadow of the law." That is, the range of possible settlements is constrained by the range of possible judgments and the trial cost.[5] In many cases, this range is narrow because knowledgeable attorneys make similar predictions. If both know the facts of the case, and the applicable statutes, precedents, and rules of evidence are clear, then each attorney is bound to advise the client to settle rather than waste the cost of a trial. Asymmetries might affect how the avoided trial costs are divided between the parties, but an impasse is unlikely. Indeed, ensuring that most trials have predictable outcomes is a major aim of legislators, judges, and the bar. The social value of the attention paid to appellate review, the role of precedent, and rigorous standards of procedure and evidence stem partly from this consideration. The judiciary's success is reflected in high settlement rates for most kinds of civil suits. For instance, only about 5% of tort cases are actually tried.

The second aspect is that a settlement negotiation resembles the used-car market studied by Akerlof. The plaintiff has a suit that the defendant might buy at the price of a settlement. If she sells, the plaintiff forgoes the *difference* between the judgment and her cost of the trial. If he buys, the defendant gains the *sum* of the judgment and his cost of the trial.

---

[5] R. Mnookin and L. Kornhauser (1979).

The key feature is that both parties' valuations of a settlement are affected by a common factor about which they are both uncertain. That is, in litigation the trial judgment plays the same role that unobservable quality plays in other transactions.

The parties' mutual uncertainty about a component affecting both their valuations is the hallmark of the winner's curse. Because they are on opposite sides of the market, as seller and buyer of the suit, the risk of adverse selection is severe and affects both parties. In practice, this risk appears in the guise of reactive devaluation and regret. Reactive devaluation occurs when an offer deemed generous by one side is interpreted by the other as evidence of weakness, justifying demands for even more favorable terms. Similarly, regret occurs when one's offer is accepted, indicating that a less generous offer might have been acceptable. The prevalence of these emotional reactions from the involved parties indicates that often the give and take of settlement negotiations is best done privately by their attorneys, who can identify a compromise from a frank exchange of views on the merits of the case.[6]

The third aspect is that prospects for settlement depend crucially on the parties' information about the judgment. Two extreme cases illustrate the possibilities. In the first, one or both parties have direct knowledge about components of the judgment. For instance, the defendant knows the trial will reveal that he is liable, or the amount of damages due to his negligence; or analogously, the plaintiff knows the value of her injury provable in court. In the second, neither has such privileged information, and the best that each can obtain is an unbiased estimate of the judgment. One's attorney is usually the most accurate estimator, because a complete assessment of the prospects at trial requires thorough familiarity with the facts of the case *and* expert knowledge of the law.

Differences in Material Information

The first case is addressed by rules of civil procedure. Each side can depose the other's witnesses, and judges often grant rights of discovery to a party claiming an informational disadvantage regarding material facts. Further, each party must disclose in advance its line of argument and its evidence. The main motive for these rules is to ensure a fair trial, but an important consequence is to promote settlements. The beneficial effect is predicted by strategic models of negotiation. The settlement rate

---

[6] This assumes attorneys have incentives to act in clients' interests, which can be false. In the short run, prolonging a dispute might increase an attorney's income. The long-term effect is negative if such actions affect adversely a reputation that attracts clients.

is lower when one or both parties know material information than when they must divulge this information.

The reasoning that underlies these predictions is a direct analog of Akerlof's analysis of adverse selection. When the defendant has superior information about his liability, for instance, the plaintiff anticipates acceptance of her settlement offer only when her prospects at trial are good. Indeed, there may be no offer that would not provoke regret after taking account of the implications of its acceptance by the other side. This is another instance of the winner's curse: the mere acceptance of one's settlement offer reveals significant information about material facts known to the other side.

One could envision signaling, as in Spence's analysis, but in fact signaling is muted in litigation.[7] A defendant with a weak case can mimic one with a strong case, so a plaintiff is unlikely to accept a defendant's assertion that the suit is without merit. The notable exception is to reveal the material facts, if this can be done credibly without prejudicing the trial. This is the role in practice of discovery, depositions, and exchanges of evidence, which allow relevant information to be disclosed according to rules of procedure. The legal system has long recognized, at least implicitly, that mechanisms for revealing information without prejudicing trials are essential both for fair trials on the merits, and for encouraging pre-trial settlements.

Nevertheless, existing mechanisms are not perfect. Major commercial litigation suffers from prolonged and costly discovery. When large judgments are at stake, finding cracks in the opposing argument can justify expenditures that might have large distributional consequences but need not promote efficiency. Or, the expense can be wasted in a fruitless search for a "smoking gun" that, were it there, would be the proverbial "needle in a haystack." A central issue is whether discovery can be abused to intimidate or harass, simply by imposing substantial expenses on the respondent. Unfortunately, few studies examine the strategic uses of discovery and other procedural privileges, and fewer outline the extent of the potential for abuse.[8] In principle, dissipative expenditures are effec-

---

[7] This is likely due to the absence of substantial delay costs, because ordinarily litigation does not interrupt productive activities. Credible signaling via rounds of serious offers and counteroffers is not very informative unless each rejection imposes a substantial cost. Other mitigating factors for plaintiffs include accrued interest on judgments, and for defendants, prospects of summary judgment or withdrawal of the suit; one study of malpractice suits noted that over 40% of claims were dropped. On the other hand, there is a strong incentive to make a serious offer at the final moment "on the courthouse steps," or earlier if trial preparation costs are large.

[8] Sobel (1989) examines a model in which discovery serves to monitor the signaling content of offers.

tive signals only if they cannot be imitated profitably were one's case weaker than it is; in this sense, the possible role of discovery lies mainly in the willingness of the respondent to sustain the disruption and cost without conceding to a settlement.

On the other hand, some disputes cannot be ripe for settlement until substantial communication of material facts occurs; discovery seems essential to settling these cases. In some kinds of litigation it is common for opposing attorneys to disclose information to minimize clients' costs and to facilitate settlement. Clients' interests are served when attorneys perceive rewards from a reputation for cooperation.

Differing Estimates of the Judgment

The second extreme scenario pertains to the last phase of litigation. At the crucial stage before trial, the parties or their attorneys are equally aware of the arguments and evidence on which the trial will depend. In considering choices between settlement and trial, each side relies on an assessment of the likely trial outcomes. This assessment is typically provided by the attorney, whose expert knowledge is essential to determining the acceptable range of settlements. The attorney's work to learn the issues in the suit and to develop the trial arguments produces a joint product: this effort establishes settlement terms *and* prepares for trial. (In English law these tasks are partly separated between a solicitor and a barrister.)

The winner's curse intervenes in this context too. Within the privacy of the attorney-client relationship, each attorney provides the client with an estimate of the expected judgment, and thus the acceptable terms of settlement. Although each side estimates the same quantity, their estimates can differ, and it is the difference that determines whether a settlement is reached. For instance, suppose they settle whenever the plaintiff demands less than the defendant offers; and, to keep matters simple, they split the difference by settling midway between the two compatible offers.[9] This scenario captures the feature that after a settlement each party realizes its offer was more generous than needed; and similarly, after settlement fails each realizes that a more generous offer might have been accepted, and might have been more profitable. This is one

---

[9] This can be interpreted as a simple approximation of offers on the courthouse steps. For some models of litigation, this procedure is actually optimal, in the sense that it minimizes the frequency of trials and thereby the expected costs of trials. Offers of this kind can be handled by "settlement escrows" of the sort proposed by Gertner and Miller (1995). The court clerk accepts sealed offers and declares the split-the-difference settlement when this is feasible – and otherwise reveals nothing.

sense of *ex post* regret that is inevitable in negotiation – with hindsight, another strategy appears better.

The other sense of regret occurs when a party is blind to the implication that the other's offer is a signal about its estimate. In particular, if the other's attorney is as accurate as one's own, then the average of their two estimates is more accurate than either alone. The winner's curse thus occurs when one ignores the inference that acceptance of the offer reveals that prospects at trial are better than one's attorney estimated. The plaintiff sees acceptance as revealing that the defendant estimated a larger judgment; the defendant sees acceptance as indicating a lower judgment; and for both, the proper inference is that the best estimate is midway between.

These are classic features of adverse selection, in which one's offer tends to be accepted more readily in less favorable circumstances. This "statistical" description omits the frequent emotional response of reactive devaluation, in which, say, the plaintiff views the settlement as less fair after seeing the defendant's offer, especially if it is large. Or if settlement fails, it is easy to blame the impasse on unrealistic estimates of the judgment or willful attempts to extract a small settlement. Our aim here, however, is to focus on fundamental strategic barriers to settlement, so we suppose the parties' strategies account accurately for the statistical effects of adverse selection.

As one anticipates, the winner's curse discourages generous settlement offers. The magnitude of the effect depends on the parameters of the particular situation. In the simple case where the attorneys provide equally accurate unbiased estimates having the familiar bell-shaped "normal" distribution, the optimal offer strategies depend only on a relative cost ratio; namely, the ratio of the total trial cost to the standard deviation of estimates. In particular, the plaintiff demands more than her attorney's estimate by a margin that depends on this ratio, and similarly, the defendant offers less. When a settlement occurs, the amount is itself an unbiased estimate of the judgment that would have resulted from a trial. The frequency of settlements is higher if the cost ratio is higher. This reflects the general pattern that settlement rates are higher when trials are more expensive, relative to the accuracy with which experts can predict the eventual judgment. This is essentially a reformulation of the hypothesis that litigants bargain in the shadow of the law.

The predictions derived from this kind of analysis accord well with data about litigation. The most important requirement of a predictive theory is to explain why most disputes settle without trial, and why settlement rates vary among different kinds of litigation. The chief prediction is that the cost ratio need not be large for the settlement rate to be in the 85% to 95% range typical for several kinds of litigation: ratios of 7 to 15 suffice. Further, the predicted settlement rate is highest for those suits with relatively high trial costs and/or estimating precision.[10] Some are nearly impossible to confirm, such as the prediction that settlements are unbiased estimates of trial judgments (since settlements preclude trials). This prediction, nevertheless, conforms to the general view that settlements are as fair as trials, and better because they are cheaper, so judges impose few impediments to settlements.[11]

Final-Offer Arbitration

These conclusions about the effect of informational disparities on settlement rates apply to other contexts. One is the resolution of disputes by private trials and arbitration. Arbitration of wage disputes is mandatory for some public-sector employees, and others contract in advance to resolve conflicts this way. The arbitrator acts as a private judge to select a settlement binding on both parties. In the version known as final-offer arbitration, each party files an offer in advance and then the arbitrator chooses between them.

A familiar instance is the procedure adopted by the baseball players' union and the owners' association for salaries of players with sufficient experience. If agreement on a player's salary is not reached by a specified date in January, then the player and the team owner file proposals from which an arbitrator selects one at a hearing in February. Over the years, the data fit a prediction based on a cost ratio that is low because arbitration hearings are inexpensive compared to litigation, and because less-formal rules of procedure, evidence, and judgment preclude estimates that are as accurate. In particular, the pre-filing settlement rate is about 75%, which is low compared to most kinds of litigation.

This quasi-judicial procedure introduces novel ingredients that, by way of contrast, reveal implicit aspects of litigation. Symmetric models of arbitration predict an additional property of unbiasedness, namely the arbitrator is equally likely to choose each proposal. In fact, players won

---

[10] The data surely include cases where a party seeks vindication in court or wants to win at any price, perhaps to sustain a reputation for invulnerability to legal challenges, so at best the fit must be rough.

[11] At a more fundamental level, strategic models based on informational disparities are consistent with the evidence that *nonbinding* arbitration "rarely achieves statistically significant reductions in total court costs or average case duration" (Institute for Civil Justice, 1993, p. 31). Similarly, Gunderson and Melino (1990) estimate the effect of non-binding mediation of wage disputes in those Canadian provinces requiring it as approximately zero. Cramton, Gunderson, and Tracy (1998) find similar effects, including nil effects from mandatory cooling-off periods.

over 40% of the cases. Another remarkable feature is that the parties' commitment in January to the proposals arbitrated in February provides a window of several weeks in which to bargain further during the interim. In fact, 80% of the cases filed for hearings settled during this interim period, yielding a 95% total settlement rate. This harvest of additional agreements presumably reflects both the additional information gleaned from the proposals submitted, and the substantial risk of losing at the arbitration hearing.

The key feature distinguishing final-offer arbitration from litigation is the link between the settlement negotiation and the hearing. Because the arbitrator chooses between proposals generated by the negotiation up to the filing date, each party has a substantial incentive to make serious proposals, and more generous proposals are rewarded with greater chances of winning. The link is manifest further in the bargaining during the interim until the hearing, when again the filed proposals generated by prior negotiations determine the risks of a final impasse. My guess is that this linkage accounts for the fact that final-offer arbitration achieves settlement rates comparable to litigation, even though hearing costs are less and the outcome is no easier to predict. To see the potential force of these linkages, imagine that the arbitration were supplemented with a penalty paid from the loser to the winner: increasing the penalty drives the predicted settlement rate to 100%.

Litigation has no linkage between negotiation and trial. References to settlement attempts are excluded from trials, and each case is judged solely on the merits. This separation precludes any possibility that the trial phase induces incentives for settlement earlier in the dispute process. This conforms to the view that the law establishes objective standards for liability and damages, but it also prevents procedural concessions to encourage settlements.

Strikes

The costs of preparing and conducting trials are a kind of inefficiency. They are inefficient because the parties are capable of settling the dispute without a trial, thereby avoiding these costs. The costs of litigation are generally deplored. My impression, however, is that emotional reactions are mild. Trials produce justice; they also pick winners and losers, and attorneys earn a livelihood. Few cases receive vigorous criticism of the costs entailed.[12] Scholars note nevertheless that legal costs

---

[12] One prominent case was *Pennzoil v. Texaco*, in which direct expenses totaled about $200 million, plus an estimated $300 million for the plaintiff's attorney's 10% share of the final settlement. In addition, the firms' share prices fell substantially, and Texaco suffered bankruptcy. See R. Mnookin and R. Wilson (1989).

are substantial. A telling statistic is that plaintiffs' net receipts from tort judgments are less than the sum of the costs incurred by both parties.[13] Surely this indicates that, in many cases, one or both parties regret afterwards that they did not make a more generous offer to settle initially.

Emotional reactions to strikes are stronger. By interrupting operations, a strike reduces employment and output. The firm loses profits immediately, and its relationships with customers and suppliers may erode, not to mention embittered relations with its workforce. The effect on union members is usually severe. To sustain the strike they must forgo regular income and deplete savings to pay bills for necessities such as groceries and mortgage payments. The waste of their talents and energies to extract a wage settlement from the firm is a tragedy from any viewpoint.

The characteristic reaction after a strike is regret. Regret is universal because afterwards it is obvious that they could have agreed initially on the same contract without incurring the costs and scars of the strike.[14] This is not to say that the strike was unnecessary, however, and indeed when the contract expires a few years later, a strike is seen again as a useful tactic.

Except for grievance strikes and disputes over work rules, most strikes are about wages or benefits. The union demands a higher wage than the firm offers, in the belief that the firm *might* be able and willing to pay more if pressure is applied. I emphasize "might" because the union cannot know what wage the firm will accept. There are always hopes that the firm settles quickly for a high wage, and also dismal prospects that a long strike yields little wage improvement. It is this uncertainty, I think, that is the root cause of subsequent regret. After a strike it is evident that initial hopes for higher wages were ephemeral, and that efforts to obtain them were fruitless. Knowing this after the fact, union members wish they had settled earlier for the same wage.

The firm also experiences a sense of tragedy. It claimed initially that it could not afford to pay the wage demanded by the union. Afterwards it laments that a costly strike was necessary to prove its claim – and interprets the final wage settlement as an act of generosity necessary to get

---

[13] Institute for Civil Justice (1993). Such statistics reflect economies of scale in litigation; larger judgments do not entail proportionately larger costs.

[14] Regret also pervades failed strikes, such as TWA's permanent replacement of striking flight attendants, and Eastern's bankruptcy and subsequent dissolution prompted by its machinists' strike. In recent years, reactions included bitterness when a firm forced a return to work by threatening to hire permanent replacements, as in the 1992 and 1994 Caterpillar strikes. In the 1985–6 Hormel strike, the firm hired 550 replacements four months before the strike ended.

the recalcitrant union back to productive work. The lament often takes the form of despair that the only way to convince the union that its claim of penury is credible is to suffer the costs of a prolonged strike. These viewpoints are two facets of the same underlying phenomenon. The firm has superior information about its valuation of the union's services, and the union knows this. Faced with this uncertainty, the union seeks to extract a wage commensurate with its value to the firm, reflecting the experience and skills of its members. Direct negotiations don't dispel the prospect that the firm is hiding the true value, attempting to garner the larger share for itself. The union sees, therefore, that it must use strong tactics. The advantage of a strike is that it imposes costs on the firm: If you reject this offer then you won't get a better one for a substantial period, and in the meantime production will be disrupted. An alternative message is: We'll accept a low wage only if you demonstrate convincingly that you can't afford a higher wage. Indeed, the firm can foresee that sustaining a strike is the only convincing demonstration.

These implicit messages indicate that a strike is a kind of communication. The strike curtails profits and wages, so the communication is costly. In fact, the costliness of rejecting an offer is necessary, because that is essential to establishing the credibility of the message. It's unfortunate that wage negotiations rely on so cumbersome a means of communication, but talk is cheap, and unconvincing to the union when the matter at stake is the livelihood of its members.

According to this scenario, a strike stems from differences in information between the firm and the union. Most often the information is asymmetric, in the sense that the firm has superior information.[15] At first glance, this hypothesis seems open to the criticism that the union has access to the firm's accounting reports, 10K filings with the SEC, and often a wealth of internal documents – why then is it unsure what wage the firm can afford? Over 85% of contract negotiations settle without strikes, so indeed the most frequent case may be that the union has enough information to avoid such disputes. To explain the remainder, there are ample sources of uncertainty about the range of wages that a strike could yield. For a craft union, a pervasive problem is that the marginal product of its services is nowhere revealed in accounting

---

[15] This common interpretation obtains some independent support from the observation that lockouts are rare compared to strikes, but this interpretation is clouded by the fact that in most states unemployment insurance is payable during lockouts. Some countries adopt measures to diminish informational asymmetries; e.g., German firms include union representatives on key committees. Other institutional factors are likely important too: Gunderson and Melino (1990) note that strikes in the U.S. and especially Canada are longer than elsewhere.

statements; in fact, standard accounting practices mask all marginal effects. All unions face the problem that the relevant magnitudes are the firm's opportunity costs in the future. Past data cannot reveal management's predictions about future factor prices, competitive pressures, new products, and new investments. Nor can they reveal the opportunity costs of forgoing plant relocation, capital-intensive technologies, and other means of substitution for the union's services. Even the feasibility and cost of training new employees to replace the union's skilled members may be uncertain.

To understand how a strike accomplishes the communication required to reach a wage settlement, we invoke the processes of signaling and screening.[16]

Strikes as Signaling

Signaling is consistent with the standard story in labor economics, and indeed justifies it. According to this scenario, the firm anticipates it can get a wage that is lower in some proportion to the length of the strike it endures. The relationship between strike duration and the wage settlement is called the union's resistance curve. Signaling implies a simple explanation for this relationship: each wage on the curve is obtainable only after enduring a strike so long that the firm would have preferred to accept a higher wage earlier if its value were higher than it actually is. This is the source of the essential credibility. Bearing the strike long enough enables the firm to argue convincingly that it cannot afford a higher wage. The implicit message is: Look, if I could afford more, then I'd have profited from conceding earlier, so believe me when I say that this wage divides the pie fairly. Signaling even incorporates an explicit determination of what "fairly" means here; namely, it is whatever the wage would result from negotiations without informational differences.[17] This reflects a common practice: often the final phase is a round of

---

[16] Unlike theories of litigation, studies of strikes commonly omit aspects derived from adverse selection and the winner's curse of the sort in Akerlof's model. The reason is that the disputants' valuations are interpreted as independent. There is no common factor to link them, and it seems implausible that one party, say the firm, has superior information about workers' reservation wages or their wages in alternative jobs.

[17] For instance, consider simple negotiations based on alternating offers and counteroffers, and suppose each party's impatience for a settlement derives from discounting. Then the wage is the best offer the other cannot afford to refuse; namely, the wage that is as good as the discounted gain from the best counteroffer. This is the implication of the standard bargaining model developed by Rubinstein (1982), who shows that there is a unique subgame-perfect equilibrium, and it has this property.

serious negotiations to determine the wage after the strike has dispelled the union's more optimistic conjectures about the firm's profitability. Other modes of signaling are possible, depending on circumstances. For instance, if the main consideration is the firm's uncertainty about the union's resolve then it is the union that signals by bearing the costs of the strike.

A peculiar aspect of signaling is that it need not involve serious negotiations until the strike nears conclusion. A recent instance was the professors' strike in Israel. This was a case in which the government was unsure what salary raises the professors would accept or the duration they would endure the strike. After an initial demand for 100% raises, and a government offer of 20%, the strike persisted for nearly eight weeks without serious negotiations; indeed, the professors' union explicitly avoided a counteroffer. Although other factors were important too, one interpretation of the climax emphasizes the role of a key vote at the Hebrew University, which revealed a 600 to 11 majority in favor of continuing the strike. Serious negotiations followed quickly, and agreement was reached to split the difference: raises of about 60% for senior faculty. I interpret this as an instance of signaling: bearing the strike, and demonstrating willingness to continue, were essential to establishing credibly that the union was unwilling to capitulate and unlikely to dissolve through dissension.

The Israeli case has the typical feature that the strike concludes with a compromise between the initial offers. This excludes some alternative forms of signaling. One possibility, for example, is that strikes are wars of attrition. A war of attrition is the predicted outcome when each party is unsure about the other's daily cost of continuing the battle: the one with the higher cost eventually realizes this and then concedes, leaving all the gains to the winner. This scenario describes well the struggle between firms competing for a market, as in a price war between products that are close substitutes, where the firm with the lower cost eventually ousts the other. But wage negotiations have different ingredients. Because the parties provide complementary inputs to production, fiercely competitive struggles would impair working relationships afterwards.[18] Moreover, strikes usually involve superior information on one side only, and the winner-take-all outcome is apparently rare. For instance, attrition models imply that average wage settlements are

---

[18] Wars of attrition between animals of the same species (competing for spoils such as food or mates) are moderated by symbolic tests of strength. One might interpret some strikes in that vein; e.g., the Israeli strike was preceded by a two-day warning strike. In general, however, economic disputes seem to offer few inexpensive options for credible communication.

unaffected by strike duration, whereas the evidence indicates that wage settlements vary with strike duration.[19]

It is important to realize, however, that some strikes fail dramatically, and embittered relations ensue.[20] After President Reagan quashed the 1981 PATCO strike by hiring permanent replacements, firms applied this tactic successfully (e.g., TWA attendants' strike) or won by threatening (Caterpillar) or partially implementing it (Hormel). In these cases the firms argued that competitive pressures precluded higher wages, and eventually took advantage of the availability of replacements; e.g., TWA hired new employees at lower wages and within eight weeks trained them to replace most of the contingent of 4500 attendants. It seems evident that whenever the union undertakes a strike under the illusion that there is a pie to be divided, when in fact competition in product and labor markets enforces a plain-vanilla market wage, the struggle reverts to something akin to attrition. Either the firm succumbs (Eastern Airlines), the strike collapses (TWA and Caterpillar), or eventually new union leadership adopts a realistic perspective (Hormel). In interpreting these prominent strikes at major firms, nevertheless, it is useful to remember that they are outliers among the thousands of strikes every year. Statistical analysis of the average run of strikes is better suited to identifying the main factors.

Strikes as Screening

An alternative interpretation of strikes is that they reflect screening. It is surely plausible that a strong, entrenched union wants to exploit its monopoly bargaining position with aggressive price discrimination. According to this strategy, the union lowers its demanded wage in steps – slowly enough and in steps small enough that the firm's best response is simply to accept, when waiting for an even lower wage is less profitable than accepting the current demand. In principle, such a strategy enables

---

[19] The pattern differs between Canada and the U.S. Using Canadian data, Card (1990a) finds no significant duration effect on wages, and with a different data set Cramton, Gunderson, and Tracy (1998) find a positive effect that they interpret as consistent with changing strike costs (e.g., inventory depletion) or the firm's uncertainty about the union's resolve. Using U.S. data, McConnell (1989) and Cramton and Tracy (1992, 1994a,b) find a negative effect consistent with a resistance curve. In any case, the resistance curve need not be steep nor easy to detect, since incentive compatibility requires only that the slope corresponds to the interest rate.

[20] A friend of mine acquires firms bankrupted by labor-management enmity, and profits by rebuilding cooperation. The bitter Hormel strike is documented in the Oscar-winning film, *American Dream*, by Barbara Kopple.

the union to obtain a wage that is higher in some proportion to the firm's privately known valuation, and to other factors affecting the firm's impatience, such as its discount rate.

One is naturally skeptical that this interpretation assigns the initiative to the union. Unlike signaling, moreover, intertemporal price discrimination relies on an explicit, and somewhat predictable, sequence of serious wage demands. Casual observation suggests the contrary; in fact, the notable absence of serious demands after the first, and the oft-emphasized reluctance of unions to compromise until the strike nears conclusion is one of the hallmarks of journalists' reports. The typical pattern instead is that compromise awaits evidence that the dispute is "ripe" for settlement, which accords better with the signaling story.

The basic difficulty must lie elsewhere, however, if one is to understand why unions are deterred from exploiting opportunities for price discrimination. I think the problem is in the implicit message from the union to the firm: Think twice before you reject this wage demand, because it will be a long while before you see one much better. This message lacks credibility unless the union can ensure the solidarity necessary to adhere resolutely to the required delay between steps in its sequence of demands. Whenever members' morale might dissolve along the way, screening risks collapse of the union's bargaining strategy.[21]

One can appreciate this risk by imagining the awkward position of the union's leader the day after their offer is rejected by the firm. When they are stressed by the demands of putting food on the kitchen table, members are persuaded easily to make another offer quickly, rather than waiting patiently for weeks. It takes a leader of considerable talent to convince them that a long delay before bettering their offer is absolutely necessary – because they must impose the requisite cost on the firm for rejecting their *previous* offer. Maintaining a reputation for punishing each rejection is essential for screening to work. If the firm finds that a rejected offer is bettered quickly, then it anticipates an even better offer soon after; the union's reputation for patience collapses and prospects for wage gains dissolve.

Other Strategic Aspects of Strikes

The exposition above focuses on the interpretation of strikes as signaling and screening. These processes implicitly convey or elicit information

---

[21] The formal description of the hazards of screening strategies is called the Coase property. The gist is that screening is ineffective when the interval between offers is short. See Coase (1972) and Gül and Sonnenschein (1988).

credibly, enabling settlement based on mutual understanding of the main economic considerations. Many other factors affect strikes too, so I mention some briefly to indicate the range of possibilities.

A significant consideration is that each party has options outside the existing bargaining relationship. For workers these options represent alternative jobs, but these are not viable options for the union collectively, so the net effect is mainly to constrain its behavior to maintain solidarity. New York and Rhode Island provide unemployment benefits to workers after eight weeks on strike. Data from these states show a pronounced effect from this increase in workers' unemployment income. Settlement rates are tilted significantly around the eight-week mark: they are higher before, and lower after this change in the economic structure.

For the firm, several outside options are important. One is the prospect of ceasing or relocating operations, or displacing a craft union's job with an alternative technology. Another is acquiring a new workforce, as when it opts to hire and train permanent replacements instead of renewing the union's contract. Each of these options puts an upper bound on the range of acceptable wages. When the union knows this bound, the problems of communication are reduced and strikes tend to be shorter. The firm is spared the burden of signaling credibly that its value is not above the bound; or, in a screening context, the union forgoes wage demands above the bound.

This is apparently characteristic of strikes motivated by informational disparities and the need for credible communication. An interesting test of this prediction is a law in Quebec since 1977 prohibiting firms from hiring temporary or permanent replacements. Similar provisions regarding permanent replacements were enacted in Manitoba (1985), British Columbia (1992), and Ontario (1993); these laws also provide reinstatement rights for striking workers. A ban on permanent replacements is proposed in a bill now before the U.S. Congress. Legislators in Quebec evidently believed that the ban on replacements would shorten strikes because it would force firms to the bargaining table (another major motive was to reduce violence). The statistical evidence suggests, however, that strikes have been substantially more frequent and longer, and wage settlements higher, as strategic models predict.[22]

---

[22] Gunderson and Melino (1990) and Cramton, Gunderson, and Tracy (1998). The latter estimate that replacement bans increased strike incidence by 50%, duration by 37%, and wages by 12% (or 4.3% when one controls for the previous wage); moreover, unions' wages increased by five times more than they increased their strike costs. Budd (1998) argues that the evidence is not definitive because Quebec implemented other policy changes at the same time; he finds weaker effects with Card's data set and different model specifications. Cramton and Tracy (1998) find from U.S. data that the risk of replacement decreases the incidence of strikes, and a ban on replacements would increase incidence by a third.

For the union, a further consideration is its option to exert pressure on the firm without forgoing wages. Laws in all states require the firm to pay wages according to the expired contract until an impasse is reached, such as a strike or lockout, and permanent replacements cannot be hired until an impasse occurs. These laws enable the union to receive wages while "working to rule." Adhering strictly to the terms of the previous contract impairs productive efficiency, especially if optimal work rules or job assignments have changed in the years since the previous contract was adopted. The union's choice between a strike and working to rule depends on both the old wage, the production losses imposed on the firm, and the risk of replacement if a strike is chosen.

A significant implication of the work-to-rule tactic is that strikes are only the more obvious part of unions' strategies.[23] Another part includes non-strike delays between the expiration of one contract and agreement on another. To the extent these involve productive inefficiencies, they are a further manifestation of the negotiation process. They can be an important part: even though the firm suffers less disruption of operations, it is bound to pay the old wage, so the pressure to settle can be as great. The union applies this option selectively, using it when the old wage is relatively high and/or the productive inefficiency of adhering to the old work rules is high. Part of the procyclical variation in the incidence of strikes can be attributed to this effect. That is, in boom times with tight labor markets the old wage is more likely to be comparatively low so the union prefers to strike rather than working to rule.[24]

The union's dual options of striking or working-to-rule turn out to be central to the interpretation of the data in terms of strategic models. Attempts to match the predictions to strike data alone fare moderately. Peter Cramton and Joseph Tracy (1992, 1994a) have shown, however, that strategic models fit the data much better when full account is taken of the frequent and sizable delays between expiration of the old contract and agreement on a new one. This is important because non-strike delays amount to a sizable fraction of the total, and more when the old wage is higher.[25] In these studies the best fit is obtained from a model in which,

---

[23] Cramton and Tracy (1994a) cite the AFL-CIO's 1986 manual for strike leaders that specifically argues the advantages of work-to-rule tactics.

[24] See Cramton, Gunderson, and Tracy (1998) and Cramton and Tracy (1992, 1994a), who use Canadian and U.S. data, respectively.

[25] Cramton and Tracy indicate that about four-fifths of delay days represent non-strike "holdouts," and they calibrate the cost as about 4% of full production, based on U.S. data. They show that during the 1980s, holdouts increased and strikes decreased substantially, possibly in response (after the PATCO strike) to firms' new tactics of threatening to hire replacements. As mentioned previously, Cramton and Tracy (1998) find from U.S. data in the 1980s that risks of replacement decreased strike incidence, and encouraged holdouts and other in-plant tactics.

if agreement is not reached quickly, the union chooses optimally between working to rule and striking, depending on how high the old wage is. In either case, the firm endures long enough to signal credibly, and then they settle on the same wage they would have agreed on initially if the union had complete information.[26]

CONCLUSION AND A CAVEAT

This examination of litigation and wage negotiation focuses on the hypothesis that costly impasses stem from informational disparities.

This conjecture stems from the presumption that strategic behavior to exploit or cope with private information is endemic. To the extent this is true, it implies limits on the efficiency of the outcomes that can be attained. Exhortations to resolve disputes by goodwill, mutual understanding, and vigorous effort fall on deaf ears if either party is wary of divulging sensitive information, or skeptical of others' good intentions. To improve efficiency it may be better to concentrate on procedural innovations designed specifically to reduce the hazards of adverse selection or facilitate credible signaling. For instance, final-offer arbitration has had notable success since it was devised by Carl Stevens (1966).

It is important to realize, however, that this hypothesis cannot be verified definitively from empirical data. Econometricians do not observe participants' private information, and the significance of aggregate data is diminished severely by enormous heterogeneity among the bargaining pairs in large samples. At most, the hypothesis is plausible to the extent it is roughly consistent with the data.

I am encouraged nevertheless by success in interpreting broad patterns, and in examining particular issues. More generally, the progress obtained from detailed studies of negotiation, auctions, and other markets indicates that strategic analysis provides new insights into price

---

[26] Cramton and Tracy (1992, 1994a,b) develop both the theory and the empirical applications of models in which the union has multiple, and possibly time-varying, threats. The predicted settlement rates from strikes and holdouts are about the same. In the U.S. in the 1980s, the declining incidence of strikes was mainly a compositional effect: the overall incidence of the two tactics remained fairly constant. Card (1990a,b) and Cramton, Gunderson, and Tracy (1998) find another strong effect in Canadian data that provides a test independent of whether it is the firm or the union who signals. Strike incidence is appreciably lower if the *previous* contract followed a long strike, and lower still if that contract's duration was short, even after accounting for the previous wage. Presumably this reflects serial correlation; e.g., if the previous strike demonstrated that the firm's profitability was low then it is again likely to be low. Kennan and Wilson (1992) analyze a model of this phenomenon.

formation and sources of inefficiencies. Multilateral trading in other markets introduces additional ingredients, but it is unlikely that the strong effects of informational disparities in bilateral bargaining are eliminated by competitive pressures. Further research will eventually produce a clear view of the strengths and weaknesses of Walrasian models as approximations of how markets work.

References

Admati, Anat, and Perry Motty (1987), "Strategic delay in bargaining," *Review of Economic Studies*, 54: 345–64.

Akerlof, George (1970), "The market for lemons: quality uncertainty and the market mechanism," *Quarterly Journal of Economics*, 84: 488–500.

Ausubel, Lawrence, and Raymond Deneckere (1993), "Efficient sequential bargaining," *Review of Economic Studies*, 60: 435–61.

Budd, John (1996), "Canadian strike replacement legislation and collective bargaining: lessons for the United States," *Industrial Relations*, 35: 245–60.

Card, David (1990a), "Strikes and wages: a test of an asymmetric information model," *Quarterly Journal of Economics*, 105: 625–59.

Card, David (1990b), "Strikes and bargaining: a survey of the recent empirical literature," *American Economic Review*, 80: 410–15.

Cho, In-Koo (1990), "Delay and uncertainty in bargaining," *Review of Economic Studies*, 57: 575–95.

Cho, In-Koo (1994), "Stationarity, rationalizability, and bargaining," *Review of Economic Studies*, 61: 357–74.

Coase, Ronald H. (1972), "Durability and monopoly," *Journal of Law and Economics*, 15: 143–9.

Cooter, Robert D., and Daniel L. Rubinfeld (1989), "Economic analysis of legal disputes and their resolution," *Journal of Economic Literature*, 27: 1067–97.

Cramton, Peter C. (1992), "Strategic delay in bargaining with two-sided uncertainty," *Review of Economic Studies*, 59: 205–25.

Cramton, Peter C., Morley Gunderson, and Joseph S. Tracy (1998), "The effect of collective bargaining legislation on strikes and wages," *Review of Economics and Statistics*, forthcoming.

Cramton, Peter C., and Joseph S. Tracy (1992), "Strikes and holdouts in wage bargaining: theory and data," *American Economic Review*, 82: 100–21.

Cramton, Peter C., and Joseph S. Tracy (1998), "The use of replacement workers in union contract negotiations: the U.S. experience 1980–1989," *Journal of Labor Economics*, 16, forthcoming.

Cramton, Peter C., and Joseph S. Tracy (1994a), "The determinants of U.S. labor disputes," *Journal of Labor Economics*, 12: 180–209.

Cramton, Peter C., and Joseph S. Tracy (1994b), "Wage bargaining with time-varying threats," *Journal of Labor Economics*, 12: 594–617.

Gertner, Robert, and Geoffrey Miller (1995), "Settlement escrows," *Journal of Legal Studies*, 24: 87–122.

Gül, Faruk, and Hugo Sonnenschein (1988), "On delay in bargaining with one-sided uncertainty," *Econometrica*, 56: 601–12.

Gunderson, Morley, and Angelo Melino (1990), "The effects of public policy on strike duration," *Journal of Labor Economics*, 8: 295–316.

Holt, Charles A., and Roger Sherman (1994), "The loser's curse," *American Economic Review*, 84: 643–52.

Institute for Civil Justice (1993), *Annual Report*. Santa Monica, CA: Rand Corporation.

Kennan, John, and Robert Wilson (1990), "Theories of bargaining delays," *Science*, 249: 1124–8.

Kennan, John, and Robert Wilson (1992), Repeated wage bargaining with private information, mimeo, University of Wisconsin.

Kennan, John, and Robert Wilson (1993), "Bargaining with private information," *Journal of Economic Literature*, 31: 45–104.

McConnell, Sheena (1989), "Strikes, wages, and private information," *American Economic Review*, 79: 801–15.

Mnookin, Robert, and Lewis Kornhauser (1979), "Bargaining in the shadow of the law: the case of divorce," *Yale Law Journal*, 88: 950–97.

Mnookin, Robert, and Robert Wilson (1989), "Rational bargaining and market efficiency: understanding *Texaco v. Pennzoil*," *University of Virginia Law Review*, 75: 295–334.

Noldeke, Georg, and Eric van Damme (1990), "Signalling in a dynamic labour market," *Review of Economic Studies*, 57: 1–25.

Rothschild, Michael, and Joseph Stiglitz (1976), "Equilibrium in competitive insurance markets: an essay on the economics of imperfect information," *Quarterly Journal of Economics*, 90: 629–49.

Rubinstein, Ariel (1982), "Perfect equilibrium in a bargaining model," *Econometrica*, 50: 97–109.

Sobel, Joel (1989), "An analysis of discovery rules," *Law and Contemporary Problems*, 52.

Spence, A. Michael (1973), "Job market signaling," *Quarterly Journal of Economics*, 87: 355–74.

Spence, A. Michael (1974), *Market Signaling*. Cambridge, MA: Harvard University Press.

Stevens, Carl M. (1966), "Is compulsory arbitration compatible with bargaining?" *Industrial Relations*, 5(2): 38–52.

1995

ROY RADNER
Economic Survival

1. INTRODUCTION[1]

Standard textbooks on microeconomic theory typically ascribe to consumers the goal of maximizing "utility," and to firms the goal of maximizing "profit" or the "value of the firm." Explicit consideration of the survival and failure of firms has scarcely been recognized by general equilibrium theory, in spite of the sophisticated development of the subject in the past forty years. The recent reawakening of interest in the evolution of economic behavior, especially among game theorists, implicitly brings with it a concern for the goal of "survival," but thus far most game-theoretic models of evolution do not bear much resemblance to even stylized pictures of economic institutions.[2]

Nevertheless, failure is a common occurrence in business. For example, during the 15-year period from 1967–1982, almost half of U.S. manufacturing firms exited from their industry each year. Even if we eliminate from each industry the group of smallest firms, producing 1 percent of the industry output, the annual exit rate was still about 37 percent. During the same period, more than 60 percent of such firms exited within their first five years in the industry, and almost 80 percent in their first ten years. (See Dunne, et al. (1988), especially pp. 503–510.) Nor is the

[1] I would like to thank P. K. Dutta, H.-L. Huynh, E. Kalai, P. B. Linhart, and M. K. Majumdar for comments on a previous version of this paper. This paper was prepared while I was still at AT&T Laboratories. However, the views expressed here are those of the author, and not necessarily those of AT&T Bell Laboratories.
[2] For exceptions, see the references in Dutta and Radner (1997).

concept of "failure" a simple one – it has many degrees and manifestations. I shall return to this point briefly at the end of the paper.

Of course, the concept of "utility" is so broad that it easily encompasses the goal of survival. For example, we could ascribe to an economic agent a "utility" of one unit per period as long as he or she survives, and zero after that. In this case, maximizing total utility would be equivalent to maximizing the time to failure. However, this is not the kind of utility function that is usually ascribed to consumers. Indeed, I shall argue here that the *explicit consideration of the goal of survival often leads to predictions of behavior that differ radically from those implied by the typical models of expected utility maximization.*

In recent decades there has been great progress in the ability of economic theory to deal with issues of uncertainty, and the connections between survival and uncertainty are particularly interesting. On the one hand, there seems to have been little disagreement among economic theorists that, in a world of *certainty and complete markets*, it makes sense to ascribe to firms the goal of profit maximization. On the other hand, in a world of *uncertainty and incomplete markets*, the very definition of "profit" becomes problematic.[3] Some authors have suggested that there is a close link between survival and the maximization of expected profit, or even that the latter is necessary for the former.[4] I shall sketch a theoretical model in which, to the contrary, *most of the surviving firms will not be maximizing expected profits.*

My plan is to discuss these issues in the framework of a sequence of theoretical models, all of which are in some sense elaborations and extensions of the classical "Gambler's Ruin Problem." Although I shall use hardly any formal mathematical notation, I must admit that the exposition will nevertheless be rather abstract, and the non-theorist will probably need some patience to get through it. I hope that the figures will provide some additional help for the geometrically minded.

I have made no attempt to provide a systematic bibliography on the subject of economic survival. Most of the exposition here is based on research that I have done jointly with Professors Mukul K. Majumdar and Prajit K. Dutta, and I would like to acknowledge as well their helpful comments on the present paper. More details about the sources of the results reported here, and other references, are given in the Bibliographic Notes at the end of the paper.

Here is an outline of the rest of the paper:

---

[3] See, e.g., Radner (1981).
[4] See Section 5 below.

2.   THE GAMBLER'S RUIN AND SURVIVAL

As every student of probability and statistics should know, the modern theory of probability dates from 1654, when Antoine Gombaud, Chevalier de la Mère, posed some some questions on games of chance to Blaise Pascal (1623–1662).

> Pascal communicated his solutions to Pierre de Fermat [1601–1665] for approval, and a correspondence ensued. At that time scientific journals did not exist, so it was a widespread habit to communicate new results by letters to colleagues. (Hald, 1990, p. 42.)

The "Gambler's Ruin Problem," which is the forerunner of the theories of survival that I shall discuss here, was evidently taken up two years later. Continuing with the account by Anders Hald:

> The correspondence of Pascal and Fermat was resumed in 1656 when Pascal posed to Fermat a problem that today is known as The Problem of the Gambler's Ruin. Through [Pierre de] Carcavi the problem was passed on to [Christian] Huygens [1629–1695] who described it in his treatise De Rationciniis in Ludo Aleae [1657] as the fifth problem to be solved by the reader. Pascal, Fermat, and Huygens all solved the problem numerically without disclosing their methods. (Hald, 1990, p. 63.)

Here is the problem:

> *Problem 5.* A and B each having 12 counters play with three dice on the condition that if 11 points are thrown, A gives a counter to B and if 14 points are thrown, B gives a counter to A, and that he wins the play who first has all the counters. Here it is found that the number of chances of A to that of B is 244,140,625 to 282,429,536,481. (Hald, 1990, p. 76.)

This problem represented a new challenge in probability theory, because the number of plays before one player wins all the counters can be unboundedly large. (In modern terminology, the underlying probability space is not finite.)

In a more general statement of the Gambler's Ruin Problem, players A and B start with some given numbers of counters, and given probabilities of winning on any one trial. James Bernoulli (1654–1705) was apparently the first mathematician to find the general formula for the probability that A wins all of the counters before B does. This formula appeared, without proof, in his posthumously published book, *Ars Conjectandi* (1713), but evidently he had discovered it much earlier. The first published proof was by Abraham de Moivre (1667–1754), and appeared in his paper, *De Mensura Sortis* (1712), and later in his book, *Doctrine of Chances* (1718). (For further details, see Hald (1990), pp. 202 ff.)

The problems I shall be discussing here correspond formally to the case in which player B has infinitely many counters; we may think of B as "Nature" or "the rest of the market." The probability that player A never loses all of his counters, i.e., that A "is never ruined," or that A "survives forever," is given by:

$$P(a) = \begin{cases} 1 - r^a & \text{if } r < 1 \\ 0, & \text{otherwise,} \end{cases} \tag{2.1}$$

where *a* denotes A's initial number of counters, and *r* denotes the odds in favor of B on any one trial. We see from the formula that if the individual trials are favorable to player A (r < 1), then the *probability of eventual ruin*, 1 − P(a), decreases geometrically from unity, when a = 0, towards zero as a increases without bound. On the other hand, if the individual trials are unfavorable to A (r > 1), or even exactly fair (r = 1), then A is sure to be ruined eventually.

The problems that follow will be different from, and more general than, the Gambler's Ruin Problem covered by this formula, in several ways. First, player A's stock of counters will (typically) be replaced by a stock of real money or other liquid assets.[5] Accordingly, I shall refer to A as an "economic agent," "investor," "entrepreneur," or "manager," and to his stock of counters as his current "fortune" or "cash reserve." Second, A may gain or lose more than one unit in any trial (period). Third, A may be able to – or be required to – withdraw money from his current stock, e.g., for consumption or to service a debt. Fourth, at each play, A may have the option of choosing – from a suitably restricted set – which game he wants to play. For example, at the beginning of every market day an investor may have the option of revising his portfolio at current market prices. *Fifth, A is "ruined" (fails, goes bankrupt, is fired) at the first time – if ever – that his stock falls below some prescribed value, which I shall conventionally take to be zero.*

---

[5] In the context of the so-called principal-agent problem, the agent's "stock" may be in units of some measure of performance, such as internal accounting profits.

Finally, most of the results I shall describe are based on a mathematical model in which "play" takes place continuously, rather than at discrete times. This model has been adopted purely for mathematical convenience, since it turns out that the relevant formulas are often simpler and crisper in a model with continuous time. In any case, we may think of the continuous-time model as an approximation to the discrete-time model when transactions are sufficiently frequent. Accordingly, I shall adopt the following general scheme, with further elaborations or variations as needed. Underlying each problem will be a stochastic process that – for the time being – we may think of as the agent's *cumulative net earnings*. Thus the increment in the earnings process over any interval of time equals the agent's net earnings during that time interval. I shall make two important assumptions about this earnings process:

1. The earnings process evolves continuously in time.
2. Conditioned on the agent's actions, the earnings in non-overlapping intervals are statistically independent.

These assumptions are not entirely innocuous, so they are worth examining for a moment. Essentially, they represent a situation in which the agent's cumulative environment consists of a sequence of small but frequent events, small in the sense that no one event has an overwhelming effect on the agent's cumulative earnings at that moment. Thus I am ruling out infrequent catastrophes such as major earthquakes, stock-market crashes, etc. One might say that I am going to discuss problems of survival in "normal times."

A strong mathematical consequence of the above assumptions is that, conditioned on the agent's actions, the agent's earnings in any time interval has a Gaussian or normal distribution.[6] Roughly speaking, in any very small interval of time, the agent's earnings in that interval will be normally distributed with mean and variance proportional to the length of the interval. If the agent has any influence over the earnings process, he effectively does so by choosing that mean and variance at each moment of time, subject, of course, to some restrictions. The typical evolution of such a cumulative earnings process is shown in Figure 1.

Following standard terminology, I shall call such a process a *controlled additive diffusion*.[7] Such processes have become standard in the modern theory of finance, following their introduction at the turn of the century by Bachelier, and later developments introduced by Samuelson (1965)

---

[6] I make no attempt to be rigorous here. See, e.g., Breiman (1968) and Harrison (1985) for details.
[7] Some authors use the term "controlled Brownian motion." See, e.g., Harrison (1985).

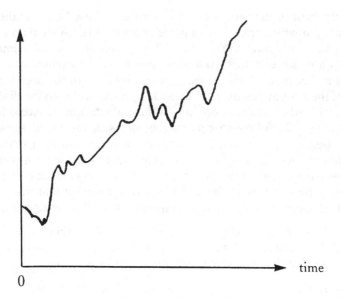

0

time

Figure 1. A Cumulative Earnings Process

and Black and Scholes (1972, 1973). (For a more recent account of applications of continuous-time processes in finance, see Merton (1990).)

I shall now give a formula for the probability of survival in the special
case of a diffusion in which the agent does not exercise any control over
the game being played, and essentially plays the "same game repeatedly."
This is the continuous-time analogue of the Gambler's Ruin Problem
solved by James Bernoulli. By this I mean that, in any time interval of
length h, the agent's earnings is a normally distributed random variable
with mean mh and variance vh, where m and v are fixed parameters.
Following standard terminology, I shall call m the *drift* and v the *volatility* of the earnings process (sometimes called the "yield" and "risk,"
respectively). The drift may be positive or negative, but the volatility is
of course non-negative. In fact, unless I indicate otherwise, I shall assume
that the volatility is strictly positive; otherwise there would be no uncertainty about the evolution of the process, which would not be very
interesting.

Suppose that the agent starts with a stock of money equal to y, and
fails (is ruined) at the first time, if ever, that his stock falls to zero. Such
a failure is illustrated in Figure 2, at time T. It can be shown (see, e.g.,
Harrison, 1985, p. 43, Corollary) that the probability that the agent
survives forever (is never ruined) is given by the formula:

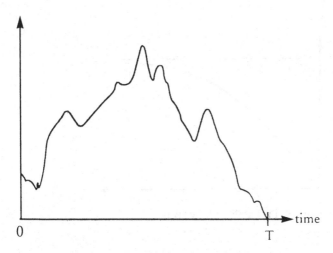

Figure 2. Failure

$$P(y) = \begin{cases} 1 - \exp(-2my/v), & \text{if } m > 0, \\ 0, & \text{otherwise.} \end{cases} \tag{2.2}$$

Note the similarity between (2.2) and (2.1). Player A's initial stock of counters, a, has been replaced by the agent's initial stock of money, y, and the odds ratio, r, has been replaced by the expression $\exp(-2m/v)$. Again, the probability of failure, $1 - P(y)$, decreases exponentially to 0 as the initial stock, y, increases without bound. Figure 3 illustrates the formula for the survival probability, with the initial stock, y, on the horizontal axis, and the survival probability, $P(y)$, on the vertical axis.

Even though the formula (2.2) is valid only for the special case in which the drift and volatility are constant, I have taken some pains to display it because it contains information that will be relevant to the more complicated problems that I shall discuss later. In particular, we see that the survival probability is higher the larger is the ratio (m/v) *whatever the initial stock, y.*

Apart from the gambling metaphor, the model I have just described might be appropriate to represent a business of a fixed size, with two kinds of assets: (1) fixed assets, which are *illiquid*, and necessary to operate the business, and (2) a cash reserve, or other liquid assets, used to pay bills and other current obligations. Net earnings in periods of equal length (e.g., a quarter) have the same mean and variance. Earnings are added to the cash reserve and/or distributed to the owner(s).

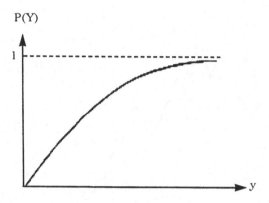

Figure 3. Probability of Survival

However, in this model, earnings cannot be reinvested to increase the scale of the business. Net earnings in any period may be negative, so the cash reserve may decrease even if there are no distributions. If the cash reserve ever falls to zero so that the bills cannot be paid, the business fails. Note that the cash reserve will typically include a line of credit, in which case the critical level that defines "failure" is really some negative number. The important point is that there is some such critical level. I shall call this the *constant size model*.

If we want to represent a situation in which earnings can be reinvested to increase the scale of operations, then we must change the model. For example, a gambler in a large casino can stake his entire current fortune on each play, at least up to some large limit. Similarly, an investor in a securities market can reinvest his earnings by buying more securities, and the prices at which he can buy securities will be independent of the scale of his purchases, at least until his fortune gets very large indeed. In both cases (up to some large limit), the agent's current net earnings are *proportional* to his current fortune; the factor of proportionality is determined by the *rate of return* on his current gamble or investment. Another feature of the gambler or securities investor is that his assets are *liquid*, so that he can remain in business as long as his fortune is positive, or at least above some minimum level. (I cannot buy or sell one penny's worth of AT&T stock, and in any case I would have to pay some minimum commission.) Suppose, for example, that the investor never spends any of his money, but continuously reinvests all of his net earnings. Since returns are multiplicative, and the agent's assets are liquid, his fortune will grow – or decline *exponentially* at a rate equal to the rate of return on the current investment. This rate of return will fluctuate, in part because of random factors and in part because of the agent's investment strategy. We can model this situation by postulating that the *logarithm of the cumulative net earnings* is a controlled additive diffusion, as described above. At any moment of time, the drift of this diffusion represents the expected current rate of return, and the volatility is its variance. I shall call this the *constant returns-to-scale model.*

These two models – constant size, and constant returns-to-scale – are the basis of the more elaborate constructions I shall describe in what follows. They are, of course, very special cases. The typical firm can invest to increase its scale, and its assets can be more or less liquid. Also, it may be subject to varying returns to scale, depending on its scale and other factors. Nevertheless, these two special cases lead to rather different results, and provide some hints as to what we can expect as rigorous analysis succeeds in exploring the rest of the map of technological possibilities.

In addition to exploring two models of technology, I shall also focus on two contrasting models of preference. In the first, it is assumed that *the agent wants to maximize the probability that he survives forever*; I shall call such an agent a *survivalist.* To make the model more interesting and realistic, I shall suppose that the agent is obliged to withdraw funds from his cash reserve, or other liquid assets, at a constant rate per unit time, e.g., in order to service a debt. (Another interpretation is that this constant rate of withdrawal is required for the agent to maintain a "satisfactory" rate of consumption.) I shall call this the model of *the indebted survivalist.* In this case the agent can influence the probability of survival by dynamically controlling the drift and volatility of the cumulative earnings process.

In the second model, it is assumed that *the agent wants to maximize the expected total discounted withdrawals.* Here the agent can dynamically control the withdrawal rate, as well as the drift and volatility of the earnings process. I shall call such an agent a *profit maximizer.*

Combining the two models of technology with the two models of preference leads to the accompanying 2 × 2 table. In the next two sections, the four blanks in the table will be filled in with descriptions of the respective optimal strategies of the agents, and their corresponding probabilities of survival.

3.   THE INDEBTED SURVIVALIST

Most firms obtain at least part of their initial capital by borrowing money. In this section I shall consider a model of an investor who wants to max-

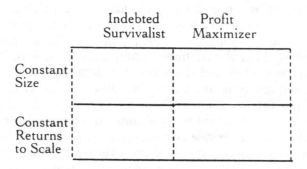

	Indebted Survivalist	Profit Maximizer
Constant Size		
Constant Returns to Scale		

imize the probability of survival, but has borrowed money and is obligated to make payments at a fixed rate per unit of time. I shall describe the rather different implications of such an obligation in the constant-size and constant-rate-of-return models.

Starting with the *constant-size model*, I need to introduce some additional concepts. Recall that the cumulative earnings process is modeled as a controlled additive diffusion. The evolution of the cash reserve is governed by the following simple accounting relation: During any time period of length h,

> end-of-period cash reserve = beginning-of-period cash
> reserve plus period net earnings less c times h,   (3.1)

where c is the constant rate, per unit time, of payout. Recall that the investor *survives* if the cash reserve never reaches zero.[8]

To help fix ideas, let us first suppose that the investor has no control over the earnings process, so that its drift, m, and its volatility, v, are constant in time. It is intuitively clear from the accounting relation (3.1) that the cash reserve is also an additive diffusion process, with the same volatility, but with drift $(m - c)$. It follows from equation (2.2) that the probability that the investor survives is

$$P(y) = \begin{cases} 1 - \exp[-2(m-c)y/v], & \text{if } m > c, \\ 0, & \text{otherwise,} \end{cases} \quad (3.2)$$

where y is the investor's strictly positive initial cash reserve (at time 0), and P(y) is the probability that the investor survives forever.

Now suppose that the investor can influence the earnings process by

---

[8] Under the assumptions of our model, the cash reserve must be a continuous function of time, and so it cannot become negative without actually taking on the value of zero.

controlling the drift and volatility through time. In other words, at each time, t, the investor can choose the drift and volatility that will govern the earnings process at that time. (Note the mathematical abstraction used here: in practice, an investor will be able to change the drift and volatility at discrete times, like every day, or every month.) Since the investor is not clairvoyant, he will at each time be able to choose the drift and volatility at best as a function of the history of the process up to that time. In fact, in the class of problems we are considering here, he need not take account of the entire history, but only of his current cash reserve.[9] The decision rule that determines his choice of current drift and volatility for each current reserve will be called the investor's *strategy*. For each strategy, there will be a corresponding probability of survival. Since the drift and volatility may vary with time, one cannot expect that the formula for the probability of survival will be as simple as (3.2). Indeed, for many quite simple strategies it will not be possible to find a (closed-form) formula at all, although numerical approximations will always be possible.

However, the investor will not be free to choose any drift-volatility pair he likes. In any situation there will be some constraints on the pairs available to him. Suppose, for simplicity, that the set of such *feasible* pairs – I shall call it A – is the same at all times. Such a set is illustrated in Figure 4, where the volatility is plotted on the horizontal axis, and the drift on the vertical axis. Three things are important about the feasible set A that is illustrated in the figure. First, notice that the volatility, v, is strictly positive everywhere in A. This means that there will be some randomness in the earnings process, whatever the choice of the investor (no risk-free investment). Second, notice that there is some part of the feasible set A where the drift, m, is strictly positive. This means that the investor can guarantee that the *expected value* of his earnings in any period is strictly positive, even though he cannot guarantee that the actual realized earnings will be so. Third, notice that the feasible set A is bounded; this means that the investor cannot make the drift of the earnings process arbitrarily large. There is some limit to how fast he can expect to make money!

What (feasible) strategy will maximize the investor's probability of survival? In our present case, the answer turns out to be quite simple: *the investor should always use the same drift and volatility, namely, the pair (m,v) that maximizes – in the feasible set A – the ratio of (m − c) to v*. This is illustrated in Figure 5, where the optimal drift-volatility pair is denoted by (m_c, v_c). Of course, in order for the investor's survival prob-

---

[9] Technically, we are dealing with a stationary Markovian dynamic programming problem.

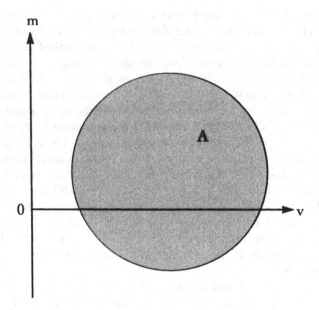

Figure 4. The Feasible Set of Drift-Volatility Pairs

ability to be strictly positive, there must be some feasible drift that is strictly larger than the payout rate, as is clear from the previous formula.

How does the optimal control depend on the payout rate c? First, when the payout rate is zero, the optimal control maximizes the ratio of the drift to the volatility; this is denoted by the point (m_0, v_0) in Figure 6. On the other hand, when the payout rate equals the maximum feasible drift, say m^*, the optimal drift is also the maximum feasible, and with the corresponding volatility, v^*, i.e., the optimal control is (m^*, v^*), also illustrated in the same figure. Of course, at this payout rate, the probability of survival is zero. Finally, it is easy to show that, between these two limits, the optimal controls increase monotonically with the payout rate. Note, however, that the *net* drift of the investor's cash reserve, $m - c$, *decreases* monotonically with the payout rate, c.

I turn now to the case of *constant returns to scale*, as described in Section 2. Recall that, in this case, if the investor were to start with a dollar, and take no payout or consumption from his fortune, then his fortune would grow exponentially at some time-varying, stochastic rate of return. Here his *cumulative rate of return*, not his actual fortune, is a controlled additive diffusion. If the investor were to start with a fortune different from one dollar, then his fortune at time t would be pro-

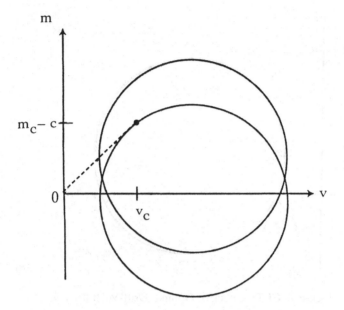

Figure 5. Constant Size: Optimal Drift and Volatility

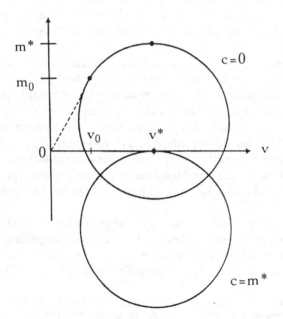

Figure 6. Constant Size: Optimal Drift and Volatility for $c = 0$ and $c = m^*$

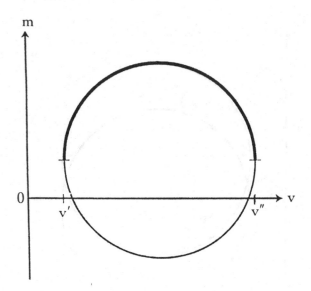

Figure 7. CRTS: Locus of Optimal Drift-Volatility Pairs

portionally different. The investor influences the cumulative rate of return by controlling its drift and volatility. Again, the choice of a drift-volatility pair is constrained to be in some feasible set,[10] say A, as illustrated in Figure 4.

Recall that, in the situation we are studying in this section, the investor must pay his creditors at a constant rate c. In any short period of time, the investor's "gross return" (before subtracting the payout) is proportional to his fortune. Hence, whatever the expected *rate* of return of his fortune, if his fortune is small enough, this expected gross return per unit time will be *less* than his payout rate, c, and *he can expect his net fortune to become even smaller*. On the other hand, if the current fortune is very large, then so will be the expected total return per unit of time (provided the drift of the rate of return is positive), and *he can expect his net fortune to become even larger*.

I shall now describe the investor's optimal policy for controlling the drift and volatility of the rate of return. First, and not surprising, whatever drift-volatility pair he chooses at a moment of time, *the drift will be as large as possible, given the volatility*. This is illustrated in Figure 7,

[10] To be precise, for the rest of this paper it will be assumed (unless stated otherwise) that the set A is closed, bounded and strictly convex, with smooth boundary, that volatility is everywhere positive in A, and that there is a point in A with positive drift.

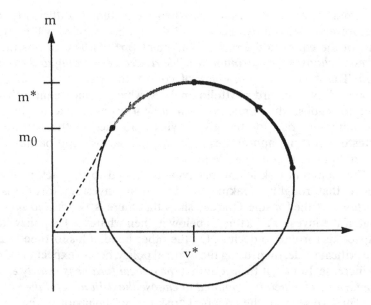

Figure 8. CTRS: Optimal Control Policy

where the upper boundary of the feasible set, A, is indicated by a heavy curve. As shown in the figure, the curve is smooth and strictly concave, first increasing and then decreasing, as the volatility increases from its lower limit, v', to its upper limit, v''. For an optimal policy, whatever the investor's choice of volatility, his corresponding optimal drift will be on the heavy curve.

We have thus reduced the problem of determining an optimal control policy to the problem of choosing the optimal volatility as a function of the current fortune, y. One can show that this optimal volatility, or *risk*, *decreases* as the fortune *increases*, i.e., *the larger the current fortune, the smaller will be the risk chosen by the investor.* This is illustrated in Figure 8 by the direction of the arrows on the curve that define the upper boundary of the feasible set. As the figure shows, when the investor's fortune is very large, his choice corresponds approximately to the optimal control in the constant-size model, namely (m_0, v_0). Keep in mind, however, that in the present case the investor is controlling the *rate* of return, not the total return.

Second, and somewhat surprising, when the investor's fortune is sufficiently small, he behaves as if he were a "risk-lover." To be precise, let v^* denote the value of v for which the corresponding drift attains its maximum feasible value, say m*. When the fortune is sufficiently small, the optimal risk will exceed v*, and the optimal control will be on the part of the curve to the right of the point (m*,v*). This means that *the investor chooses the maximum feasible risk corresponding to the optimal drift.* This behavior contradicts, of course, the well-known "efficiency property" of standard portfolio analysis, which would require that the investor choose the *minimum* volatility corresponding to the drift, i.e., the minimum risk for the given "yield." In fact, in the limit, as the investor's fortune approaches zero, his optimal risk approaches v″, the maximum risk that is feasible for him.

This apparent risk-loving behavior is related to the fact, mentioned above, that, roughly speaking, the drift in the investor's fortune is pro-*portional* to the fortune. One can show that there is a *critical fortune* such that, if the investor's fortune is below it, then whatever his policy, he can expect his fortune to decline. On the other hand, if his fortune is above the critical value, then, using the optimal policy, he can expect his fortune to increase. In fact, it turns out that *the critical fortune is exactly equal to the fortune at which it is optimal to choose the drift m* and the volatility v*.* Thus we see that the apparent "risk-loving" behavior of the investor when his fortune falls below the critical value has nothing to do with his attitude towards risk. The interval between zero and the critical fortune is a kind of *trap*, from which the investor tries to escape by taking sufficiently high risks, and the smaller his current fortune the greater the risk he must take.

Another insight into the investor's apparent attitude toward risk is obtained by examining the function that gives the maximum probability of survival, starting from any current fortune. Since the investor is constantly changing the drift and volatility of the rate of return, there is no simple formula for this probability. It turns out to be convenient to measure the "state of the system" by the *logarithm* of the fortune, rather than by the fortune itself; I shall call this the *logfortune*. Figure 9 illustrates the maximum probability of survival, P(z), given that the initial logfortune is z. As we would expect, P(z) increases with z, approaching 1 asymptotically as z increases without bound. What is perhaps less expected is that P is *S-shaped*. The point z* at which the "S" changes direction is, in fact, the logarithm of the critical fortune, i.e., the *critical logfortune*. In mathematical language, P is *convex* on the interval from 0 to z*, and *concave* after that.

Now imagine that the investor is at time 0, with an initial logfortune z. Suppose that he adopts a drift for the rate of return process during a short time interval from 0 to h. If the interval is sufficiently small, then the probability that the investor fails in the interval 0 to h will be

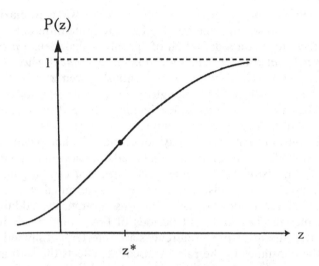

Figure 9. CRTS: Optimal Probability of Survival

negligible. Therefore, the investor will want to control the process *so as to maximize the expected value of the probability P at the end of the interval.*

Those of you who have some familiarity with the theory of economic choice under uncertainty can now appreciate the significance of the shape of the function P. Since P is convex below the critical logfortune, z^*, the short-run behavior of the investor will appear to exhibit a love of risk in that region, whereas when his current logfortune exceeds z^* then his short-run behavior will exhibit apparent risk-aversion.

How do the optimal control and probability of survival depend on the payout rate? First, one can show that the optimal control is determined by the *ratio*, c/y, of the payout rate to the current fortune. It follows from what we know about the dependence of the optimal control on the current fortune that *the optimal volatility increases monotonically with the payout rate,* and that *the optimal drift first increases from m to m*, and then decreases.* Furthermore, as the payout rate, c, decreases to zero, for any given fortune the probability of survival increases towards unity; in other words, the entire curve P(z) shifts upwards.

4.   THE PROFIT-MAXIMIZING INVESTOR

Up to this point I have focused on the implications of the hypothesis that the investor wants to maximize the probability of surviving forever. I shall now switch to the hypothesis that the investor wants to maximize profits, and we shall see that the implications are quite different.

We first have to fix on a definition of "profit." I shall define *profit* to be the *expected total discounted income from the investment,* where future income is discounted at some fixed, exogenously given, rate. Although this may seem straightforward enough for some listeners, some comments may be in order for others. By "income" from the investment I mean money withdrawn from the capital stock or cash reserve for the purpose of consumption, debt repayment, and/or other payments to (other) investors. Thus money that is reinvested does not count as current income to the investor. Income may reflect *realized* capital gains, but since the investor's horizon is infinite, there is no terminal value of the capital stock. If the income is used for consumption, the addition of discounted income from different periods of time corresponds to the hypothesis that the investor's preferences are intertemporally independent, and the constancy of the rate of discount reflects the stationarity of his preferences (a constant rate of impatience).[11] Finally, taking the expected value reflects the investor's neutrality towards risk. Thus this definition of profit is not innocuous, and it will have strong implications for the investor's behavior. On the other hand, this is a fairly standard definition of the "profit" of a firm.

As in the previous section, the investor's optimal behavior will depend on his investment "technology." Again, I shall consider the two polar cases of constant size and constant returns-to-scale. However, this time I shall first discuss the *constant-returns-to-scale model.* The reason for this switch in order is that the CRTS model will require very little of our time. The combination of profit maximization and CRTS results in a poorly posed optimization problem: *either the investor can make an infinite profit, or he will want to terminate his investment and withdraw all of his liquid capital at the very beginning.* I believe that this phenomenon is well known in the case of certainty, and it can also be shown to exist in the uncertain world of our model, but I shall not discuss it further here.

So I turn now to the *constant-size* model. Recall that, in this model, the "productive" capital stock is fixed and illiquid. Its cost is sunk, and so – for the purpose of characterizing the investor's optimal policy – it will not be necessary to subtract it from the profit. At any time, the current net earnings can be divided between a part that is added to the cash reserve and a part that is withdrawn. The amount that is "added" to the cash reserve can even be negative, as long as the cash reserve is strictly positive. On the other hand, the amount withdrawn in any period

---

[11] See Koopmans (1986).

must be positive or zero. Thus we have the following simple accounting relation in any period

end-of-period cash reserve = beginning-of-period cash
reserve plus period net earning less amount withdrawn. (4.1)

This process continues until the first time, if ever, that the cash reserve falls to zero (call this the failure time), after which the earnings, cash reserves, and amounts withdrawn are all zero, i.e., the enterprise ceases to exist. The *profit* from the enterprise is defined to be the *expected total of the discounted withdrawals*.[12]

In the model of this section, there may be more than one investor in the background, although these will not be described explicitly. For this reason, I shall call the decision maker the *entrepreneur*. In addition to managing the firm, the entrepreneur may also have money invested in it. The entrepreneur's *policy* will have two parts: (1) a *control policy*, for controlling the drift and volatility of the earnings process, and (2) a *withdrawal policy*. In Section 3, we saw a particularly simple example of a withdrawal policy, namely, a constant rate of payout (as long as the enterprise is solvent). As we shall see, this is not a profit-maximizing policy. In fact, the profit-maximizing withdrawal policy is also simple, but quite different.

To prepare you for the description of the optimal (i.e., profit-maximizing) policy, I shall first describe a special class of withdrawal policies, which I shall call *overflow policies*. Imagine that the cash reserve is stored in a tank, as illustrated in Figure 10. Incoming rain adds to the water level in the tank (positive net earnings), but evaporation decreases it (negative net earnings). If the tank ever goes dry, the firm fails. Near the top of the tank is a hole that feeds into a pipe; the pipe, in turn, empties into a bucket. Whenever the water level reaches the hole, any excess water (net earnings) flows into the pipe, and is thus withdrawn into the bucket; this corresponds to a withdrawal of funds from the cash reserve. The capacity of the tank up to the level of the hole, say b, is a parameter of the overflow policy, which we might call the *overflow level*.

The next two figures illustrate how the cash reserve will fluctuate with an overflow policy. Figure 11 shows a typical evolution of the cash reserve with no withdrawals, i.e., the cumulative earnings. Figure 12 shows how the cash reserve would evolve with the same net earnings, but with an overflow withdrawal policy.

If the entrepreneur uses an overflow policy, then the cash reserve will

---

[12] Note that it is implicitly assumed in (4.1) that the cash reserve earns zero interest. However, this assumption could be relaxed.

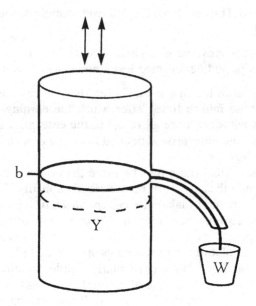

Figure 10. Overflow Withdrawal Policy

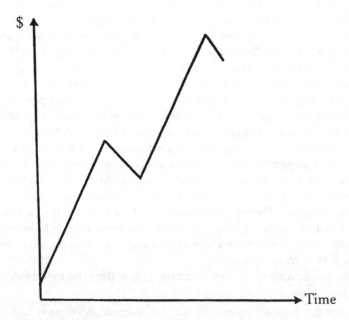

Figure 11. Cash Reserve: No Withdrawals

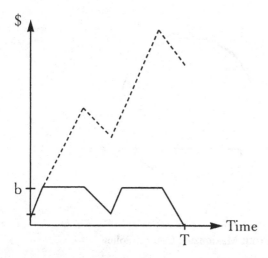

Figure 12. Cash Reserve: Overflow Withdrawal Policy

fluctuate between zero and the overflow level, but will never exceed the latter (see Figure 13). Money is withdrawn from the cash reserve only when the reserve level reaches the overflow level, and then only if a further accumulation of positive net earnings would raise the cash reserve above it. Furthermore, it can be shown that, with an overflow policy, the cash reserve will eventually reach zero in finite time, and hence the firm will not survive forever.[13]

The first important result about the profit-maximizing policy is that *the optimal withdrawal policy is an overflow policy*, for a suitably chosen overflow level, b. This characterization has an important corollary, namely, *a profit-maximizing firm will fail in finite time*! Although a rigorous proof of this requires the use of advanced mathematical techniques, some heuristic remarks may make it plausible. Recall that the cash reserve is not directly productive, but it is indirectly productive in that it provides insurance against a run of bad luck that would lead to failure. The larger the cash reserve, the greater is the protection that it provides, and hence the greater is the expected value of *future* withdrawals. However, this indirect (insurance) productivity of the cash reserve is subject to decreasing returns. The larger the cash reserve, the smaller is the *marginal* benefit – in terms of expected future profit – from a further increase in the reserve, compared to the benefit of an immedi-

[13] In fact, it can be shown that the expected time to failure is finite.

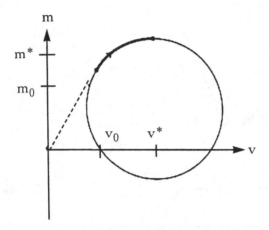

Figure 13. Profit-Maximizing Control Policy

ate withdrawal. On the other hand, it can be shown that, in order to have a positive probability of surviving forever, the firm must accumulate a larger and larger cash reserve, without bound; but beyond a certain point such accumulation is no longer profitable.

I turn now to the other part of the entrepreneur's policy, namely, the *control of the drift and volatility of earnings*. We shall see that there is a marked contrast with the behavior of the indebted investor of the previous section. The optimal policies are similar in that the entrepreneur always chooses the maximum possible drift for any given volatility; in other words, he always chooses a point on the upper boundary of the feasible set. But here the similarity ends. First, the optimal control lies between the pair that maximizes the ratio of the drift to the volatility, i.e., the yield/risk ratio – the familiar point (m_0, v_0) – and the pair that maximizes the yield – the point (m^*, v^*) in the figure. Thus the optimal control is always "efficient" in the sense of standard portfolio theory. Second, the optimal volatility is an increasing function of the cash reserve, which is just the opposite of the survival-maximizing control policy of the indebted investor. Third, it follows that the optimal drift is also an increasing function of the cash reserve. This direction of monotonicity of the drift and volatility is illustrated by the arrow in the upper boundary of the feasible set in the figure.

5.   SURVIVAL AND SELECTION

Although economists may admit that, *a priori*, different firms may have different goals and behaviors, it is often argued that market forces will tend to weed out all but the firms that display a certain specific behavior. In particular, it has been argued that firms that maximize profits (and are the most "efficient") will have the greatest chances for survival, and hence in the long run most of the existing firms will be maximizing profits.[14] I shall call the proposition in this more specific form the *Neoclassical Selection Hypothesis* (NSH). Thus Milton Friedman has written in his *Essays in Positive Economics*:

> ... under a wide range of circumstances individual firms behave *as if* they were seeking rationally to maximize their expected returns ... and had full knowledge of the data required to succeed in this attempt ... unless the behavior of businessmen in some way or other approximated the behavior consistent with the maximization of returns, it seems unlikely that they would remain in business for long. (Friedman, 1953, pp. 21–22.)

Although some authors have criticized the NSH – notably Sidney Winter (see, e.g., Winter, 1982) – I think that it is fair to say that the issue has not received a thorough and systematic treatment. It is, of course, tautological that in the long run most of the existing firms will be those with the largest probability of survival, but the results of the previous two sections might cast some doubt on the validity of the more specific NSH. After all, we have seen that (1) firms that maximize (expected) profits are sure to fail in finite time, whereas there are policies that produce a positive profit and yet have a positive probability of surviving forever. If both kinds of firms are present initially, then after a long time most of the surviving firms will be of the latter kind, and hence not be profit maximizers.

But, one might say, won't the competition for investment funds force each firm to pay the highest possible return? If this were the case, all existing firms would be profit-maximizers, and all would fail in finite time, although some would last longer than others.

Nevertheless, Prajit Dutta and I have argued that the NSH can be wrong under quite plausible conditions. I can only very briefly summarize the argument here. Successive cohorts of investors and potential new firms enter the capital market every period. The investors want to maximize their expected discounted returns. The firms are diverse in technology and behavior. In particular, if we call the maximum expected rate of return that a firm can offer its *potential rate of return*, then firms are diverse in their potential rates of return. At the market equilibrium, all new firms that are actually financed *offer the same rate of return to*

---

[14] See, for example, Alchian (1950), Friedman (1953), and other references cited in Dutta and Radner (1997).

outside investors. Firms whose potential rates of return are less than the equilibrium rate will not be financed. Firms whose potential rate exactly equals the market rate can be financed, but must maximize profit to do so, and hence will fail in finite time. A "supramarginal" firm, whose potential rate exceeds the market rate, will have some freedom to pursue goals other than profit maximization, for example, the goal of survival, in which case it will have a positive probability of surviving forever. The result is that, if each cohort contains some supramarginal "survivalists," then as time goes on, *the relative frequency of profit-maximizing firms becomes negligible*.

What is happening, of course, is that the supramarginal firms are capable of earning "rents," which they can use in pursuit of various goals, e.g., survival. In this sense the capital market is "imperfect," in contrast to a so-called "perfect" capital market in which there would be an infinite supply of firms that offer the highest possible rate of return. I don't know what kind of capital market Milton Friedman had in mind, but I have no doubt in my own mind that the "imperfectly competitive" case is the normal one. In fact, it is quite common to call a market such as the one for investment funds I have described here "competitive," since the firms, although finite in number, are price-takers in the market for investment funds.

6.   CONCLUDING REMARKS

The models I have described here are admittedly special, and need to be generalized in various directions. First, we need richer models of the technology and of the capital market. Second, my picture of "failure" is too stark. There are various forms and gradations of bankruptcy. There are also other crises that the firm may confront, such as hostile takeovers. Many of these crises may result in a change of management, but not in the disappearance of the firm itself.

Third, these considerations lead naturally to another set of issues that concern the separation of ownership and management. The models I have discussed here are perhaps suitable descriptions of a firm with a single entrepreneur/manager who raises investment funds from outside lenders and/or investors who, however, have no control over the firm except to force it into bankruptcy when it runs out of cash. They are less suitable as descriptions of a publicly held firm with shareholders and a board of directors, and a management team reporting to them. In the latter case, we should deal more directly with the agency problems that such a structure entails. Both casual observation and game-theoretic research suggest that the threat of dismissal may be an effective ingredient in a potentially long-lasting principal-agent relationship.[15]

Nevertheless, I hope that I have been able to communicate the idea that the survival motive has interesting implications for behavior under uncertainty, implications that sometimes differ radically from the implications of profit maximization. I also hope that I have raised doubts in your mind about whether the connection between profit maximization and survival is as straightforward as it is assumed to be.

7.   BIBLIOGRAPHIC NOTES AND REFERENCES

I have already noted that the early history of the analysis of the Gambler's Ruin Problem is described fully by Hald (1990). Modern treatments for the case of discrete time can be found in many textbooks and treatises on random walks and Markov chains, e.g., Spitzer (1976). Likewise, the analysis of the ruin problem for the case of a controlled diffusion is well known; I have relied here on Harrison (1985), who, however, prefers the term "controlled Brownian Motion."

Regarding the indebted survivalist, the optimal policy for the constant-size technology is easy to derive, although I cannot find a convenient published reference. My exposition of the results for the case of constant returns to scale is based on Majumdar and Radner (1991). Further results about survival under production uncertainty under various conditions have been derived by Majumdar and Radner (1992) and Mitra and Roy (1993).

The fact that the problem of profit maximization is not well posed in the model of constant returns to scale has been pointed out by Radner and Shepp (1996). The characterization of the profit-maximizing policy in the constant-size model was first given by Dutta and Radner in 1993 (Dutta and Radner, 1997). They dealt with the case in which the set A of feasible drift-volatility pairs is compact and strictly convex; the rate of withdrawal can be unbounded (as was implicitly assumed here), or bounded above by some exogenously given number. A more explicit characterization of the optimal policy can be derived if the set A is finite; in this case it is sufficient to consider the extreme points of the convex hull of A; see Radner and Shepp (1996). It is conjectured that the analysis can be extended to the case in which A is only assumed to be compact. The results for the constant-size model can be generalized to models with variable but decreasing returns to scale (Dutta and Radner, 1997; Radner, 1998).

---

[15] See Dutta and Radner (1995) for a survey.

Section 6 is also based on Dutta and Radner (1997). That analysis was inspired, in part, by the now extensive theoretical literature on the evolution of strategies in games, and more particularly by Dutta and Sundaram (1992) and Blume and Easley (1992).

References

Alchian, Armen (1950), "Uncertainty, Evolution, and Economic Theory," *J. of Political Economy*, 21, 39–53.

Black, Fisher, and M. Scholes (1972), "The Valuation of Option Contracts and a Test of Market Efficiency," *J. of Finance*, 27, 399–418.

——— (1973), "The Pricing of Options and Corporate Liabilities," *J. of Political Economy*, 81, 637–659.

Blume, Lawrence, and David Easley (1992), "Evolution and Market Behavior," *J. of Economic Theory*, 58, 9–40.

Breiman, Leo (1968), *Probability*, Addison-Wesley, Reading, Mass.

Dunne, Timothy, Mark J. Roberts, and Larry Samuelson (1988), "Patterns of Firm Entry and Exit in U.S. Manufacturing Industries," *Rand J. of Economics*, 19, 495–515.

Dutta, Prajit K., and Roy Radner (1995), "Moral Hazard," in R. Aumann and S. Hart, eds., *Handbook of Game Theory*, Vol. 2, North-Holland, Amsterdam, pp. 869–903.

——— (1997), "Profit Maximization and the Market Selection Hypothesis," Columbia University, New York (unpublished).

Dutta, Prajit K., and Raghu Sundaram (1992), "Survival and the Art of Profit Maximization," Dept. of Economics, U. of Rochester (unpublished).

Friedman, Milton (1953), *Essays in Positive Economics*, University of Chicago Press, Chicago (reprinted by Phoenix Books Division, 1966).

Hald, Anders (1990), *A History of Probability and Statistics and Their Applications before 1750*, John Wiley and Sons, New York.

Harrison, J. Michael (1985), *Brownian Motion and Stochastic Flow Systems*, John Wiley and Sons, New York.

Koopmans, Tjalling C. (1986), "Representation of Preference Orderings over Time," Ch. 4 in C. B. McGuire and R. Radner, eds., *Decision and Organization*, U. of Minnesota Press, Minneapolis, 2nd ed., pp. 79–100.

Majumdar, Mukul K., and Roy Radner (1991), "Linear Models of Economic Survival under Production Uncertainty," *Economic Theory*, 1, 13–30.

——— (1992), "Survival under Production Uncertainty," in M. K. Majumdar, ed., *Equilibrium and Dynamics*, Macmillan, London, pp. 179–200.

Merton, Robert C. (1990), *Continuous-Time Finance*, Basil Blackwell, Oxford.

Mitra, Tapan, and Santanu Roy (1993), "On Some Aspects of Survival under Production Uncertainty," *Economic Theory*, 3, 397–411.

Radner, Roy (1981), "Equilibrium under Uncertainty," in K. J. Arrow and M. Intriligator, eds., *Handbook of Mathematical Economics*, Ch. 20, pp. 923–1006.

—— (1998), "Profit Maximization with Bankruptcy and Variable Scale," *J. of Economic Dynamics and Control*, 22, 849–867.

Radner, Roy, and Lawrence A. Shepp (1996), "Risk vs. Profit Potential: A Model for Corporate Strategy," *J. of Economic Dynamics and Control*, 20, 1373–1393.

Samuelson, Paul A. (1965), "Rational Theory of Warrant Pricing," *Industrial Management Rev.*, 6, 13–39.

Spitzer, Frank, L. (1976), *Principles of Random Walk*, Springer-Verlag, New York, 2nd ed.

Winter, Sidney G. (1982), "Competition and Selection," in J. Eatwell, J. Milgate, and P. Newman, eds., *The New Palgrave*, Vol. I, Stockton Press, New York, pp. 545–548.

1996

NANCY L. STOKEY

Shirtsleeves to Shirtsleeves:
The Economics of Social Mobility

It is an honor to be here today to give this lecture, for several reasons. First, the speakers who have preceded me in this lecture series form a very distinguished group, and it is an honor to join them. Second, Northwestern University is where I began my career. It was a wonderful environment for me and I have many fond memories, so it is nice to be back. And finally, Nancy Schwartz, in addition to being an outstanding scholar, was a kind and generous friend to me when I first arrived at Northwestern, and I am glad to have this opportunity to pay tribute to her.

I.   INTRODUCTION

My topic today is intergenerational mobility, and I want to begin with a brief discussion of why I think it is an important issue. I will discuss three reasons: one that is moral or philosophical and two that are pragmatic and policy oriented.

First the philosophical question. We are all brought up with the notion that the United States is a land of equal opportunity. Now the fact that we talk about equal opportunity rather than equal outcomes means that we are willing to accept at least some inequality. In fact, as a society we are evidently willing to accept a substantial degree of economic inequality. In part this is because we believe economic incentives are needed to

I am grateful to James Heckman, Larry Jones, Robert E. Lucas, Jr., Casey Mulligan, Derek Neal, Christopher Phelan, Peter Rossi, and Paul Wolfson for helpful comments, to Yizu Yeh for research assistance, and to the National Science Foundation for financial support.

induce people to expend effort. Society's production of goods and services depends on the willingness of individuals to go to school, to study, to acquire skills, to practice, to work, to take risks, to plan, and to innovate. These activities are difficult or risky or both, so individuals are willing to engage in them only to the extent that they expect to be rewarded. The demise of the former Soviet bloc is in part a triumph of the capitalist philosophy that economic incentives are necessary, and the evidence seems to be that such incentives necessarily lead to a substantial degree of inequality.

But we care about the sources of inequality as well as its extent, which is why we distinguish between equal opportunity and equal outcomes. To what extent is the claim that our society provides equal opportunity justified? How can we tell?

I am going to take the position that if economic success is largely unpredictable on the basis of observed aspects of family background, then we can reasonably claim that society provides equal opportunity. There still might be significant inequality in income across individuals, due to differences in ability, hard work, luck, and so on, but I will call these unequal outcomes. On the other hand, if economic success is highly predictable on the basis of family background, then I think it is difficult to accept the claim that our society provides equal opportunity. In this case accidents of birth – unequal opportunity – are primary determinants of economic status.

Consequently, on a first pass we can judge whether there is equal opportunity by looking at parents and their children to see whether the economic success of the children is determined in large part by the success of their parents. If it is, then we can go on to ask what the mechanisms are by which this happens and whether there are any changes in social or institutional arrangements that would lead to more equality of opportunity.

To think concretely about the causes and consequences of social mobility, it is useful to have a couple of specific issues in mind. Two that are much in the news recently are school funding policy and immigration policy.

Local funding of public primary and secondary schools, which was the standard method of financing in this country for many years, led to highly unequal spending across school districts. In most states a substantial portion of the revenue is now collected and apportioned at the state level, resulting in much more equal expenditures per pupil across districts. Is this likely to have much effect on equality of opportunity? More generally, how do various institutional arrangements affect the educational outcomes of children from various types of families? For example, how important are funding arrangements for public schools, the availability of college scholarships and loans, the availability of publicly supported universities, and so on in determining educational outcomes for various types of children?

The number of new immigrants entering the U.S., both legal and illegal, has increased dramatically since the passage of the Immigration Act of 1965. Many of these immigrants have substantially less education and lower earnings than the native born population, and the debate about whether our immigration policy should be tightened has become very heated. A sensible discussion of the long-run consequences of a restrictive or a liberal policy involves many issues. One of these is what the children and grandchildren of these immigrants are likely to look like in economic terms. How long will it take for the families of the current immigrants to be assimilated economically? How many generations will be required before their descendants are similar to the native born in terms of educational and economic attainment?

II.   INEQUALITY AND MOBILITY

A.   Measuring Inequality

We must be careful to distinguish between inequality and immobility: they are not the same. To provide a rough idea about the extent of inequality in the U.S. and how it has changed over time, Figures 1a–1c display the distribution of earnings of men aged 35–40 in the U.S. for the years 1960, 1980, and 1990. Earnings, which are the sum of wage and salary income, self-employed income, and farm income, are measured in current dollars, in log form, and the data are from the Censuses for those three years.

The figures clearly show a substantial increase in nominal income from year to year: each of the later distributions is shifted to the right. These shifts reflect both inflation and real growth. Over the 20-year period between 1960 and 1980, the average inflation rate was about 4.4% per year and the average real (deflated) earnings for this group grew at about 2.9% per year. Between 1980 and 1990 most of the change was due to inflation: during the 1980s the average inflation rate was about 5.2% per year and average earnings for this group grew at about 1.5% per year.

The figures also show an increase in inequality from year to year: each of the later distributions is more dispersed. To get a sharper picture of how much inequality increased over this period, it is useful to compare individuals at various percentiles. This is done in Table 1. As shown there, in 1960 a man at the 75th percentile had earnings that were 134% of the

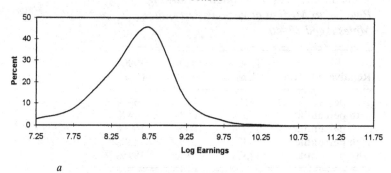

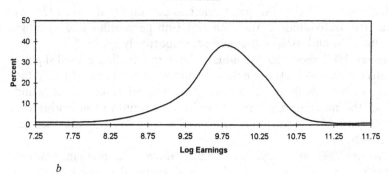

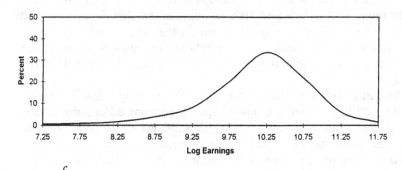

Figures 1a–c. Distribution of Log Earnings for Men Aged 35–40

Table 1. *Changes in Inequality: Earnings
Relative to Median at Various Percentiles,
Males Aged 35–40*

Relative position	1960 Census	1980 Census	1990 Census
10th percentile	41%	38%	36%
25th percentile	73%	65%	64%
50th percentile	100%	100%	100%
75th percentile	134%	136%	143%
90th percentile	173%	178%	197%

median, and one at the 90th percentile had earnings that were 173% of
the median. Individuals at the 25th and 10th percentiles had earnings
that were 73% and 41% of the median, respectively.

Between 1960 and 1980 individuals above the median gained slightly
in relative terms, while those below the median lost ground. In 1980 the
earnings of individuals at the 75th and 90th percentiles rose to 136% and
178% of the median, respectively, while the earnings of individuals at
the 25th and 10th percentiles fell to 65% and 38% of the median,
respectively.

Between 1980 and 1990 individuals above the median enjoyed
another gain in relative terms, while those below the median suffered
a further loss. In 1990 the earnings of individuals at the 75th and
95th percentiles grew to 143% and 197% of the median, respectively,
while those at the 25th and 10th percentiles fell slightly, to 64% and
36% of the median, respectively. Overall, the most significant change
was the very large increase in the relative earnings of those in the
upper tail of the distribution, but all of the groups showed substantial
changes.

Thus, although the 1960, 1980, and 1990 earnings distributions in
Figure 1 all have roughly similar shapes, the means differ substantially
and dispersion grew to some extent. The same general conclusions hold
for earnings for other groups, for wage rates, and for household incomes.
To adjust for growth in average income, it is convenient to measure earnings, wage rates, and so forth, in logarithmic form and as deviations from
the cohort mean. In terms of Figure 1 this simply means relabeling the
horizontal axis so the mean of each distribution is zero and choosing any
convenient (but constant) units for the scale. Throughout the rest of this
lecture, whenever I talk about earnings, wage rates, income, or con-

sumption, I will be measuring it in this way: as a percentage deviation from the cohort mean.

So measured, the distributions still show a noticeable increase in inequality over the past three decades. Although these changes are important, they will not be the main focus of my talk. Moreover, it is not at all clear that they represent a long-run trend. Earlier decades show both increases and decreases in inequality, with neither predominating. For example, during the 1940s there was a very sharp compression of the wage distribution that was only slowly reversed over the subsequent 35 years (Goldin and Margo, 1992, figure 1). Taking a longer view, then, earnings inequality in the U.S. has shown considerable fluctuations over time, but no obvious long-run trend, and for convenience I will take it to be constant.

B.   What Is Mobility?

To measure *immobility* it is useful to have a stylized model of the relationship between fathers and sons. Figure 2a shows an idealized earnings distribution for an age cohort of fathers. It is constructed to have a mean of zero and a variance of unity. Suppose, for illustration, that each father has exactly one son. As we just saw, the data suggest that roughly the same idealized earnings distribution represents the sons. The mean income of the sons is higher, but the shape of the distribution is about the same.

Assume that the earnings of each son (measured as a percentage deviation from the cohort mean) is determined in the following way. The son inherits a fixed fraction – the same fraction for everyone – of his father's relative position. In addition, each son's earnings has an idiosyncratic random component, which we can interpret as ability or luck. The degree of *persistence* or immobility in the society is measured by the fraction of the father's relative position that his son inherits. I will refer to this number, which lies between zero and one, as *beta*. Low values for beta indicate low persistence (high mobility); high values indicate high persistence (low mobility).

Suppose that each son inherits three-quarters of his father's relative position, so beta equals 0.75. Take fathers with earnings at the 10th, 50th, and 90th percentiles and consider their sons. (Remember that each one of our idealized fathers has one son.) We can pull these three groups of sons out and look at each group separately. These three groups are shown in Figure 2b. Notice that there is almost no overlap between the top and bottom groups. In this society if you went to two picnics with these two groups, it would be very easy to figure out which group was which.

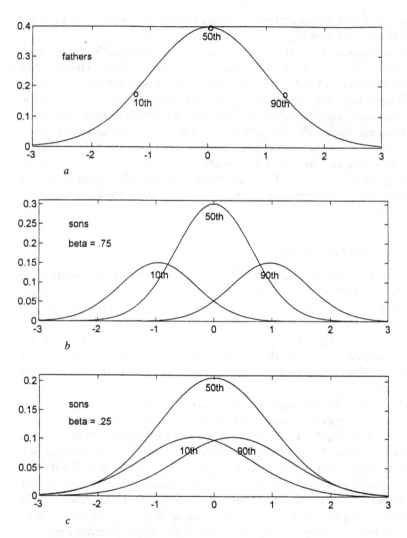

Figures 2a–c. Effects of Intergenerational Persistence

Alternatively, suppose a son inherits only one-quarter of his father's relative position, so beta equals 0.25. If we do the same experiment, we get Figure 2c. In this case the earnings distributions for sons of fathers at the 10th and 90th percentiles have substantial overlap. In this society it would be hard to distinguish the two groups of sons.

If there were complete mobility, that is, if a son inherited none of his father's relative status (beta = 0.0), then all groups of sons would look exactly alike. If there were complete immobility, each son would inherit exactly his father's relative position (beta = 1.0). This would be a perfect caste society.

Notice that in societies with more persistence, a father's earnings are more useful in predicting his son's earnings, and vice versa. Notice, too, that the degree of immobility – as measured by beta – can change without changing the degree of inequality – as measured by the variance of the distribution. Similarly, the degree of inequality can change without changing the degree of immobility.

C.   Pitfalls in Measuring Social Mobility

Opinion among economists about the extent of social mobility has changed dramatically in the past decade, and it is interesting to see why this is so. Ten years ago a survey of the available empirical studies would have led to the conclusion that there was very little persistence in economic status. A number of studies, using data from the U.S. and several western European countries, all found persistence coefficients of 0.20 to 0.25. The evidence today, as we will see in just a moment, is that these estimates are far too low. Two important problems marred the early studies.[1]

The first problem was that the samples were nonrepresentative, and this biased the results. To illustrate the problem, consider the society depicted in Figure 2b, where the persistence coefficient between the earnings of fathers and sons is 0.75. Figure 3a displays earnings data from this society in a different way, with sons' (normalized, log) incomes plotted against their fathers'. In this figure the persistence coefficient is represented by the slope of the regression line.

Suppose that a sample from this population is constructed by taking young men, sons, who are high school graduates and who joined the army. A sample like this might be used because the data are easy to obtain. Then many of the sons with very low earnings or very high earnings do not appear in the sample: the former did not finish high school and the latter did not join the army. To make the point very clearly, suppose that none of the sons with earnings below a certain minimum or above a certain maximum appear in the sample, and that all the others do. The resulting sample appears in Figure 3b. Clearly, a regression line fit to the sample group is flatter than the regression line for the population. That is, the estimated persistence coefficient, the slope, is too low.

[1] See Corcoran et al. (1990) and Solon (1992) for a further discussion.

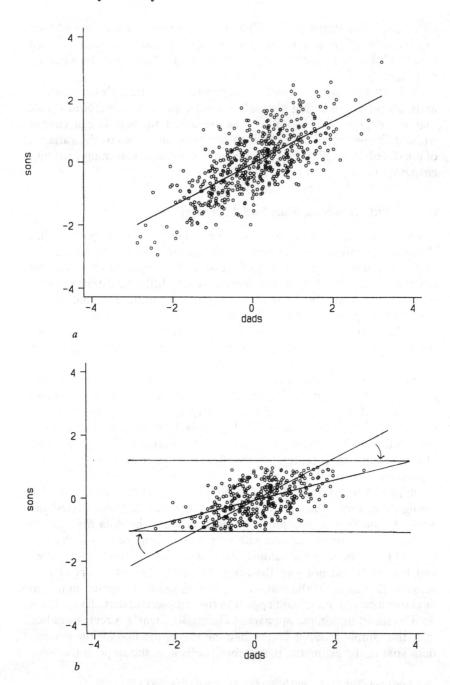

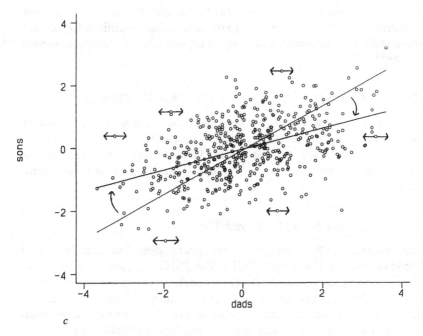

c

Figures 3a–c. Effects of Selection Bias and Measurement Error

The example here is stark, but clearly the principle is very general: if the sample is chosen in a way that makes the sons similar to each other, then it is hard to discern the similarity between fathers and sons. The slope of the regression line fit to the sample is too low, and we underestimate the degree of persistence. This is the problem of sample selection bias.

The second problem was that fathers' earnings (or wage or income) were poorly measured. For the purpose of estimating persistence coefficients, we want to compare the *lifetime* earnings of fathers and sons. But earnings in any one year typically have a large transitory component: a spell of unemployment or poor health might reduce income, and overtime hours or moonlighting might raise it.

As before, suppose that Figure 3a represents the true relationship between the lifetime earnings of fathers and sons. If fathers' earnings are measured in only one year, the transitory component for that year scatters the points to the left and right. Figure 3c shows the sample that results and the corresponding regression line. Again, the regression line for the sample is flatter than the true regression line, and the estimated persistence coefficient is too low. One method for removing – or at least reducing – measurement error is to observe fathers' earnings for several years and take an average. Other more sophisticated techniques are also available.[2]

III.   RECENT ESTIMATES OF PERSISTENCE

Next I want to review several recent empirical studies, to give a sense of what the best current estimates suggest about the degree of intergenerational mobility. I will look at five studies, all using U.S. data. The first three look at representative U.S. samples; the last two focus on immigrant groups.

A.   Evidence from U.S. Family Data

The first study is by Gary Solon (1992), who uses data from the Panel Study on Income Dynamics (PSID). The PSID is a nationally representative survey of about 5,000 families, conducted annually since 1968. It contains data on the wage rates and earnings of individual family members, total family income (including nonlabor income), some components of consumption, and many demographic variables. In addition, information about assets (wealth) was collected in two years.[3]

This study has been running for a long enough period so that the children of the original PSID households are now adults. Consequently it is a good source of data on the earnings and income of parents and children. A nice feature of these data is that the earnings, wages, income, and so on, of the parents are self-reported values collected contemporaneously. In this respect the information should be quite accurate. Data on earnings and income collected retrospectively are likely to contain much larger reporting errors, especially if the information is collected from the children.

---

[2] Because a regression line is fit by minimizing the sum of squared deviations in a vertical direction, selection bias and measurement error enter asymmetrically for fathers and sons. Specifically, using a nonrepresentative sample of fathers does not bias the slope of the regression line, although it may increase the standard error of the estimated coefficient. Similarly, measurement error for the sons does not introduce bias, although it will reduce the goodness of fit. Therefore, we need to worry about selection bias for the sons but not the fathers and about measurement error for the fathers but not the sons.

[3] Although the original PSID sample was chosen to be representative, attrition has introduced some biases. Studies have found that low and high income individuals – both parents and children – are more likely to leave than those with middle incomes. Thus, the sample used here to some extent underrepresents fathers who are poorly educated or have low earnings.

Table 2. *Effects of Selection Bias and Measurement Error on Measured*
Persistence of Earnings

	Trimmed sample	Single-year income	Two-year average income	Three-year average income	Four-year average income	Five-year average income
Solon	0.21	0.30	0.36	0.37	0.39	0.41
(PSID)	(0.08)	(0.07)	(0.08)	(0.08)	(0.09)	(0.09)
Zimmerman	n.a.	0.40	0.47	0.53	0.54	n.a.
(NLS)		(0.06)	(0.07)	(0.07)	(0.08)	

Source: Solon 1992, p. 402 and table 2; Zimmerman 1992, table 6.

Solon looks at sons in the cohort born between 1951 and 1959. The
1984 earnings of the sons are related to their fathers' earnings in 1967–71,
so the sons are 25–33 years old when their earnings are measured and
the fathers are 27–68 years old in the first year their earnings are measured. Observations where earnings are zero are dropped, and if a family
has more than one son, only the oldest is included. All the regressions
have around 300 observations, and all control for the age of the father
and the age of the son.

Table 2, which shows the persistence coefficients for a variety of
regressions of son's earnings on father's earnings, clearly displays the
effects of selection bias and measurement error. In the first column the
sample is trimmed to include only sons who have at least 12 years of education, and the earnings of the fathers are measured in 1967. The other
columns use the full sample, and each entry is calculated in the following way. For single-year measures of father's earnings, Solon estimated
five regressions, using father's earnings in each of the years from 1967 to
1971 as the independent variables. For two-year measures of father's
earnings, he estimated four regressions, using father's average income in
1967–68, 1968–69, and so on. The coefficient in the second column here
is the average of Solon's five single-year estimates, the one in the third
column is the average of Solon's four two-year estimates, and so on.

The effects of selection bias and measurement error are striking. It is
clear how earlier studies could have arrived at low estimates of persistence. For the trimmed sample, the persistence coefficient is 0.21, which
is in the range of the early estimates. Eliminating selection bias, by using
the entire sample, raises the estimated coefficient to 0.30. Reducing the

measurement error in father's earnings, by averaging reported earnings over several years, further increases the estimated coefficient. When father's income is averaged over all five years, the coefficient is 0.41.

Results from a second study confirm these conclusions. David Zimmerman (1992) conducted a similar analysis using data from the National Longitudinal Survey (NLS). The NLS, which was initiated in 1966, has data on wage rates, earnings, and the Duncan index (which is a measure of occupational status) for up to 15 years (through 1981) for about 900 father-son pairs. The average age of the fathers in 1965 was 49.7, and the average age of the sons in 1981 was 33.8. Zimmerman uses observations only where both father and son are fully employed, that is, working at least 30 hours per week for at least 30 weeks out of the year, and if a family has more than one son, only the oldest is included. All the regressions include experience variables for fathers and sons.

Zimmerman regresses son's earnings in 1981 on single-year measures of father's earnings in 1965, 1966, 1968, and 1970, on two-year average earnings in 1965–66, 1966–67, and 1968–69, and so on. The coefficients reported in Table 2 are the average of four estimates with single-year earnings, of three estimates with two-year average earnings, and so on. Zimmerman finds the same pattern that Solon does, although his coefficients are somewhat higher. For single-year measures of father's earnings, the average regression coefficient is 0.40. Averaging father's income over two or more years produces steady increases in this value. For a four-year average of father's earnings over the period 1965–68, the persistence coefficient is 0.54.

Table 3 presents what I believe are the best current estimates of persistence coefficients for several different measures of status: (individual) hourly wage, (individual) earnings, (family) income, and (family) consumption. In each case the coefficients are estimated using instrumental variables, another technique for dealing with measurement error. All the regressions include age or experience variables for both fathers and sons to control for life-cycle effects. Two sets of estimates are from the studies by Solon and Zimmerman. The third study is by Casey Mulligan (1997), who also uses the PSID data. He uses more recent waves of that data set (up to 1989), which allows him to use several more birth cohorts. More important for the results here, he uses different instruments.

In Solon's regressions the father's status is measured in 1967 and the son's in 1984, and the instrument is father's years of education. In Zimmerman's regressions the father's status is measured in 1966 and the son's in 1981, and the instrument is the Duncan index. Mulligan measures parental variables in 1967–72 and looks at the adult children in 1984–89. The children must be born between 1951 and 1961, and there

Table 3. *Instrumental Variables Estimates of Persistence*

	Wage (individual)	Earnings (individual)	Income (family)	Consumption (family)
Solon (PSID)	0.45 (0.10)	0.53 (0.14)	0.53 (0.12)	
Mulligan (PSID)	0.50 (0.05)	0.48 (0.07)	0.71* (0.06)	0.77* (0.05)
Zimmerman (NLS)	0.57 (0.12)	0.68 (0.13)		

* Includes daughters.
Source: Solon 1992, table 4; Mulligan 1997, table 7.3; Zimmerman 1992, tables 9 and 10.

may be several adult children from one family. In addition to wages, earnings, and income, Mulligan looks at consumption, and the persistence coefficients for the two family measures, income and consumption, include daughters. In these regressions the children may be household heads, wives of heads, or cohabitors of heads. There are about 700 observations (sons) in the wage and earnings regressions, and about 900 observations (sons and daughters) in the income and consumption regressions. His instruments are average earnings and family income in similar demographic groups, and for the consumption regression income is also used.[4]

Although the estimates in Table 3 vary quite a bit across status measures and across studies, several patterns are clear. First, the instrumental variables (IV) estimates for persistence in earnings and in the other status measures exceed those in Table 2. Apparently, averaging five contiguous years of data on earnings still leaves substantial measurement error. Second, income and consumption apparently are more persistent than wage rates and earnings. There are several possible explanations for this. First, parents may adjust their bequests in response to a child's

[4] The instruments Mulligan uses (nine in total) are average 1970 earnings and family income in the same sex/race/one-digit occupation category, in the same sex/race/schooling category, and in the same two-digit industry, and average 1970 per capita personal income, per capita earnings, and earnings per worker in the same county. A dummy variable for daughters is included in the regressions for income and consumption. Mulligan's consumption data are for food eaten at home and away from home, rent, and the value of owner occupied housing. The data are averaged for the available years and then weighted according to calculations from the Consumer Expenditure Survey to estimate total household nondurable consumption. No adjustment is made for family size.

earnings. That is, parents may increase their bequests to low-wage children and reduce their bequests to those with high wages. Assortative mating and persistence in family size may also be factors.

The estimates in Table 3 suggest that persistence coefficients for various status measures are at least 0.50 or 0.60, and perhaps even higher. This is quite a change from the early estimates of 0.20 or 0.25. Monday morning quarterbacking is easy. It is also fun, so I will indulge in saying of those who accepted the low estimates at face value: they should have known better. Why? There were two clues. The first is Figure 2. If the true persistence coefficient were 0.25, then the sons of fathers with high earnings would be quite difficult to distinguish from the sons of those with low earnings. Moreover, in this case the persistence coefficient between grandfathers and grandsons would be $0.25^2 \approx 0.06$. Grandfathers whose earnings were twice the mean or one half the mean for their cohort would have grandsons whose earnings were, on average, only 12% above or below the mean, so the two groups of grandsons would be virtually indistinguishable from each other. Everyday observation suggests that both conclusions are wrong.[5]

B.   Evidence from U.S. Immigrants

The next two studies, both by George Borjas, look at immigrant groups and examine the extent to which status differentials across ethnic groups persist from one generation to the next. This work is interesting for several reasons. First, as an additional and entirely different source of information about persistence, it provides a check on the estimates in Table 3. If the children of immigrant families regress to the mean at the same rate as children of native born parents, then the persistence coefficients for ethnic groups should be the same as those for the PSID and NLS families. Persistence for ethnic groups as groups may be higher than persistence for families, however, if "neighborhood effects" that operate within ethnic groups are present. There is a great deal of controversy about the importance, if any, of such neighborhood effects in determining the educational and economic success of children. One problem that has always plagued attempts to measure them is the difficulty of identifying the relevant neighborhood. For the immigrant families in these studies, the ethnic group serves as the neighborhood. If ethnic neighborhood effects are present, earnings differentials across

---

[5] Moreover, studies of persistence for occupational prestige – a Duncan index or similar measure – had found much higher coefficients. For example, see Corcoran and Jencks (1979).

ethnic groups will display more persistence than earnings differentials across families.

In his first study, Borjas (1992) measures the extent to which the wage rates and occupational status measures of the children and grandchildren – both sons and daughters – of immigrants are influenced by the attainment of both their parents and their ethnic groups. Borjas looks at first and second generation Americans, that is, those with parents or grandparents born outside the U.S. (African Americans and Native Americans are excluded.) Two data sets are used.

The General Social Surveys (GSS) consists of a series of cross sections collected between 1977 and 1989. Borjas pools information on persons aged 18–64 from each wave, obtaining a total of about 6800 observations. The data include information on the occupation of each respondent and his or her father, the family's (self-reported) ethnic background, and whether the parents and/or grandparents were foreign born. There is no direct information about the wage rates, earnings, or income of the respondent or parents, so Borjas looks at mobility in the Hodge–Siegel–Rossi score of occupational prestige, which is similar to the Duncan index. About 30 ethnic groups are represented.

The National Longitudinal Survey of Youth (NLSY) has panel data collected between 1979 and 1987. Information is available about the respondent's hourly wage rate in 1987, the birthplace (U.S. or foreign) of both parents, the (self-reported) ethnic background, and father's occupation in 1979. There is no direct information about the father's wage rate or earnings, so the analysis uses his occupational earnings, which are obtained by matching his occupation code with the average earnings for his occupation, using data from the 1970 Census. The respondents are 22–29 years old when their wage rates are measured. There are about 3700 observations in the sample, and about 20 ethnic groups are represented.

Ethnic group status is the average value of the measure – occupational prestige or occupational earnings – within the ethnic group in the father's generation. Summary statistics for both data sets show wide variation across ethnic groups in both status measures.

Before looking at the results it is useful to think about how we should interpret the coefficients from regressions that include the status of both the father and the ethnic group. If there are no ethnic neighborhood effects, then presumably the status differentials for (immigrant) ethnic *groups* will have the same degree of persistence as the differentials for (native or immigrant) *families*. If ethnic neighborhood effects are present, then ethnic groups will show *more* persistence as groups than families do.

Table 4. *Ethnic Group Influence on Economic Status*

	Father only	Father +	Ethnic group =	Total
Occupational prestige – GSS	0.20 (0.01)	0.18 (0.01)	0.46 (0.22)	0.64 (0.23)
Wage – NLSY	0.35 (0.03)	0.33 (0.03)	0.28 (0.10)	0.61 (0.13)

Source: Borjas 1992, table III.

If all variables were perfectly measured, the estimated coefficient for the parental variable would measure persistence within families, and the sum of that coefficient and the one for the ethnic group variable would measure persistence within ethnic groups. But the regression coefficient on the ethnic group variable may be positive even if neighborhood effects are absent. If father's status is measured with error, as it surely is in both of the data sets here, then the coefficient on the father's status will be biased downward, for the reasons discussed before. In this case the coefficient for the ethnic group variable will pick up some of the unmeasured effect of father's status as well as the ethnic group effect. Consequently, the sum of the coefficients on the father's status and the group's is an estimate of the persistence in status differentials displayed by ethnic groups as groups, whether or not there are neighborhood effects. *If* there are no neighborhood effects, it is also an estimate of persistence within families.

Table 4 displays the results of regressions of child's status on father's status only and on both father's and ethnic group's. All the regressions include dummy variables for gender, for those with immigrant parent(s) (as opposed to grandparents), for those enrolled in school (in the NLSY), and for the year of the survey (in the GSS). The regressions with both father's and ethnic group's status also include age, age squared, and regional dummies.

The persistence coefficients are modest when father's status is the only regressor: 0.20 for occupational prestige (which is measured in levels) and 0.35 for the (log) wage rate. Adding the ethnic group measure to the regression has very little effect on the coefficients on father's status and it adds a significant effect of its own. For occupational prestige, total persistence rises to 0.64, with the ethnic group measure contributing over two-thirds of the total. Total persistence rises to 0.61 for the wage rate, with the ethnic group measure contributing almost half of the total.

Thus, ethnic group differentials in occupational prestige and wage rates show very high levels of persistence. The estimates, 0.64 and 0.61, are at the upper end of the range of coefficients for wage rates and earnings in Table 3. It is not surprising that persistence of economic status differentials would be as high in families of recent immigrants as in the whole population. Borjas's estimates suggest that the persistence coefficients for the ethnic groups as groups may be even a little higher.

The last study, also by Borjas (1994), looks at persistence of economic differentials by ethnic group for descendants of turn-of-the-century immigrants. During the Great Migration of 1880–1910, almost 18 million immigrants entered the U.S., an enormous influx. The U.S. population in 1880 was only 50 million, while by 1910 it had grown to 92 million (Maddison, 1982, table B2), an increase of 42 million. Of this increase, over 40% was directly due to immigration. In addition, there were indirect contributions, as the early waves of immigrants had families. Geographically, the immigrants were concentrated in the northeast and north central regions, and were more likely than native whites to live in large cities. Very few immigrants lived in the South and very few went into agriculture.

Borjas uses the 1910, 1940, and 1980 Censuses to look at these immigrants, their children, and their grandchildren, to see on average how quickly – or slowly – ethnic groups were assimilated economically. In particular, he looks at persistence in wage rate differentials for the 32 ethnic groups that constituted the bulk of the Great Migration.

First Borjas uses data for working men aged 25–64 from the 1910 Census to construct an average earnings measure for each ethnic group. Although wage rates are not directly available, the 1910 Census does report a detailed industry/occupation code (420 categories). Borjas imputes earnings for each individual by matching these occupation codes with the occupational earnings measures for the year 1900.[6]

The 1940 Census has information about birthplace of parents, so Borjas can accurately identify second generation Americans, that is, those with at least one parent born outside the U.S. He looks at second generation men aged 25–64 who are in the civilian sector and not in school. Both reported hourly wage and occupational hourly wage by three-digit occupation are available. Ethnic affiliation for these men is

---

[6] No occupational wage is available for farmers, who constitute about 25% of the native born population but only a very small fraction of the immigrants. Thus, the immigrants are in effect compared with the nonagricultural native white population.

Table 5. *Persistence in Ethnic Group Wage Differentials*

	1940 (one generation)	1980 (two generations)
Reported wage	0.60 (0.14)	0.20 (0.05)
Occupational wage	0.67 (0.19)	0.27 (0.09)

Source: Borjas 1994, tables 5 and 6.

defined by father's place of birth, unless only the mother was born outside the U.S. There is only a modest amount of marriage between ethnic groups, however, so in most cases the precise method for identifying ethnic affiliation is not crucial. Borjas looks only at those individuals in the 32 nationality groups of the Great Migration, but these are 98.3% of the second generation group.

In the 1980 Census there is no information about birthplace of parents or grandparents, so instead Borjas looks at individuals by self-reported ancestry. Of nonblack natives, 80% fall into the 32 ethnic groups of the Great Migration. Borjas uses these individuals, thereby excluding only those who are black or those who report either no ancestry or American or an ethnic affiliation outside the 32 groups. Obviously, this sample contains most of the grandchildren of the Great Migration, but it is contaminated by the inclusion of many others. In particular, it contains second generation Americans, third generation Americans whose immigrant grandparents came after 1910, and fourth and higher generation Americans who still report an ethnic identity different from American. In addition, intermarriage across ethnic lines is more frequent among the parents of this group. As before, Borjas looks at men aged 25–64 who are in the civilian sector and not in school, and focuses on reported wage rate and occupational wage by three-digit occupation.

Table 5 displays the coefficients for regressions of (log) wage and occupational wage of the second and "third plus" generation Americans – those in the 1940 and 1980 Censuses – on the (log) occupational earnings of their ethnic group in the 1910 Census. All the regressions include age, age squared, regional dummies, and an urban dummy. There are about 11,000 observations in the 1940 sample and about 250,000 in the 1980 sample.

For the regressions using the 1940 Census, the coefficients are 0.60 for the reported wage and 0.67 for the occupational wage. Thus, the persistence of relative status for ethnic groups in this data set is very similar to those reported in Table 4 (the sums) and also very similar to the high end of the range of values for families reported in Table 3.

For the regressions using the 1980 Census, the coefficients are 0.20 for the reported wage and 0.27 for the occupational wage. These coefficients are much smaller than the values $-0.60^2 = 0.36$ and $0.67^2 = 0.45$ – that one would expect on the basis of the one-generation results. This is not surprising, since the sample from the 1980 Census is contaminated in the ways described above.

IV.   SOURCES OF PERSISTENCE

A.   A Model of the Family

Thus, the evidence is quite strong for a high degree of persistence. What are its sources? I want to think about a simple model of the family, developed and studied by Gary Becker and Nigel Tomes (1979, 1986), John Laitner (1992), Glenn Loury (1981), Casey Mulligan (1993, 1997), Jesus Navarro (1992), and many others.

Consider individuals with finite lifetimes who care about their children. To simplify the problem, I will adopt two conventions that are standard in this area, ignoring marriage and population growth. That is, I will assume that each parent, a mother, has exactly one child, a daughter, who in turn will have exactly one child when she becomes an adult, and so on. In addition I will assume that tastes are identical within and across families.

Thus, families consisting of mother and daughter, and perhaps grandmother as well, are organized into "dynasties." There are no family ties between different dynasties, and each dynasty has a constant number of living members. A period is one generation – about 30 years – and each individual lives for two or three periods.

Consider a typical 30-year period, during which the mother makes all the decisions. The mother has an endowment of time that she can allocate to various activities, including work, leisure, and child-rearing. She also has income, the size of which depends in part on her work decision. The mother can allocate her income to various uses, including current consumption by all family members, investments in her daughter's health, education, and so on, and financial bequests to her daughter. The investments include everything that will affect the daughter's earning ability later in her life, so they encompass a wide variety of specific items: prenatal care, good nutrition, health care, and educational toys, as well as expenditures on college tuition.

The motive for the mother's investment in and bequests to her daughter is altruism: the mother cares about her daughter's well-being as well as her own consumption. The daughter in turn cares about *her* daughter's well-being, so the utilities of the granddaughter and all later descendants are included indirectly. This model suggests two channels of persistence in income differentials: direct bequests of wealth and investments, such as schooling, that affect the child's earnings. How important is each of these?

B.   Inherited Wealth

Inherited wealth is often what people think of first when they think about persistence: the Astors, the Rockefellers, and the Mellons. How important are inheritances of tangible assets for persistence in economic status? First, note that *earnings* are very persistent. Since labor income is two or three times larger than nonlabor income, the persistence in earnings is itself a very large part of the persistence in income. Table 3 suggests that differences in income are more persistent than differences in earnings, however, so something more is going on. The data on inheritances is rather meager, but there are two studies that allow us to draw some conclusions. The first focuses on the very wealthy; the second is a representative sample of estates.

The first is a study by Paul Menchik (1979) that looks at the probate records of about a thousand Connecticut residents who died in the 1930s and 1940s leaving estates of $40,000 or more in current dollars. For about 300 of these people the death records of children were located in Connecticut, and for 200 of these cases the estate of the other parent was identified. This produced a sample of 146 sets of parents with about 200 children. Menchik compares "midparent wealth," an average of the estates of the two parents, adjusted to avoid double counting, with the child's wealth at death.

The mean midparent wealth was about $800 thousand, the median about $200 thousand. For the children, the mean and median were $1,000 thousand and $150 thousand (all in 1967 dollars). Clearly, this is a very wealthy group. The coefficient in a regression of child's wealth at death on parents' wealth at death is 0.69, so evidently there is a great deal of persistence in wealth transfers in the upper tail of the distribution.

The second study is by Nigel Tomes (1981), who looks at data from a 5% random sample of estates probated in Cleveland, Ohio, in 1964–65, yielding about 650 estates. The mean estate was $12,000. Disposable personal income per capita at that time was about $2,400, so the average estate was about five times per capita income. About 40% of the estates were less than $500, however, so for a large fraction of the population inheritances are negligible.

Thus, while inherited wealth may be a significant contributor to persistence in the upper tail of the income distribution, for the rest its importance is modest and for the bottom half it is apparently of little or no consequence. It is persistence in earnings that has the greater influence, because earnings are the bulk of national income and because earnings are important in all ranges of the income distribution.

C.   Human Capital

The other channel for persistence in economic status is the investment that parents make in their child's earning capacity. These investments in the child's human capital are guided by two factors.

The first is the expected rate of return on such investments. Empirical estimates of these rates of return are high: 17–22% for lower education, 15–16% for high school, 12–13% for college, and 7% for graduate school (Willis, 1986). Thus, investments in primary, secondary, and tertiary education all have rates of return that are significantly higher than the average rate of return on financial assets. Consequently, if parents want to increase the income of a child, investments in the education of the child are a more efficient mechanism for doing so than bequests of tangible assets. Parents will leave bequests only if the possibilities for investing in the child's education have been exhausted.

The second factor affecting the investment decision is the set of resources available to the parents. Recall that investments take two forms: direct investments of the parents' time and investments in goods and services such as formal education that must be purchased in the market. The parents' decisions about both types of investment will be influenced by their wage rate(s), their nonlabor income, their skill in educating the child – which may be especially influenced by the mother's education, and the total endowment of time – which depends on whether the father is present. Both modes of investment are important: indeed, the evidence is growing that family influences in very early childhood are critical determinants of the child's success both in school and later in life. Investments in formal education are easier to measure, however, so I will focus on that decision. In particular, I will look at the relationship between family income and schooling.

The evidence is strong that family background and family income have an important effect on the probability of staying in school, at every level of education. That is, family income has a significant effect on the decisions to complete elementary school, attend and graduate from high school, attend and graduate from college, and attend graduate school.[7] The effect at every stage is statistically significant and quantitatively important.

The theoretical model described above suggests that the influence of family income on investments in the child's education should be strong for low income families and should decline as family income rises. For low income families, investments in the child's education offer a high rate of return, so additional dollars of income will be invested there. High income families will exhaust the attractive opportunities for investing in the education of their children and invest additional savings in financial assets. The available evidence, while modest, is consistent with this prediction.

Tomes (1981) finds that family income has an important effect on the child's educational attainment only in poorer families. Specifically, he finds that among families that leave minimal size bequests to their children, family income has a significant effect on the child's educational attainment. Among families that leave substantial bequests, however, family income has no effect. Mulligan (1996) finds the same pattern in the PSID-SRC sample: parental income has a larger impact on son's educational attainment among families making small bequests. (The results change, however, if the whole PSID is used.)

The simple model described above highlights the inefficiency in educational investment created by a system where parents finance the education of their children. Since educational investments depend on the parents' income, and incomes vary across parents, education will vary across children for reasons that are unrelated to differences (in ability, for example) in the children themselves. The absence of markets for loans to invest in children is the source of the inefficiency.

There are a number of possible interpretations of this inefficiency. One is that low income families find it difficult to send their children to college: not only is the tuition cost high, but the child's entry into the labor force is delayed. Consequently, even if the investment in a college education is financially attractive, in the sense of having a high rate of return, the family may be liquidity constrained and hence unable to make the investment. This underinvestment is inefficient, and it can be remedied at least partially by offering scholarships and loans to low income students.

Another interpretation is that many of the critical investments are made very early. The idea here is that a well prepared student from a low income family could go to college without undue financial hardship. Such

[7] See Cameron and Heckman (1996) for a survey of the evidence.

students might not be able to afford to attend elite – and expensive – private institutions like Northwestern and the University of Chicago, but there are many alternatives. Illinois and all its neighbors have excellent public universities, as well as community colleges, that charge very modest tuition. In addition, many scholarships, loans, and work opportunities are available.

According to this interpretation, the main reason that so few children from low income families go to college is that so few are well prepared to do so when they finish high school. Their reading, writing, and quantitative skills are poor, and, given this starting point, a college education is not a particularly good investment. The cost of going to college is not the main problem, and offering more college loans may not help very much. Instead, the problem is underinvestment at a much earlier stage: children from lower income families attend lower quality schools, and therefore are less successful in acquiring the cognitive skills that are important for subsequent education. In the rest of this lecture I want to present some evidence that I think supports this point of view.

In a recent paper Derek Neal and William Johnson (1996) look at some data that reveal a great deal about the source of black–white wage inequality. I want to describe their results here because I think they are also very suggestive about the sources of wage inequality between children from high and low income families.

Using data from the National Longitudinal Survey of Youth (NLSY), Neal and Johnson look at the performance of black and white high school students on the Armed Forces Qualification Test (AFQT), a set of four tests measuring word knowledge, paragraph comprehension, mathematics knowledge, and arithmetic reasoning. Extensive research on the AFQT shows that it is a good predictor of (objective) performance in a variety of military tasks, and that it is not racially biased. Moreover, it apparently is a measure of acquired skill, not innate ability: scores improve with age and years of education, and black–white gaps widen with age.[8]

The tests were administered to a group of 15–23-year-olds in the summer of 1980. Neal and Johnson look at the 15–18-year-olds, a group that had not yet started college or entered the labor force full time. For these young adults the test measures the verbal and mathematical skills they had acquired by late high school.

The NLSY surveyed the same group again 10 years later, in 1990 and 1991, and obtained measures of their hourly wage rate. At that time the

[8] It is also interesting that on this test developed to predict performance of military tasks, women have higher average scores than men!

blacks and Hispanics in the group had significantly lower average wage rates than the whites, and this was true for both men and women. By itself this is not surprising. Moreover, Neal and Johnson find that educational attainment explains only a small fraction, about 20%, of this wage gap.

What is surprising is that the AFQT test scores 10 years earlier explain a large fraction of the wage gap: 75% for men and 100% for women. That is, the wage gap between blacks and whites in their middle to late twenties can be almost fully explained on the basis of skills they had – or hadn't – acquired by the time they had finished high school. A very modest part of this skill differential works indirectly, by influencing the decision to attend college.[9]

Thus, cognitive skills at the end of high school are a critical determinant of future wages, and policies directed toward raising those skills may be the most valuable tools for raising the earnings of children from low income families. What are such policies? An obvious solution would seem to be to provide better schools. Doing this may be harder than it seems, however.

V.   SCHOOL QUALITY AND STUDENT PERFORMANCE

The evidence on school quality and student performance is surprisingly mixed. I don't think anyone doubts that there are enormous differences among schools, and I expect that if you polled the parents of school-age children in, say, the Chicago area, there would be considerable agreement about which schools were better than others. What is difficult, however, is to find robust connections between student performance and any of the obvious indicators of school quality. In particular, the most widely used measures, such as expenditures per pupil and teacher–pupil ratios, have no power in predicting student performance.

It is clear that on average, students from the public schools in the North Shore suburbs of Chicago perform much better than students from the public schools in the city. They perform better on standardized achievement tests, a higher fraction finish high school, a higher fraction start college, they have higher earnings, and so on. But the families living on the North Shore are also quite different from families in the city: in particular, they are better educated and have higher incomes. And we

---

[9] These results are consistent with several earlier studies. For example, see Corcoran and Jencks (1979) and Crouse (1979).

know that parents have a very large direct influence on the performance of their children.

Thus, while measurable indicators of school quality are higher in many suburban schools – teacher–pupil ratios, teacher salaries, and expenditure per pupil are all higher – it is impossible to attribute any of the superior performance of the students to these factors. After taking family effects into account, these measures of school quality have no discernible impact on student performance. The evidence on this point is quite striking, so it is useful to review it more closely.

One common method for trying to assess school performance is to use a production function approach. The idea is to relate an "output" measure to various "inputs." Assume the output is an end-of-year score on a standardized test. (It could also be the fraction of students continuing to the next grade, the graduation rate, or the college entrance rate.) The inputs include the student's beginning-of-year test score, family characteristics such as family income and parents' education, peer characteristics such as average income and average education in the community, school characteristics, and teacher characteristics. Since the beginning-of-year test score is one of the inputs, this type of analysis can be used to determine how much "value added," as measured by improvement on the test, is contributed by each of the other inputs.

How can school quality be measured? That is, what school and teacher attributes might appear in such an analysis? Instructional expenditures are about two-thirds of school budgets. Clearly, these expenditures are dictated by class size and teacher salaries, and under the present system teacher salaries are determined by experience and educational attainment. Thus, the typical measures of school and teacher quality are the teacher–pupil ratio, teacher educational attainment, teacher experience, teacher salaries, and expenditures per pupil.

In a very interesting survey article, Eric Hanushek (1986) tabulates the results of 147 published studies that attempt to find a link between student performance and these measures of school and teacher quality. He finds that the vast majority of the effects reported in these studies are statistically insignificant, and among those that are statistically significant a sizable fraction have the wrong sign. Only teacher experience has some success in explaining student performance, and even there the evidence is not overwhelming. Moreover, it is unclear whether the correct interpretation is that experience is useful or that unsuccessful teachers tend to switch careers.

Does this mean that all teachers and all schools are alike? Hanushek rejects this idea emphatically and so do I. The problem is not that all teachers are equally effective, but that we are looking at the wrong measures of teacher quality. In other studies Hanushek (1971, 1992) looks at "teacher effects." This concept will be familiar to parents. If a family with school-age children moves to Evanston or Wilmette, it is not difficult for the parents to elicit opinions from other parents about which teachers in, say, the local elementary school are the better teachers. And I conjecture that there would be a fair amount of agreement among parents about who they are.

Hanushek looks for systematic data of this type. Consider first the problem of evaluating teachers within a school. Using the value added approach described above, we can relate the performance of the students to the specific teacher(s) that student had during the year. Performance must be adjusted for family variables if these vary systematically across classrooms. Since other characteristics of the school are the same for all the students, as are neighborhood effects, these can be neglected. Each teacher's performance can then be measured by looking at the average value added for the students in his or her class(es), and teachers can be compared according to the average gains in the performance of their students. If the average gain is higher for some teachers than for others, year after year, we probably want to say that those individuals are better teachers. This type of analysis is an obvious way for school principals to rate teachers.

Are teacher effects important? That is, is there systematic evidence that some teachers are better than others in improving the cognitive (and perhaps other) skills of their students? The formal evidence is weak, because there are few studies that look at the same teachers over multiple years. In an early study Hanushek (1971) found nontrivial teacher effects for second and third grade teachers: having the best teachers rather than the worst would raise the student's performance by about 0.2 grade levels per year. In another study, Hanushek (1992) finds even stronger effects for elementary school teachers. There, having a good teacher – one who is one standard deviation above the mean – rather than a bad teacher – one who is one standard deviation below the mean – adds one to one-and-a-half grade levels to the final achievement test score. Both data sets are small and nonrepresentative, however, so the evidence must be viewed as tentative.

Moreover, Hanushek has very little success relating teacher performance to measurable teacher characteristics. In the first study the only characteristic that is useful is the teacher's score on a verbal test, which might measure communication ability or general intelligence. In the second study Hanushek finds weak evidence that teachers with higher I.Q. scores are more successful and that experience is valuable. Beyond this, almost nothing can be said.

Is it surprising that it is hard to predict teacher performance on the basis of easily observable attributes? I don't think so. Consider other types of service professionals: surgeons, lawyers, hair stylists, and so on. No one believes that all surgeons are equally good. If we have to choose a surgeon, however, we do it not by looking at his years of education or grade point average, but by looking at his past performance. We evaluate surgeons on the basis of their success in performing operations. The same is true for many other occupations. For the most part individuals are evaluated on the basis of performance; for teachers this has been rare. It would not be hard to do, but the current structure of the public school system does not encourage – or even allow – administrators to do it.

As noted above, comparisons across school districts are difficult because demographic factors vary. If two parallel school systems operate in the same city, however, this problem is greatly reduced. This observation suggests that comparisons of public schools and Catholic schools will provide a useful source of information about school quality. Many such comparisons have been made, but they have been hard to interpret for another reason. In Chicago or any other large city, students in the Catholic schools perform better than students in the public schools: their test scores are higher, a higher proportion go to college, and so on. Nevertheless, it is hard to distinguish how much of this is due to the superior quality of instruction in the Catholic school system and how much is simply self-selection.

Suppose that it is widely believed that the Catholic schools provide better instruction than the public schools. Then parents who are especially concerned about their children's education will put them in Catholic schools, which they can do even if they are not Catholic. Consequently, compared with the public schools the Catholic schools will have students whose parents are, on average, more concerned about the school performance of their children. But a higher level of parental concern itself raises the performance of the children, independent of school quality. Thus, the performance of Catholic school students will exceed the performance of public school students because of the effects of the parents, even if the quality of instruction is identical in both school systems. Or, if the quality of instruction is actually somewhat higher in Catholic schools, the measured differences in student performance will overstate the effect of school quality.

In a recent study, Derek Neal (1997) manages to avoid the problem of selection bias by using instrumental variables, with information about the availability of Catholic schools as the instrument. Neal focuses on high schools. He finds that most Catholic high schools – 69% of the schools and 79% of the students – are in urban areas (counties with populations over 250,000), and that it is in urban areas where they have a significant impact.

Specifically, Neal divides his sample, the NLSY, into four subgroups: urban versus suburban, and white versus black and Hispanic. His performance measures are high school graduation rates, college graduation rates, and, for the men in the sample, hourly wage rates at ages 27–34. He finds that for the suburban schools there is no significant difference between the performance of Catholic and public schools students. In the urban areas, however, he does find significant differences.

For white students, the gain in terms of graduation rate is modest: transferring to a Catholic school raises the probability of graduation from 75% to 85%. For black and Hispanic students, the gain is enormous: transferring to a Catholic school raises the probability of graduation from 62% to 88%. For college graduation rates, the gains are also substantial. Among urban high school graduates, attending a Catholic school raises the probability of college graduation from 31% to 42% for white students and from 16% to 30% for minority students. Finally, Catholic schooling has little effect on the wage rates of white men in the sample but does have a substantial effect on the wages of men in the minority group.

Neal also presents evidence suggesting rather strongly that the source of the effect for blacks and Hispanics in urban areas is the poor quality of the public schools available to them. For these students the Catholic schools offer an education that is comparable in quality to the one available in a typical suburban public school.

VI.   CONCLUSIONS

The evidence is quite strong that in the U.S. today there is a great deal of persistence in economic status from one generation to the next. The current estimates need to be refined, but clearly there is much less social mobility than we thought just a decade ago. The persistence coefficient for relative status seems to be at least 0.50 and perhaps as high as 0.60 or 0.70. If equal opportunity is interpreted to mean that children from rich and poor families have similar chances for economic success, then our society is very far from providing it.

It this cause for concern? Equity and efficiency are often seen as conflicting goals and the ethical question is posed in terms of a tradeoff: how much efficiency is one willing to sacrifice for more equity? The evidence I have presented here suggests that this view is misleading, at least for the inequality associated with social immobility in the earnings distribution. If earnings are based on productivities, and if productivities are influenced by schooling and other investments, then there is not necessarily a conflict between equity and efficiency: the average earnings of children from low income families can be raised without reducing the earnings of others.

Thus, high persistence at the bottom of the earnings distribution *is* cause for concern, because it is a signal that large, high return investment opportunities are being missed. Although genetic factors might explain a modest degree of persistence, it is difficult for me to believe that the very high degree of persistence we observe is primarily due to those factors. Instead, high persistence suggests that there is substantial underinvestment: that improvements in the quality of education for children from families at the bottom of the income distribution could enhance both equity and efficiency.

The evidence shows very clearly that cognitive skills acquired by the end of high school have a dramatic impact on subsequent earnings, and a comparison of public and Catholic high schools in urban areas strongly suggests that schools differ substantially in terms of their effectiveness in developing the cognitive skills of their students. The difficulty in finding a relationship between student performance and the school attributes that are easy to measure – expenditure per pupil, teacher salaries, and so on – should not necessarily be discouraging. Perhaps it only shows how easy it is to spend money badly. Formal evidence and casual observation both suggest that teachers vary, perhaps dramatically, in their effectiveness. Thus, school systems that identify and reward effective teaching are likely to produce students with better skills. Altering the incentive structures in the education sector might have a significant effect, then, with no change in expenditures.

Even if additional resources are required, however, the evidence suggests that it is an investment that is well worthwhile. Equal opportunity is an ideal that has inspired many generations, and the returns from moving toward it appear to be very high.

References

Becker, Gary, and Nigel Tomes. 1979. An equilibrium theory of the distribution of income and intergenerational mobility, *Journal of Political Economy*, 87: 1153–89.

Becker, Gary, and Nigel Tomes. 1986. Human capital and the rise and fall of families, *Journal of Labor Economics*, 4: S1–39.

Borjas, George. 1992. Ethnic capital and intergenerational mobility, *Quarterly Journal of Economics*, 107: 123–50.

Borjas, George. 1994. Long-run convergence of ethnic skill differentials: the children and grandchildren of the great migrations, *Industrial & Labor Relations Review*, 47: 553–73.

Cameron, Stephen V., and James J. Heckman. 1996. Life cycle schooling and educational selectivity: models and evidence, manuscript, University of Chicago.

Corcoran, Mary, et al. 1990. Effects of family and community background on economic status, *American Economic Review*, 80: 362–6.

Corcoran, Mary, and Christopher Jencks. 1979. The effects of family background. In Christopher Jencks, ed., *Who Gets Ahead?* New York: Basic Books.

Crouse, James. 1979. The effects of academic ability. In Christopher Jencks, ed., *Who Gets Ahead?* New York: Basic Books.

Goldin, Claudia, and Robert A. Margo. 1992. The great compression: the wage structure in the United States at mid-century, *Quarterly Journal of Economics*, 107: 1–34.

Hanushek, Eric A. 1971. Teacher characteristics and gains in student achievement: estimation using micro data, *American Economic Review*, 61: 280–8.

Hanushek, Eric A. 1986. The economics of schooling: production and efficiency in public schools, *Journal of Economic Literature*, 24: 1141–77.

Hanushek, Eric A. 1992. The tradeoff between child quantity and quality, *Journal of Political Economy*, 100: 84–117.

Laitner, John. 1992. Random earnings differences, lifetime liquidity constraints, and altruistic intergenerational transfers, *Journal of Economic Theory*, 58: 135–70.

Loury, Glenn C. 1981. Intergenerational transfers and the distribution of earnings. *Econometrica*, 49: 843–67.

Maddison, Angus. 1982. *Phases of Capitalist Development*, New York: Oxford University Press.

Menchik, Paul L. 1979. Inter-generational transmission of inequality: an empirical study of wealth mobility, *Economica*, 46: 349–62.

Mulligan, Casey B. 1993. *On Intergenerational Altruism, Fertility, and the Persistence of Economic Status.* Doctoral dissertation, University of Chicago.

Mulligan, Casey B. 1997. *Parental Priorities and Economic Inequality*, Chicago: University of Chicago Press.

Navarro, Jesus Ignacio. 1992. *A Model of Bequests and Intergenerational Mobility.* Doctoral dissertation, University of Chicago.

Neal, Derek A. 1997. The effects of Catholic secondary schooling on educational attainment, *Journal of Labor Economics*, 15: 98–123.

Neal Derek A., and William R. Johnson. 1996. The role of premarket factors in black-white wage differences. *Journal of Political Economy*, 104: 869–95.

Solon, Gary R. 1992. Intergenerational income mobility in the United States. *American Economic Review*, 82: 393–408.

Tomes, Nigel. 1981. The family, inheritance, and the intergenerational transmission of inequality, *Journal of Political Economy*, 89: 928–58.

Willis, Robert J. 1986. Wage determinants: a survey and reinterpretation of human capital earnings functions. In Orley Ashenfelter and Richard Layard, eds., *Handbook of Labor Economics*, Vol. I. Amsterdam: North-Holland.
Zimmerman, David J. 1992. Regression toward mediocrity in economic stature, *American Economic Review*, 82: 409–29.

DAVID M. KREPS

Anticipated Utility and Dynamic Choice

Imagine you are about to play a repeated strategic-form game against a randomly selected Stanford MBA student. You may not talk to her before or during the play of the game – interactions are computer-mediated. To the extent that it matters, her exposure to game theory has consisted of two lectures in the autumn quarter of her first year (which prominently featured an informal account of the folk theorem, based on the prisoners' dilemma); subsequently, she has specialized in courses in finance and accounting.

The game is played repeatedly, with a constant termination probability: You play once and learn (to an extent specified below) the outcome of the first round of play. Then a two-digit random number is drawn: If it is 00, the interaction is over; anything else and you play again. Hence after each round there is a 0.01 chance of the interaction ending and a 0.99 chance of it going on for at least one more round.

The stakes per round are on the order of tens of dollars, enough (I hope) so you and she will take the game seriously, but not so large that risk aversion or liquidity constraints play an appreciable role. Your name and hers will be shielded so that reputation effects (outside of this encounter) can be ignored.

It remains to specify the game itself. In fact, I want you to think of this situation for four different experimental treatments:

Treatment A. The game is the Prisoners' Dilemma, with cooperative-outcome payoffs of $50 apiece, noncooperative-outcome payoffs of $0

Comments by Eddie Dekel, Faruk Gul, and Ehud Kalai were very helpful. The financial assistance of the National Science Foundation (Grant SBR-9511208) is gratefully acknowledged.

	Fink	Cooperate
Fink	$0,$0	$80,$-30
Cooperate	$-30,$80	$50,$50

a

	Column 1	Column 2
Row 1	$130,$-30	$0,$0
Row 2	$100,$5	$-30,$35

b

Row 1	$-10	$55	$0
Row 2	$0	$80	$10
Row 3	$20	$70	$5

c

Figure 1. (Pieces of) Three Strategic-Form Games

apiece, and off-diagonal payoffs of $80 for the noncooperator and $-30 for the cooperator. (The game is depicted in Figure 1a.) After each round of play, you learn what actions each side took.

Treatment B. The game is the 2 × 2 game depicted in Figure 1b, with payoffs in dollars. Each of you knows this; you each have read the same description of the situation. After each round of play, you learn what actions each side took.

Treatment C. The game is a 3 × 3 game. You select the row, and your payoffs are given as in Figure 1c. You have no idea what the payoffs are for your opponent. After each round of play, you learn what actions each side took, although you don't learn your rival's payoffs. (Her situation is symmetric.)

Treatment D. You have three possible actions (in the stage game). You have no idea how many actions your rival has, nor what her payoffs are, nor what your payoffs are. After each round, your payoffs are reported to you, but you don't learn what action your rival took. (Your rival's situation is symmetric.)

I'm interested in the following questions: First, how would you play in these situations? What sort of analysis would you do, if any? Since you are likely to be a specialist in this sort of problem, how do you think a nonspecialist (say, a Kellogg student, playing against a Stanford GSB counterpart) would behave? How should we model the behavior of such subjects? Suppose it is not you but the person sitting next to you that is playing this game. Suppose that I tell you (but not the person playing) that, in fact, the stage game being played has a prisoners' dilemma structure: Both players have a dominated strategy that together does better for both than any equilibrium payoffs. How likely is it, do you think, that the two sides will arrive at some cooperative outcome (where each does better than at any Nash equilibrium)? Of course, in all these questions I'm especially curious about how the treatment conditions matter.

1.   A TRIBUTE TO NANCY L. SCHWARTZ – MODELING DYNAMIC CHOICE

Nancy L. Schwartz, in her too brief but brilliant career, made two sorts of enduring contributions to microeconomics that make these fit questions for a lecture in her memory. First, she was one of the pioneers who, in the early and mid-1970s, started a revolution in economics. Specifically, together with her colleague Mort Kamien, she brought to the subject of Industrial Organization the careful and rigorous study of the dynamics of competition. The revolution she helped create continues to this day, as the language of noncooperative game theory and the concepts of information economics combine to help us come to grips with an ever widening array of topics in economics, from macro-policy to international trade to internal organization to the evolution of economic institutions.

The style of analysis that she helped pioneer is, of course, built upon models of individual maximizing behavior. The "individual" in question is sometimes a firm, pursuing maximal profits or net worth, and sometimes a consumer, pursuing maximal utility. Since dynamics are an essential ingredient in the topics being discussed, we immediately must come to grips with individual dynamic choice behavior.

Axiomatic decision theory, the foundation of choice behavior in economics, is by and large a static theory of choice. An individual decision maker (she) confronts an opportunity set from which a choice must be made, and by positing that her choices either obey standard axioms of revealed preference or arise from preferences that are complete and transitive, we conclude that her choices are as if she were maximizing some numerical index of well-being.[1]

---

[1] Some alternatives to the standard theory (e.g., regret theory) are constructed around informal dynamic considerations, and some dynamic stories are used to justify the

When her choices are dynamic – stretched out through time – the standard practice is to regard her as a vastly competent strategic thinker and doer: First, she understands the world she inhabits sufficiently well so that she comprehends all the strategic options at her disposal. Second, she is able to map each strategy into its consequences for her. She evaluates strategies according to those consequences – we (implicitly) invoke a (static) axiomatic model of choice applied to consequences, deriving a utility function for the consequences, and we assume that she will choose whichever strategy gives a consequence of largest (available) utility. And then she flawlessly carries out the strategy so chosen. In effect, dynamic choice becomes the static choice and then dynamic implementation of an optimal strategy.

This methodology for modeling dynamic choice is deeply ingrained in economic theory – so ingrained that many graduate micro-theory textbooks don't even bother to point it out. And yet this methodology colors what our models tell us. Especially combined with the common prior assumption, issues such as the deregulation of industries, the economy's response to a change in the Fed's policy, and the evolution of the economies of formerly socialist states are confronted with theoretical tools that almost perforce assume that participants fully comprehend the challenges and opportunities of their new environment, the responses to those challenges and opportunities of their fellow participants, and the macro-implications of those responses. And, understanding all those things, the participants act optimally.

Of course this is fantasy. We model these situations to reduce our own ignorance of what will happen. If we are ignorant to begin with, and, more important, if our models lead to real controversy as to what will happen, it isn't too much to believe that the participants in these "experiments" and others like them must feel their own way. But then it takes quite a leap of faith to suppose that models based on strategically sagacious individuals will capture all or most aspects of reality.

I doubt that many readers will be startled by these contentions. (In particular, previous Schwartz Lectures – notably Truman Bewley's lecture on Knightian Decision Theory – began similarly.) Theories built on the edifice of hyperrational individuals – for current purposes, those with phenomenal strategic skills – are of course subjected to suspicious empirical testing, both casual and formal. Common sense is a handy and ever-present guide: I think it safe to say that IO types by and large agree that we learn a lot by applying equilibrium analysis to a settled industry with a few participants who know each other well; however, only the

standard axioms (see in particular Menachem Yaari on Dutch Books), but formal treatments of dynamics are (a) rare and (b) rarely actually used in applications.

most fervent believer in equilibrium analysis would think to learn something from an equilibrium analysis of capacity expansion in an industry characterized by a brand new product with as-yet poorly understood market potential, many new players, and very large minimum efficient scale of production (relative to demand).[2]

Moreover, these questions have attracted substantial (and growing) attention. The literature on boundedly rational behavior is growing rapidly; Northwestern and especially MEDS have been home to some of the most important and influential work on adaptive learning, the foundations of equilibrium, and choice that admits the limitations faced by real-life subjects. Which brings us back to Professor Schwartz's second enduring legacy: As one of the creators of MEDS, she shares in the credit that comes to Northwestern for that marvelous research institution.

So I probably don't have to convince many of you of the importance of continued study of dynamic choice. Some of you may hope and expect that the outcome of such study will be to justify the standard approach as a good positive model. Others of you – probably limited to those who don't consider themselves economists – believe that such study should abandon the economists' fascination (fetish?) with purposeful behavior altogether. For myself, I take a "middle" position: I believe that dynamic choice differs from the paradigmatic static-choice-of-an-optimal-strategy in ways that are of consequence and (hence) need to be addressed by our models, but still I think there is much to be learned by hewing to the economists' general attachment to purposeful (individual) behavior.

If no one needs to be convinced of these platitudes, what is left to discuss? My modest aims in this essay are twofold. While I applaud the efforts of several colleagues (names will be forthcoming) to model more realistically how dynamic choices are made, I want to suggest a modest redirection in some of their efforts, toward models in which decision makers actively and consciously deliberate. Such models are advanced not as the only way to go, but as a direction that ought to be further explored. While developing this basic theme, some commentary on various examples and general forms in the literature will be provided. Following this, I will discuss through the example above a class of problems in the sort of models I'm advocating, problems that I'm unsure how to solve, hoping that members of the audience will be spurred into action.

At this point a warning is in order. This essay proved to be very hard to construct. Not to put too fine a point on it, my computer contains five abandoned efforts – abandoned because the corresponding talks would have been mind-numbingly technical and run to three hours or so, qual-

---

[2] See Porter and Spence (1982).

ities which I was exhorted by Ehud Kalai to avoid. Hence I present a talk/essay that risks going too far to avoid these sins: This effort is more journalistic than precise, with a fair number of unsupported (but, I hope, not unsupportable) assertions. For those seeking formalism and rigor, the abandoned drafts will be resurrected at least in part in Kreps (1998). But don't misunderstand: In the end, I don't have satisfactory answers to most of the questions I raise. My primary objective both in this essay and in Kreps (1998) is to ask questions that will, I hope, provoke my colleagues.

2. ATTEMPTING TO COOPERATE, CONTINUED

To whet your appetite, let me begin by relating the results of an informal survey I took. I quizzed perhaps fifteen people about the problem(s) set at the start. The subjects of my survey were economists or economics-oriented sociologists and social psychologists; some at Stanford and some more broadly placed. I did not tell the subjects that each game had the character of a prisoners' dilemma embedded in it except as they could devine this (in treatments A and B themselves). It hardly needs saying that this is a highly sophisticated audience and (as important), if anchoring bias has any validity, an audience whose behavior is more likely to conform to models in the literature than would the behavior of, say, randomly selected physicists or MBA students or managers. So this can be nothing more than appetite whetting (and quite possibly for the wrong dish entirely).

The answers I got were fairly broadly distributed, as to both general "strategy" and specifics.[3] However, averaging over the responses I heard

---

[3] I will identify (neither) my subjects nor their responses, except for the following quiz: Among my early victims were five eminent colleagues – Eddie Dekel, Faruk Gul, Bengt Holmstrom, Ariel Rubinstein, and Robert Wilson – who were asked how they would play the prisoners' dilemma game (treatment A). In fact, this was something of a pretest, and the stakes and continuation probability were lower for these eminent pretest subjects; the continuation probability was never lower than 0.9, however. The five responses I obtained all began with cooperation and then went on as: (a) the grim strategy; (b) cooperate two rounds, then play tit-for-tat until the fourth incidence of finking and then move to the grim strategy; (c) N tits for the Nth tat, which is to say, fink N times in a row the Nth time the rival initiates finking; (d) perfect tit-for-tat; and (e) tit-for-two-tats (respond to two rounds of finking with finking, and then restore cooperation after the rival cooperates twice in a row). (I've tried to arrange these roughly in order of how kind they are.) The quiz is, Which eminent theorist gave which of these five answers? (Added after the talk: Eddie Dekel correctly observes that the individual who chose the grim strategy may have done so anticipating that I would write this footnote, seeking to cultivate a wide reputation for being unforgiving in such circumstances.)

(with my own biases doubtless active in the weighting function), I noted the following general tendencies.

(1) No one seriously attempted a full analysis, formulating a Bayesian prior on the full dynamic strategy employed by the rival and optimizing against it. Especially in treatment A (the classic prisoners' dilemma), there was vague talk about justifying the chosen strategy by this means: "My strategy" (went the typical response) "is meant as a best response against a mix of students, some of whom will cooperate from the outset, and others of whom will try to take advantage." In cases where this sort of response was given, I also didn't check rigorously whether the purported justification was tight, but in all such cases it sounded pretty reasonable.

(2) Moreover (and along the same lines), enunciated "strategies" almost always had something of the character of trial balloons. "I'd try xxxxx for a while, and then reassess." In such answers, "xxxxx" was not usually something like "row 1" or "alternating row 1 and row 2." Instead, it was usually something more sophisticated, on the order of "two tits for a tat" (especially in treatment A). But the point is, with a few exceptions, trial balloons were advanced with the intention of reevaluating later if needed.

(3) There was typically a lot of variation in the character of responses to the four different treatments, holding the individual respondent fixed. Of course, given my subject population, most subjects approached treatment A as a problem in game theory, heavily influenced by the Axelrod tournaments and subsequent literature. The trial-balloon strategies had names (or were hybrids of things that had names). There was a lot of confidence in the subject's ability to narrow down the rival's behavior to one of a few possible patterns (all of which have names in the literature). Overall, both anchoring bias and the overconfidence bias of "experts" were blatantly present in how my subjects responded regarding treatment A (as if further evidence for these two biases is needed).

Treatment B gave less definite responses. Note that the stage game is strategically equivalent to the classic prisoners' dilemma.[4] But (of course) this doesn't give the column player much improvement over her maxmin strategy. Accordingly, the Row players (my subjects) tended to more forgiving strategies than in the first treatment; "n tits for a tat" in treatment A became "one tit for two tats" here. And, in a lot of cases,

---

[4] Permute the columns in Figure 1b. Then Column's payoffs in Figure 1b are those in Figure 1a, except that Column gets an additional $45 in Figure 1a if Row chooses Row 2; and Row's payoffs are the same, except that Row gets an extra $50 in Figure 1b if Column chooses Column 1.

the subject regarded the essence of the matter as a bargaining game: The MBA was "entitled" to some fraction of Row 2–Column 2 outcomes (the rest being Row 2–Column 1), with the fractions to be worked out in the course of play.

Skipping treatment C for the moment, responses were very different in character for treatment D. The dominant initial response to game D was unhappiness at being given too little to go on. (I agree: This treatment is too unstructured for much useful analysis.) But a fairly prevalent secondary reaction was that game-theoretic reasoning had to give way to loose decision-theoretic reasoning, with the multi-armed bandit being the dominant "paradigm." A typical response was to pick a row at random and keep using that row as long as your payoff is above, say, $40. If your payoff goes below $40, choose another row at random. Keep this up for a while – if you settle into consistent payoffs above $40 per round, be satisfied; if you never can settle into such a situation, choose a more reasonable aspiration level based on what payoffs you observe, and continue. (The $40 figure in this response was pretty clearly a residue of the scale of payoffs in earlier games.) But I also heard on several occasions a general strategy of experimenting randomly for a while and (only) then thinking through what strategy to employ.

For treatment C, the modal response mixed game-theoretic and decision-theoretic considerations, although I think game-theoretic thinking was more prevalent: The modal idea was to try to "teach" the rival to play Column 2, so (with somewhat random starting strategies) a fairly typical plan of action by the respondent was to: "reward" the play of Column 2 by playing the same strategy again; "punish" Column 1 or 3 by shifting (somewhat randomly) to either Row 2 or Row 3; and (if play seems to get stuck away from Column 2) offer occasionally a possible "olive branch" in the form of Row 1. (All the scare quotes signify that without seeing something of Column player's payoffs, there is no reason to suppose that any of these terms are apposite. Going back to earlier points, subjects who spoke in this fashion did so under a working hypothesis that Column's payoffs made this terminology appropriate, a working hypothesis that would be abandoned if it turned out to be unsupported by the evidence.)

One final observation (which perhaps has a lot to do with my subjects' profession and that of the hypothetical rival): In treatments A, B, and C, responses very often were rationalized with a perceived asymmetry in roles: The subjects tended to speak (and, I assume, think) in terms of training or teaching their opponent how to behave; little heed seemed to be paid to the notion that one's rival might conceive of her role as that of teacher.

3.   A MODELING STRATEGY: SHORT-RUN
RATIONALITY, LONG-RUN THEORIZING

I reiterate that the "data" related above are as unscientific as can be: The subject population is far from ideal (if we want to explore seriously how to model the dynamic game-playing behavior of anyone except for self-regarded specialists); the population was small; and the "interviews" were conducted without any particular protocol but instead with (at least) a subconscious desire to elicit answers that would justify my pet theories about dynamic choice. With those caveats, I will assert that I find something quite provocative in these . . . let me call them . . . directed reflections of my colleagues; viz., the style of reasoning that they employed. By and large, my subjects tried to: (1) construct a relatively simple model of the situation; (2) find a strategy that fit that model, and then (3) apply the strategy until the model proved inadequate, at which point another model, informed by experience, would be attempted.

Of course, we see satisficing rearing up here. If the model is adequate (in the sense that it isn't grossly controverted by experience) and the payoffs are acceptable, the decision maker turns off his or her processor. Indeed one colleague (an organizational sociologist) justified this with a theory – since another party was involved, if an acceptable stable pattern of behavior emerged, abandoning that pattern would only confuse the other party, possibly making matters very much worse for a long time to come. Indeed, this colleague turned this into a criterion for his early strategy for play: He wanted to avoid falling too early into a pattern that might be misinterpreted.

How do we turn these vague observations into a paradigm for modeling boundedly rational dynamic choice behavior? At this point, reluctantly, I'm going to have to use some symbols: We want to model the choice behavior of an individual who, at date t, must take some action a_t from a given set A_t. This is done based on knowledge the individual may have about currently prevailing conditions, and also based on the individual's past experiences. Notwithstanding real-world considerations such as framing effects, as a modeling strategy I want to assume that the individual's preferences over available actions are "rational" in the weak sense of being complete and transitive (and, as necessary, continuous), so that the choice is made as if the individual were maximizing some function $u_t: A_t \rightarrow R$, which, of course, reflects the individual's past experiences and current thinking. I will call u_t her *anticipated utility* from the action a_t.

The theorem guaranteeing the existence of u_t is universally interpreted by economists as saying only that the decision maker's choices are made *as if* she were maximizing this function. Economists typically eschew the notion that the decision maker is (necessarily) computing or comparing utilities. But my term *anticipated utility* connotes active reflection by the decision maker. This is intentional; I want further to advocate models where the decision maker "constructs" her anticipated utility function in much the manner we teach MBA students to do analysis: She models the situation, using first-principle thinking about the structure of the situation, with parameters fitted from past observations.

4. EXAMPLE: LEARNING RATIONAL EXPECTATIONS EQUILIBRIUM

This very brief description is probably inadequate to convey what I have in mind, so let me give an example from the literature.[5] Suppose you must repeatedly choose how to invest an endowment of $1000, where your options are to divide the endowment between a riskless investment and a risky asset. The riskless asset returns $1.02 for every $1 invested. The risky asset has a random return – I will denote by θ_t its return (per share) in period t. You must make this investment (with a fresh $1000) in periods $t = 0, 1, 2, \ldots$, where your objective in each period is to maximize the utility of your return; that is, for a utility function $U: R \to R$, you seek to maximize the expectation of

$$U\big(\theta_t x_t + 1.02\big(1000 - p_t x_t\big)\big),$$

where p_t is the dollar price of a share of the risky asset and x_t is the number of shares of the risky asset you purchase (so that $1000 - p_t x_t$ is invested in the safe asset). Never mind where this objective comes from; there is a story to go with it – see below – which isn't germane at the moment. The complicating feature is that while you began with a prior assessment on the distribution of θ_t, you have noted (over time) a positive correlation between θ_t and p_t; that is, when the price of the risky asset is high, it has tended to return more per share. You suspect that this happens because there are investors in the market who have (superior) private information about θ_t; when that information is optimistic (respectively, pessimistic), those investors increase their demand at any price, shifting out their demand schedules, and thus raising (on average) the equilibrium price of the risky asset. (You are a price taker in this market, as are all other investors.)

---

[5] While I chose this example because of other points I will make with it, I would be remiss if I did not say that, as far as I know, it is seminal for the sort of model I have in mind. If earlier references to this sort of model could be supplied to me, I'd be grateful.

Clearly, you can improve your investment strategy if you can disentangle the statistical relationship between p_t and θ_t. But how can you do so? If you were hyperrational, with full understanding of the structure of the economy and all its inhabitants, you might compute the equilibrium price functional, taking into account the private information of those who have it. But as you are not hyperrational (I assume), a seemingly natural thing to do would be to collect data on past prices and returns. That is, at date t, you assemble the data

$$\left(p_0, \theta_0\right), \left(p_1, \theta_1\right), \ldots \left(p_{t-1}, \theta_{t-1}\right),$$

and you use those data to formulate a hypothesis on the relationship. To be more specific, had you just completed a course in basic econometrics, you might be led to a parametric hypothesis, such as that

$$\theta_k = a + bp_k + \varepsilon_k,$$

for some constants a and b and some (i.i.d.) error term ε_t, and you might then apply ordinary least squares estimation to estimate a, b, and the residual variance of ε_t. Then, letting $\hat{a}$, $\hat{b}$, and $\hat{\sigma}_\varepsilon^2$ be your estimates based on the data through date $t - 1$, you might formulate your demand so that if the equilibrium price is p_t, your assessment of θ_t is $\hat{a} + \hat{b}p_t + \varepsilon_t$, where ε_t is a mean zero, variance $\hat{\sigma}_\varepsilon^2$ Normal variate.

Of course, there are many other things you might do. Depending on your personal model of the economy you inhabit, you might use a nonlinear specification. Depending on how and how well you were trained in inference and econometrics, you might try some fancier estimation technique, and you might adopt a Bayesian approach. As time passes (and you use the data that are provided to reestimate the coefficients in your model), you might run tests of the linear model; perhaps nothing fancier than looking graphically at the distribution of the residuals, or perhaps something more precise, and at some point (if the evidence turns bad) you would probably reject the linear model and try something else.

If you do any of these things, you are acting in a fashion that accords with the general model of dynamic behavior outlined in Section 3. That is, you are using some first-principles knowledge about the economy (there are many investors, you are small among them) when you take the approach that you are a price taker. In other contexts, you might use a model in which you had some strategic impact on prices, or on the behavior of others, or on what you would learn (to be used for later purposes).[6] Based on those principles and your basic understanding of your

---

[6] However, taking the latter sorts of things into account can be complex – see Section 6.

situation, you create a model of your situation. You fit the model based on past observations, and you use the model to compute (within the model) the effect on your utility of various actions you might take; that is, you compute your (anticipated!) expected utility for each portfolio choice based on the estimated model you have created. (In real life, you might also subject the recommendations of your modeling exercise to a smell test – at least you would if you had been properly educated about the normative uses of analysis. But in creating a formal model of your behavior, I would probably skip this last bit and assume you follow the "recommendations" of your model.)

I should probably interject at this stage a problem in terminology manifest in the last sentence. I have used the term *model* twice there, meaning two different things. As an economist, I am modeling the actions of individual investors (and then, presumably, considering the aggregation of those actions in a market or some other institutional context). My model of those individual actions involves models created by the individuals. Perhaps it would be clearer if I used a term such as *meta-model* for my efforts, and (simply) *model* for the efforts of those who populate my meta-model. But the term *meta-model* is pretentious, so I will refrain and hope that my meaning is clear from the context.

The situation and model of individual behavior just described appeared in the literature in the early 1980s, around the issue of learning rational expectations equilibrium in competitive economies with private information. To set the context, we must go back to 1975 or so, when the basic equilibrium concept first appeared.

Imagine (as in the story told above) a two-stage economy in which a number of consumer–investors must decide in the first stage what portfolio of financial assets to hold; in the second stage the assets pay terminal dividends, which are consumed. Let $h = 1, \ldots, H$ index the consumer–investors; let $n = 1, \ldots, N$ index the assets; and let $d_n \in R$ be the dividend paid by asset n (with d the vector of asset returns). Let asset 1 be the numeraire, let p_n be the relative price of asset n, and let $e^h \in R^n$ be the initial endowment of consumer–investor h, so that this consumer-investor faces the budget constraint $p \cdot x^h \leq p \cdot e^h$, where x^h is the vector of post-trade asset holdings of h. We assume h seeks to maximize the expected utility of the terminal dividends he receives; that is, the consumer–investor's problem is to

$$\text{maximize } E\Big[U^h\big(d \cdot x^h\big)\Big], \text{ subject to } p \cdot x^h \leq p \cdot e^h,$$

where $E[\cdot]$ denotes the expectation operator (over the random d), and any appropriate nonnegativity constraints are thrown into the formulation.

The key to the story is, How does consumer–investor h take expectations? We assume that consumer–investors share a common prior assessment about d, but that h (prior to trade) gets a private signal s^h that gives some indication about d. If h is naive, he will then formulate his demand based on the maximization of $E[U^h (d \cdot x^h) \mid s^h]$, where now we have in mind the conditional expectation over d, based on the common prior, conditioned on the realization of s^h. But (at least in well-behaved parametric specifications) if consumer–investors all act in this way, after we impose market clearing, we find that equilibrium prices p, which depend on the vector s (because this vector affects individual demand schedules), will be correlated with dividends.

Grossman, Grossman and Stiglitz, Hellwig, and others, in a number of papers published in the mid- to late 1970s proposed that sophisticated and/or experienced consumer–investors would understand this relationship between equilibrium prices p and dividends d and take it into account in formulating demand. A *rational expectations equilibrium* consisted of consumer demands and an equilibrium price function $p(s,\zeta)$ such that, for every realization of the signals s and any other "noise" in the economy ζ, markets would clear at the price $p = p(s,\zeta)$ if consumer–investors formulated their demands based on the maximization of $E[U^h(d \cdot x^h) \mid s^h, p(s, \zeta) = p]$.[7]

This notion of a rational expectations equilibrium, formulated as above, was criticized on many fronts. One (then) unanswered question was, Could investors really make the very sophisticated inferences necessary? We who live in the age of Nash equilibrium take it for granted that they could and would do so on account of their sophisticated hyper-rationality; that is, fully understanding the economy they inhabit, they "compute" the equilibrium price functional, with inspired guesses involved in case the economy admits more than one equilibrium. (In this age of Nash equilibrium, we would ask the related question, What is the mechanism by which the market finds an equilibrium price from supply and demand, where net trades are conditioned on that price? This important question, which was addressed in subsequent literature, will not be discussed here.) But early proponents of this equilibrium notion weren't

---

[7] The "noise" term ζ is found in many parameterizations to prevent equilibrium prices from being fully revealing of s or, at least, of a sufficient statistic of s (sufficient for d). I have not written down the market-clearing condition because, in these parameterizations, market clearing involves this noise term; for example, the sum of consumer–investors net trades must equal ζ, interpreting ζ as the result of so-called noise or liquidity traders. If you are entirely new to this notion of a rational expectations equilibrium, it will probably help to see a concrete example worked out. Examples are provided by Grossman (1976), Grossman and Stiglitz (1976), and Hellwig (1980).

quite bold enough to rely entirely on hyperrational sophistication and instead felt the need to justify the rational expectations equilibrium notion by asserting informally that experience could proxy for sophistication: As long as the economy was sufficiently stationary, consumer–investors would, through observation, come to understand the equilibrium relationship.[8] This story isn't quite so obviously true (unless one had in mind an economy in a stationary state owing, say, to the sorts of random deaths and births found in Fudenberg and Levine [1993]), because as consumer–investors learned the equilibrium relationship, they would change that relationship. But an intuitive if informal argument (which I heard first from, and will thus attribute to, Joe Stiglitz) held that *as long as the economy converged to a steady state*, the steady state would have to be a rational expectations equilibrium, because consumer–investors would certainly learn the steady-state relationship.

In the early 1980s, a number of authors studied formal models of the learning process. I will first relate something of a bastardization of the models of Bray (1982) and Radner (1982). The two-stage economy described above for a single rational expectations equilibrium repeats (i.i.d.-style) at dates $t = 1, 2, \ldots$, with no wealth carry-over from one date to the next.[9] At each date t, investors are all aware of past equilibrium prices and security dividends, and they imagine that the statistical relationship between these is linear. Being good (if somewhat un-teched-up) econometricians, they employ ordinary least squares regression on past data, to estimate the coefficients of the relationship, just as I imagined earlier you might do. And then they formulate their demand at date t (contingent on the equilibrium price – the price-setting mechanism is not spelled out) using their estimates. Note the misspecification in their models; they are estimating the supposed equilibrium relationship with a model that supposes time-unvarying coefficients, while in fact the coefficients that prevail at date t depend on time and history, because time and history affects the estimates used by the consumer–investors and thus affects their demand schedules.

Blume and Easley (1982) propose a different sort of anticipated-utility model for the same context. In their model (again, I'm taking artistic license with the details for expositional purposes) the consumers begin with the hypothesis that the relationship between prices and returns is

---

[8] Comparisons with the more recent literature that seeks to justify Nash equilibrium with learning stories are obvious.

[9] The models employed a single risky asset and constant absolute risk aversion utility functions, so wealth carry-over per se was actually unimportant. But the *spirit* of no interaction between periods *except for the learning process* is key, hence I have chosen to highlight it in slightly misleading fashion.

generated by one of a finite number of possibilities, of the form $d = f_i(p,\zeta)$, for $i = 1, \ldots, I$. They are unsure which of these possibilities prevails, and so (at the start) entertain a prior assessment on which is the correct model. At date t, given the information so far generated (through time $t - 1$), they use Bayes' rule to update those priors: Let $\pi_i^h(t)$ denote the posterior probability of consumer–investor h that f_i gives the true relationship at date t, with the dependence of this posterior on past data suppressed. Then (at date t) the consumer–investor formulates his demand at price p based on his own information s_t^h and based on this posterior. In other words, while the consumer–investors of Bray and Radner's world are work-a-day econometricians, those in Blume and Easley's model are Bayesians with fairly dogmatic (finite support) prior beliefs.

To reiterate, these are precisely the sort of dynamic choice (and then market aggregation of those choices) models I advocate generally: The consumer–investors are insufficiently (hyper)rational to think through the equilibrium. Instead they use a model of the economy they inhabit, a model derived adaptively from past observations. And they formulate their current decisions – or, equivalently, their anticipated utilities for the various investment choices they could make – using this model as a surrogate for the unfathomable (by them) truth.

Bray, Blume and Easley, and Radner employ this sort of model to answer two questions: As time passes and the consumer–investors obtain more and more data upon which to base their estimates, will those estimates (and hence the economy) settle down to some stationary relationship? And if the economy does settle down in this sense, will it be to a rational expectations equilibrium? Because their models differ, we don't expect precise answers to the first question to be the same, but in spirit they get the same answer: The economy will settle down if the actual equilibrium relationship isn't too sensitive to the learning process.[10] But, perhaps surprisingly, they disagree on the second question. Bray and Radner confirm Stiglitz's intuitive argument: If the economy settles down, it settles to a rational expectations equilibrium. Blume and Easley show by example that posteriors can converge to a

---

[10] Typically they deal in models where some fraction of the consumer–investors are fully informed and the rest are uninformed. The fully informed need not, and do not, try to disentangle the equilibrium relationship. In these specifications, the number of "learners" (more precisely, their total risk tolerance) is a surrogate for the impact of learning on the equilibrium relationship. Readers who wish to chase down this particular subject should consult (together with these seminal papers) work by Marcet and Sargent (1989a,b), which provides the cleanest treatment of the question, Will the economy settle down?

degenerate distribution on one model that is not a rational expectations equilibrium.

5. COMMENTARY

I'll return to this conundrum in a bit, but let me leave it until the end of this section to make several comments on the general modeling strategy I'm advocating.

(1) While learning rational expectations equilibrium is the earliest example of this form of modeling with which I am familiar, it is far from the only one. The literature on learning in games, in particular, concerns a number of models of this sort.

The literature that concerns (variants of) fictitious play is the most obvious citation. The story there is a lot like the problems with which this essay begins: repeated play of a strategic-form game. But (in fictitious play) the players are assumed to be myopic; they use history to formulate an assessment about the action their rival is about to take, and select their own action to maximize their immediate payoff.[11] The assessment is, essentially, proportional to the past actions of the rival; that is, if the rival has played Column 1 fifty-five times in one hundred rounds of play, on the hundred-and-first round, Row assesses probability 0.55 of Column 1. Similar learning models involve Cournotian conjectures (the rival is predicted to do in round t whatever she did in round $t - 1$). See also Milgrom and Roberts (1991) for a general definition of adaptive learning in this context.

In contrast to models based on fictitious play, Fudenberg and Levine (1993) and Kalai and Lehrer (1993, 1995) study models where the players are not myopic, entertain a full-scale Bayesian prior on the strategy used by their opponent(s), and compute anticipated utility "properly" given that prior; that is, they solve the full infinite-horizon dynamic programming problem. The models don't quite involve hyperrationality in that the prior does not necessarily coincide with objective reality but still, solving the infinite-horizon optimization problem requires formidable analytical skills (except in trivial cases).

A different sort of contrast can be found in Erev and Roth (1997), who study models of reinforcement learning. In these models, anticipated utility is computed fairly mechanically; for example, the anticipated utility associated with a particular action is the sum of all rewards

---

[11] Myopia is justified in several ways: Players may discount very heavily; or the interaction may involve large numbers of players and random matching. With regard to the latter justification, see Ellison (1997).

received using that action. Erev and Roth's models don't quite conform to the general structure laid out in Section 3, in that they have random choice models; the probability of choosing action *a* is proportional to its "anticipated utility." (There are standard tricks for turning random choice models into more traditional models with deterministic choice, by imagining that utility is subject to random shocks, for example.)

One can even (roughly) interpret evolutionary models of game playing in this light: Players are assumed to stick with a particular strategy for a random (exponential) length of time, but every so often rethink what they are doing. When they rethink, they look around at colleagues, and they imitate the strategy of a colleague with probability proportional to how well the imitated strategy has just done.

Marimon, McGratton, and Sargent (1990) use a Holland-classifier algorithm to study issues connected with the endogenous emergence of a common medium of exchange. This model is similar to reinforcement learning as in Erev and Roth; that is, the "score" associated with a particular action depends on payoffs received from using that action in the past, and the probability of taking an action is proportional to its score.

Sargent (1997) provides a very stimulating analysis of the conquest of inflation in the United States (over the period from 1980 to 1990) using precisely this sort of model.

In a series of papers, Gilboa and Schmeidler (1995, 1997, among others) have studied so-called case-based decision theory. These models are similar to those of Erev and Roth and Marimon, McGratton, and Sargent, in that actions are scored based on past experiences with them and with similar actions, but the model involves deterministic choice: The action taken is the action with the highest current score. Gilboa and Schmeidler's general analysis is notable on at least two scores: They axiomatize this form of dynamic decision making, and they score actions based on how that action *and similar ones* have performed; that is, they include in their notion of how the decision maker models his environment the idea that the decision maker will decide (exogenously in their models) that certain actions are similar, and make inferences about values (or, in my terminology, anticipated utilities) accordingly.

(2) The model of fictitious play illustrates very cleanly the two "aspects" of this general scheme for modeling dynamic choice: models of behavior at a single point in time; and the dynamic process by which those models are adapted to circumstances. To be pedantic, in the model of fictitious play, a player at any date forms a probability assessment over the actions his rival(s) will take and chooses his own action to maximize his immediate expected payoff, given that assessment. And the adaptive dynamics lie entirely within adaptation of the player's assessment of the

actions of his rival; that is, the assessment at date t is essentially proportional to empirical frequencies of past actions.

(3) The literature on learning in games, running the gamut from the very highly sophisticated behavior in Kalai and Lehrer (1993) through fictitious play to the reinforcement learners of Erev and Roth (1997), illustrates well the notion that an appropriate model of dynamic behavior must be sensitive to the computational and cognitive skills of the parties being modeled, their levels of experience, the information they are provided by the institutions within which they act, and (even) the complexity of what they must learn. The discussion of this point in Erev and Roth (1997) and Cooper and Feltovich (1997) should not be missed; these two papers come to different conclusions (based on different data samples) about the relative merits of fictitious play versus reinforcement learning, but they identify the root cause of the different conclusions in differences in the sort of factors listed above.

Indeed, I contend that full equilibrium analysis, with hyperrational agents, is different in degree and not in kind from the type of models I am advocating. When the environment is simple enough, or the individuals involved are sophisticated and/or experienced enough to be expected reasonably to be able to compute anticipated utilities based on a common equilibrium view of their environment, we should model them as doing so. (I will return to this theme, and stand it a bit on its head, in the concluding remarks.)

(4) At the talk from which this essay is extracted, Nancy Stokey raised the inevitable objection to this way of modeling dynamic choice; viz., it so multiplies the range of possible models that almost anything could be predicted on the basis of such models, and insofar as anything can be predicted, nothing is learned.

My response to this critique is, "Yes, but. . . ."

Yes, it is true that almost any conclusion one wishes to reach can be reached with a model built along the general lines given here. If we permit economic analyses to be built around individual behavior that is restricted so little, we permit a lot of contradictory analysis.

But the forms of model we use are analogous to languages we employ to write stories; they are not the stories (models) themselves. Allowing more flexibility in the "language" of economics permits the composition of more and more varied models. Inevitably this means more models can be created that are nonsense. But it also (potentially) means that more models can be created that are sensible and sensitive to real-world phenomena. And it is the specific model, not the language, that should be subject to empirical testing, both formal and informal. The assumptions and conclusions of a particular model must be checked against reality at the level of a smell test at least, although (one hopes) something more systematic can be employed.

Recall Frank Fisher's (1989) critique of game theory as applied to Industrial Organization. Fisher distinguished between exemplifying theory – theoretical models constructed to show logically consistent possibilities – and generalizing theory – theories that cut across a broad range of models, to establish conclusions that hold generally. An example establishing the possibility of a Giffen good is exemplifying theory; the Theorems of Welfare Economics are examplars of generalizing theory. Fisher asserted that Industrial Organization didn't need game theory to create exemplifying theory; Chamberlain, writing before game theory, already noted that in multi-period competition almost anything was possible, and all that game theory added along this dimension was unnecessary high-tech gloss. And since game theory has proven so flexible a language, it has provided little or nothing in the way of generalizing theory.

I don't want to spend time in this essay debating Fisher's evaluation of game theory's contributions to I.O. (The curious should see Kreps [1990, chapter 4].) But his dichotomy is helpful in responding to the Stokey criticism: The sort of models I am advocating will certainly make the task of exemplifying theory easier. This, of course, weakens the impact of a piece of exemplifying theory *per se*. However, there are empirical phenomena that are (at least) hard to exemplify with hyper-rational individuals but that are easily exemplified with individuals who are limitedly rational in the sense of this essay. (See Kreps, 1998.) To come to grips with these phenomena, I assert we need additional flexibility in modeling dynamic choice that matches the reality of individual dynamic choice.

On the other hand, to the extent that one grants the validity of models with this sort of individual behavior included, generalizing theory *that generalizes across these models as well as across the standard hyper-rationality-based models* becomes more difficult. But if one doesn't believe in hyperrationality, then generalizing theories that require it become suspect. That is, allowing these sorts of models into the tent provides our (few) generalizing theories with higher hurdles to clear, but these are hurdles that ought to be cleared if the theories are to be accepted.

What Fisher decries – a decline in the number of generalizing theorems as the universe to be generalized becomes richer – is inevitable *and desirable* if we believe that the universe is richer than we are accustomed to assuming. Assuming that preferences all exhibit weak gross substitutes allows us to prove that general equilibrium is unique – a nice piece of generalizing theory in terms of the strength of the conclusion, but not a useful one, given the strong assumption needed to obtain it. So what substitutes for fewer generalizing theorems? Presumably the answer is more empirics, directed at the assumptions and the conclusions of specific models.

I don't want to go too far in this direction. Economics has gotten a lot of mileage out of adherence to the twin rubric of rational (purposeful) behavior and equilibrium. A wholesale abandonment of those standards is unwarranted. But careful, limited, and circumspect abandonment ought to be attempted (at least) before it is condemned as heresy.

(5) While economists may think these models stray too far from the paradigm, other social scientists may think they have not gone far enough.

In assuming that current choices (from currently available options) are rational, I've dismissed things like framing effects applying at that level. This is not done because I think framing effects are unimportant, but because I want to direct attention to a different array of choice-theoretic considerations; viz., those that have to do with dynamics. This is somewhat disingenuous: To the extent that dynamics complicate the decision problem, they (probably) make it more likely that the decision maker will be subject to framing effects. For example, as the decision maker casts around for a simple model of her environment, the set of options presented to her may influence the model she builds. Suppose her choice set consists of a and a', which differ chiefly along dimension X. If these are her only two options, she is likely to concentrate her thinking and model building exercises on models that feature dimension X. But if her choice set consists of a, b, c, d, and a', she may be led to models that feature a different critical dimension, models that reverse the "apparent" relative values of a and a'. Tversky and Kahneman (1981), among others, teach us that when it comes to cognition and choice, process can powerfully determine content. Notwithstanding this and similar considerations, I pass on framing effects for immediate action choices today.

(6) The extent to which parties analyze and deliberate is surely not exogenous or fixed through time. I noted already a strong whiff of satisficing behavior in my informal survey. If matters are proceeding satisfactorily, the parties involved may abandon analysis as too costly. Bray's consumer–investors are apt to abandon their OLS analysis before reaching the theoretical limit that she studies. A complete and completely satisfactory model of dynamic choice will undoubtedly include this endogenously induced form of satisficing. I have nothing pertinent to say about it today and so only mention it in passing.

(7) On the other side of the coin, if we model a party as employing a

particular model in her deliberations, we ought to give her credit for being smart enough to dispose of the model when it performs abysmally. Or, put differently, failing to do so can lead to some pretty anomalous results.

This point is best illustrated by juxtaposing the papers of Bray (1982) and Blume and Easley (1982). The question posed in these two papers is the same: What is the long-run behavior of an economy with privately held information, if investors attempt to learn from history what is the equilibrium relationship between prices and assest returns? As noted above, Bray concludes that if the economy settles down, it will be to a rational expectations equilibrium. Blume and Easley show by examples that, in their model, things can settle down to a relationship that is not a rational expectations equilibrium. Why the difference?

In Bray's model, if a stationary state is attained in the economy she deals with, a stationary and linear relationship between prices and private information will emerge. And thus, with probability one, her OLS-plying investors will learn that relationship. Hence if a stationary state emerges, it must be a rational expectations equilibrium; it will be learned and optimally acted upon, and rational expectations equilibria are the fixed points of this sort of map.

When Blume and Easley get convergence to an equilibrium that is not a rational expectations equilibrium, it is because the equilibrium that emerges is not in the support of the investors' (dogmatic) Bayesian prior. Hence no matter how much evidence accumulates, the investors never assess positive probability for the true relationship. Doing the best they can, investors have increasing faith (asymptoting in complete belief) in the model in the support of their prior that comes closest to the truth, which, if they believe it with certainty, gives rise to another (out-of-the-support) relationship. If we suddenly allowed the consumer–investors in Blume and Easley's model to admit the truth to the support of their Bayesian posteriors, the consumer-investors would begin to believe in this model, and the truth would shift once more.

The point is simple. If the investors in Blume and Easley did a "smell test" on their initial (misspecified) model of the world, they would find, as time passes, that their model stinks. A statistical relationship emerges that their model gives absolutely no chance of being correct. I'm sure that Blume, Easley, and any other sensible economist in this situation would conclude that the model is no good, and abandon it. I suggest that insofar as we chase down the very long horizon implications of these models, we ought to give the actors in our models credit for equal levels of good sense.

(To add a final remark on the Stokey critique [item 5, above]: Here is a good first example of how I think we might successfully increase the flexibility of our language and still get some generalizing theory out. Blume and Easley are exemplifiers *par excellence*: They show how the Stiglitz conjecture might fail. And, at the same time, their theory points to assumptions that guarantee the veracity of the Stiglitz conjecture: If we suppose that the econometric/Bayesian models of the consumer–investors are asymptotically empirical, which means that their beliefs come into concert with long-run empirical frequencies, then with the right level of continuity assumed about consumer–investor response rules [continuity in the weak topology], the Stiglitz conjecture can be proved in general. That is, Blume and Easley show us that things can "go wrong," and their example gives us enough of an indication of how, so that we can tell what assumptions are needed to ensure that it doesn't happen.)

6. INTERTEMPORAL LINKAGES

Having advocated a design for modeling dynamic choice (at least, for some contexts), I will now indicate why implementing this design will not be uniformly easy.

The economy Bray models is simple in several respects. The consumer–investors are price-takers, hence they believe (and act as if) their immediate decisions have no impact on the terms of trade they face, on the actions (now or in the future) of their fellow investors, or on the information they will receive that might guide their own future actions. In other words, today's outcome can affect tomorrow's decision because of what is learned today, but today's *decision* has no impact on tomorrow's decision or outcome.

In other contexts, the current decision can affect subsequent outcomes. In imperfectly competitive settings, today's decision can affect the actions of others (who meet cooperation with cooperation, or weakness with aggression, or spite with spite), and thus affect tomorrow's outcome.[12] And today's decision can affect the information received today that is relevant for tomorrow's decision (and thus for tomorrow's outcome). Both of these intertemporal linkages can make dynamic decision making extremely complex.

Let me illustrate briefly with two examples.

---

[12] It is not imperfect competition per se that is crucial, but that a decision maker, in formulating her immediate decision, takes this effect into account. In models of learning to play games based on fictitious play, a player's immediate action may affect what her rival will do subsequently. But it is *assumed* (and sometimes justified by a large-numbers, random-matching assumption) that the player is myopic: Her immediate decision is taken without regard to any such effects.

Walking in the Woods

Imagine you have taken for the next 30 days (indexed $t = 1, \ldots, 30$) a vacation home sitting on the edge of a forest. You are determined to spend your mornings working at the computer, but for the next month, your work-day will end at noon, when you will pack a daypack and go walking in the forest.

The choice problem I wish to discuss is, What should you take in your daypack? Presumably you wish to carry useful things: water, food, a poncho, insect repellant, sunscreen, and so on. But the more you put into your daypack, the heavier it will become, and the less enjoyable will be your walk. You must trade off the utility of what you carry and its weight.

So how do you choose what to take? More to the point, how should we (as economists) model your dynamic choice behavior, where the dynamics involve a process of adaptive learning?

Notation is unavoidable: Let X be the set of all possible things you might put into your daypack on any given day. Let Z be the set of all subsets of X, so that Z is the set of "packed daypacks" you might carry. Let $w: X \to R$ be a function that gives the weights of the items – that is, the weight of x is $w(x)$ – and extend w to the domain Z by the rule $w(z) = \Sigma_{x \in z} w(x)$. It is useful to decouple the items and weight aspects of a particular daypack, so I assume that we have your preferences defined on the space $Z \times R^+$, where the interpretation is that (z,w) represents a daypack whose contents are given by z and whose total weight is w. In the end, of course, you must choose among $\{(z,w) \in Z \times R^+: w = w(z)\}$, but having your preferences defined on the larger domain will make the theory go a bit more smoothly. (Realistically, the weight of the pack will change as the walk progresses; for example, as you drink water, you reduce the weight of what you are carrying. That is too realistic for this parable, and I ignore such considerations.)

Following my earlier discussion, I will assume (for the sake of modeling) that your preferences at date t over the space $Z \times R^+$ are "well-behaved," that is, complete and transitive, and (say) continuous in w. Thus we can represent those preferences by a function $u_t: Z \times R^+ \to R$. It seems entirely natural to suppose that more weight is worse than less and that more items are better than fewer (holding weight fixed); that is,

$$u_t(z,w) > u_t(z,w') \text{ if } w < w' \quad \text{and} \quad u_t(z,w) \geq u_t(z',w) \text{ if } z \supseteq z'.$$

I assume these properties throughout.

The issues are: What more can be said about static preferences? What sorts of analysis/heuristics can we reasonably suppose of the decision maker? How do past events/outcomes affect static preferences via the decision maker's models?

Of course, any decision maker who takes this problem seriously enough to model the problem explicitly will defeat the purpose of the vacation. In the context of the specific story I've spun, I would expect a pretty rough-and-ready heuristic, along the lines of: Take one of everything, and start removing stuff from the daypack if, after two or three days, it hasn't been used.[13] But the symbols of the story are easily adapted to settings where the decision might be taken more seriously; for example, interpret X as pieces of capital equipment that might be held by a producer so that $z \in Z$ are ensembles of capital actually held, and $w(z)$ represents the rent associated with z. Or think of X as individuals possibly employed by an organization; $z \in Z$ then becomes different employment rosters, and $w(z)$ can be thought of as the wages paid. (Note that in such contexts, it would be natural to assume that u_t is some sort of reduced-form profit function, with w entering quasi-linearly.) Thus I will proceed to the questions posed in the previous paragraph under the assumption that the decision maker takes this problem more seriously than might seem natural.

An obvious "model" is one with state-dependent utility. The decision maker supposes: The state of the forest at date t is represented by some random variable ϕ_t; conditional on ϕ_t, the value of bundle z at weight w is some $U_t(z, w, \phi_t)$; and the overall expected utility from (z,w) is

$$u_t(z,w) = \int U_t(z,w,\phi)\mu(d\phi),$$

where μ is the decision maker's (subjective) assessment of the state of the forest. I neither preclude nor insist on ϕ representing some tangible "state of the world"; that is the decision maker might want to consider ϕ as a description of temperature, precipitation, and so on, in the forest, or he might want to regard ϕ as a canonical random variable that directly indexes the values of (z,w).[14] Indeed, even if the decision maker attaches tangible meaning to some aspects of ϕ, there might still be some residual uncertainty in his mind about the value to him of (z,w); see Kreps (1992). The sequence $\{\phi_t\}$ might reasonably be taken to be an i.i.d.

---

[13] This particular rough-and-ready choice heuristic can lead to decidedly suboptimal outcomes. See Kreps (1998).

[14] In the latter case, it might make more sense to write $u_t(z,w) = \int_R \phi_t \mu(d\phi; z,w)$; that is, the measure on utility ϕ is indexed by the daypack's contents and its weight. For the afficionado: Note how much easier it is with this second way of writing the model to formulate a condition such as asymptotic empiricism.

sequence if the decision maker is familiar with the general conditions of the forest or, perhaps more reasonably given persistence in weather conditions, the sequence might be taken to be a Markov process. In addition, it is reasonable to suppose that the decision maker, by sticking his head out the window at 11 a.m. or by reading the weather report in the morning paper, can get a partial reading on ϕ_t; we might want to speak of $\mu(d\phi|\psi_t)$, where ψ_t are conditions observable from the cabin prior to setting out on date t. (Having mentioned these possible modeling complications, I will not carry through with them in subsequent discussion.)

But what if the decision maker is unaware of the general conditions of the forest. The story, after all, is that the decision maker is new to this forest. Thus he may be unsure of the distribution of ϕ_t or, equivalently, he might assess subjectively that $\{\phi_t\}$ is exchangeable (instead of i.i.d.). Taking the former modeling perspective, we would write

$$u_t\big(z,w\big) = \iint U_t\big(z,w,\phi\big)\mu\big(d\phi\big)\eta\big(d\mu\big),$$

where η is his subjective assessment of the distribution μ of ϕ_t. Then as time passes and he gains experience, the impact of that experience would be captured by the evolution of η. That is, we should write $\eta(d\mu|I_t)$ where I_t is all the information accrued up to time t. Natural heuristics for the evolution of $\eta(\cdot|I_t)$ are suggested immediately; that is, the decision maker might take a "Bayesian" approach, or he might use something like fictitious play: Start with a prior formed from a set of equally likely scenarios for the value of each z, and after each date add to this set the value function that applied on that date; to decide what to do on date t, give equal probability to the elements of the original prior and the $t - 1$ additional value functions experienced on the $t - 1$ previous dates.[15]

There is, however, one problem with this model, which is the reason for introducing this story. The model (and its evolution) sketched in the previous two paragraphs assumes implicitly that when the decision maker takes his stroll on day t with z_t in his daypack, he comprehends the value on that day, under conditions ϕ_t, of every $z \in Z$. This is not wholly ludicrous – even if one's daypack lacks a poncho, the experience of rain on the trail will be evidence that a poncho would have been useful – but it is not hard to imagine that the information the decision maker will receive at date t about the value of various items or collections of items he might carry is affected by what he is actually carrying. To take

---

[15] I apologize to readers who find this too-brief description hard to follow. But the details aren't important, and they take many pages to relate fully. If you do not divine what I'm saying from this rough rendition *and* you are interested in the details, see Kreps (1998).

for the sake of definiteness a concrete alternative to the information-is-free case implicit in what I've done so far, suppose that at date t, carrying z_t, the decision maker comprehends what is the value to him of z' in conditions ϕ_t, for every $z' \subseteq z_t$, and he learns *nothing* about the value of z' for $z' \cap z_t = \phi$.

This changes the story dramatically. In particular, I think that without further simplifying assumptions, it renders the story practically intractable. Now there is a value-of-information calculation to perform; that is, the decision maker may regard it unlikely that object x is worth carrying given its weight, but unless he carries x, he won't learn how valuable it might be. Hence (perhaps) he will carry x for a few days, just to get some information.

In terms of the formal model, to $\int\int U_t(z,w,\phi)\mu(d\phi)\eta(d\mu)$ (where U_t is the immediate payoff from holding the bundle z), we should add a term that reflects the increase in future payoffs from holding z. To keep the notation at all manageable, we first need to assume something about how the decision maker trades off "utility" today versus utility tomorrow: I will assume for the remainder of this discussion that he wishes to maximize a discounted sum of day-by-day utilities, or $\Sigma_{t=1}^{30}\alpha^t\mathbf{E}[U_t(z,w,\phi_t)]$, for $\alpha < 1$ and $\mathbf{E}[\cdot]$ representing a general expectation. Then we would have $u_t(z,w) = \int\int U_t(z,w,\phi)\mu(d\phi)\eta(d\mu) + U_t'(z)$ where $U_t'(z)$ is a (relative) measure of the value of information for future purposes gained from carrying z today. But this is a very formidable value to measure indeed.

One can get a sense of how formidable this term is by considering two relatively simple cases. At the extreme of simplicity, suppose that, on first principles, we know that $U_t(z,w,\phi)$ takes the form $\Sigma_{x\in z} v_t(x,\phi) - w$. That is, immediate utility is quasi-linear in weight and, on the same scale, linear in the values of the various single objects. Then the decision whether to carry x depends only on the distribution of $v_t(x,\phi)$ vis-à-vis $w(x)$. In particular, there is no interaction whatsoever between x and any other x', or between x and the total weight being carried. Thus the decision to carry x or not can be separated from the same decision for other members of X. And now, following from the analogy of the multi-armed bandit problem, it is easy to argue that (with the constant discount rate) if x is ever dropped from the daypack, it will never be added back. The precise calculation of the value of information from carrying x (given a prior on μ) is not impossibly hard, and if it is still too hard to carry out, reasonable heuristics (involving the distribution of $v_t(x, \phi)$ above $w(x)$, the length of time until the vacation ends, the precise value of α, and so on) are available.

But all this depends on the strong linear separability assumption (for each day's utility). Items from x are neither substitutes for one another nor complementary. This assumption may be reasonable in some contexts, but certainly it is too strong for most, and so we move on to simplifying assumptions a bit less stark than this one.

For example, suppose that the items of X are perfect substitutes. That is, one and only one $x \in z$ will be brought out of the daypack. Absent the value of information, the "natural" model is then

$$u_t(z,w) = \int\int \max_{x \in z} v_t(x,w,\phi)\mu(d\phi)\eta(d\mu),$$

where $v_t(x,w,\phi_t)$ gives the value of the object x if w is being carried in circumstances ϕ_t.[16] An analogy with the classic multi-armed bandit problem may now appear feasible. Recall that in the multi-armed bandit problem, the arms of the bandit are (by fiat) perfect substitutes; only one can be selected at each date. Combined with the independence of the arms, this allows for computations of the value of information one arm at a time, via the Gittens Index. But the analogy is false. Although the items are perfect substitutes ϕ_t by ϕ_t, integrating over all possible states, items may become complementary. To take a concrete example, suppose that X contains a large Swiss Army knife, a small Swiss Army knife, and a can opener. Suppose that the small Swiss Army knife has a blade only, and that in any conceivable circumstance the decision maker will need (only) a can opener or a knife blade, but not both. The small knife and the can opener may be perfect substitutes (and perfect substitutes for the large knife) for each value of ϕ. But as substitutes for the large Swiss Army knife, reckoned while there is still uncertainty about ϕ, the small knife and the can opener are complementary – together they are a fine substitute for the large knife. This means that the value of information about one of them depends on the other. For example, with two periods left to go, it may be worthwhile to carry both knives in order to learn more about the value of the small knife, because the small knife and the can opener together are almost as good (given their weight) as the large knife (given its weight).

I can't prove to you that the value-of-information calculations that are required in this case are impossibly hard, or that simple and reasonable heuristics for the value of information aren't available in theory. But the complexity of the problem, where the value of information about each

---

[16] Afficionados will recognize this form of utility as having something of an axiomatic basis, from Kreps (1992) and/or Dekel, Liman, and Rustichini (1997). In this regard, note that citing Kreps (1992) is largely inappropriate – that paper is descriptive and not normative in orientation. But Dekel, Lipman, and Rustichini (1997) has a normative interpretation and so provides an axiomatic basis for this representational form.

item depends on what is known about all the others, is enormous. In particular, no item-by-item calculation of value (corresponding to the Gitten's index) is going to be possible. (That, at least, can be proved.) Even quite simple information-based intertemporal linkages give us a lot to think about.

Learning to Cooperate

Returning to the problem with which this essay began, to this we add a second intertemporal linkage, namely the effect the decision maker's actions today have on the actions of others tomorrow. (The use of *add* is intentional here; see the discussion following.)

Take the game in Figure 1a, the classic Prisoners' Dilemma. Under the circumstances described, it is fairly apparent that what one player does in round t will affect subsequent actions by his rival. (If this were not true, then it would be patent that the best thing to do in each round would be to choose the dominating strategy.) Moreover, a value-of-information calculation is impounded in this: To learn how one's rival will react to, e.g., an occasional unprovoked fink, one must fink occasionally. Perhaps more to the immediate point, suppose play bogs down in noncooperative play of repeated finking by both sides. You might wish to know your rival will respond to cooperation; that is, will this be reciprocated? But the only way to find out is to cooperate, which (potentially) comes at significant immediate cost.

How should we model dynamic behavior in this sort of setting? There is a large literature on learning to play games, which is of almost no help whatsoever. At one extreme are papers in the spirit of fictitious play or that use reinforcement learning. In these papers, the players are (generally) myopic, concerned (only) with the immediate payoff they will receive. Accordingly, cooperation cannot emerge when the stage game is as in Figure 1a; players will be led rather strongly to playing their dominating strategy (how strongly depends on the specific model). In other words, the intertemporal linkages are wiped out by fiat.[17] At the other extreme are Kalai and Lehrer (1993) and Fudenberg and Levine (1993),

---

[17] In Fudenberg and Kreps (1994), although players are "largely" myopic, they still experiment to gain information about what their rivals will do; the stage game is an extensive-form game, and experimentation is undertaken to reach otherwise unreached parts of the game tree. In other words, the story is one of value of information, and not the influence current actions have on other players. And models of when-to-experiment are never proposed concretely; there is only a blanket assumption that players experiment "enough," where (moreover) the prescription for "enough" is known to be more than is optimal in, say, a multi-armed bandit problem with a positive interest rate.

who assume that the players in their models are able to solve the extraordinarily complex dynamic programming problems engendered when a player has a full Bayesian prior on the (infinite horizon) strategy of his rival(s).[18] Their analyses, under the assumption that players solve these problems, are characteristically insightful. But those analyses do not provide guidance concerning how to model the behavior of a player who (a) confronts a fixed opponent whose behavior may be influenced and must be discovered, and (b) is incapable of solving the immensely complicated dynamic programming problem involved in finding an optimal dynamic strategy given a subjective assessment on the strategy his rival will use.[19]

What lies in the middle ground between myopia and full dynamic optimization? The only reference I can point to is Cho (1996).[20] Cho imagines that each player assumes that his rival is playing a linear strategy in which the action at date t depends on the sign of a linear function of all past outcomes; each player uses the history of play to estimate the coefficients of the strategy and then plays a "best response" taking into account the complexity of the computations involved.

Let me sketch another middle-ground model: Suppose each player believes his rival is playing a time-invariant Markovian strategy, where the probability selected for cooperation (in the Prisoners' Dilemma game from Figure 1a) is fixed as a function of the previous period's outcome. There are four possible previous outcomes, CC, CF, FC, and FF (listing the player's action first and his rival's second), and thus the strategy supposed of one's rival is a four-tuple $(p_1, p_2, p_3, p_4) \in [0,1]^4$, where p_1 is the probability that the rival will select C following CC, and so on. Each player emulates fictitious play in estimating the p_i; for p_2, for example, the player considers all past occurrences of FC, and p_2 is the frequency that C from the rival followed those occurrences. (Suitable modifications are made in case FC has never happened.)

---

[18] Kalai and Lehrer (1993) concerns directly the problem posed here; repeated play of a fixed game against a fixed opponent. Fudenberg and Levine (1993) concerns repeated play of an extensive-form game against a sequence of randomly selected opponents drawn from a large population in a steady state. Hence Fudenberg and Levine do not consider the impact of one player's decision on the actions of his rival(s); they are concerned instead with the value-of-information temporal linkage.

[19] The dynamic programming problem is much less complex when the discount factors are small. But the need to learn what an opponent is doing and how he can be influenced is reduced directly with the complexity of the problem.

[20] The literature on this topic is growing rapidly, and I'd be grateful if readers could point me to other references.

Given an estimated strategy for the opponent (p_1, p_2, p_3, p_4), it is relatively simple to compute a dynamic best response to it: By standard and simple results from dynamic programming, if the rival is using a strategy that has one-period memory and is time homogeneous, such a strategy is optimal (as well) for the player in question. We could assume that the players at each date use a best response given their current estimates of $(p_1, \ldots, p_4)$ for their rival, or that they play a best response with probability approaching one but experiment occasionally with suboptimal actions to gain more information about how their rivals would react to otherwise rarely observed circumstances. (The value-of-information/experimentation aspects of a player's overall strategy will have to come from outside this particular model, since the model presumes counterfactually that the player knows the strategy of his rival. That is, the model against which the player optimizes operationalizes the idea that today's action will affect one's rival's future actions, but it does this so simple-mindedly that value-of-information considerations are entirely lost.)

I leave it to you to verify that $(1,0,0,1)$ versus $(1,0,0,1)$ is a stable attractor of the corresponding dynamic system, leading to cooperation, as long as the CC payoff is large enough relative to the sum of the FC and CF payoffs. (For details and a second construction of this sort, see Kreps, 1998.)

While this model does lie in the middle ground between full dynamic sophisticated optimization and myopia, it is not, to my mind, a very satisfactory model. The model constructed by the decision maker(s), on which basis he is (meant to be) selecting his static action, is premised on the clear counterfactuals that (1) he knows his rival's strategy and (2) that strategy is time homogeneous, even as he is changing from one date to the next what he himself "knows" and does. In a sense, this isn't that different from the Bray model, where ever-changing estimates are treated (in terms of static choice) as true parameters, or models of learning based on fictitious play. But for both those purposes, a distribution on the unknown parameter integrates out in terms of static decisions. That is simply not true in this context. (Compare best responses to: [1] You believe that your rival is using the strategy $(1,0,0,0)$ with probability 1/2 and is using $(0,1,1,1)$ with probability 1/2; and [2] your rival is certain to be using $(1/2,1/2,1/2,1/2)$. In the first case, you begin cooperatively and, with probability 1/2, you cooperate forever. In the second, you fink in each period for sure.)

Thus the best thing I can say about this model is that it is an example of a model of the general sort I am advocating that lives in the middle ground between dynamic ultra-sophistication and myopia. The middle ground is inhabited. The task before us is to populate this middle ground with more sensible models.

7. CONCLUDING REMARK – THE INSTITUTIONAL RESPONSE TO COMPLEXITY

Where does this leave us? Dynamic choices are crucial to some of the most important economic phenomena. The standard paradigm for dynamic choice has been of enormous service to economic modelers. But increasingly in the literature, we see attempts to move away from the standard paradigm. As part of the portfolio of our models, I find interesting and would like to advocate further work on models where the decision makers are reasonably smart; where, if you will, they are model builders more or less the way that we are.

But how do they (and will we) deal with intertemporal linkages? Perhaps because economists have typically reduced dynamic choice problems to their static equivalents, I don't think we know many good modeling heuristics for such linkages short of the usually unimplementable "Do it (hyperrationally) right." So (seemingly) first we have to work out sensible heuristics for these sorts of problems. Only then will we be able to study (sensibly) the interactions of individuals who face these sorts of complicated dynamic choice problems.

This may be merely the jaded view of an over-the-hill theorist, but I am compelled to record the conjecture that sensible and widely applicable heuristics to deal with intertemporal linkages will not be easily found. Decision makers will not do well (in the sense of behaving sensibly) in circumstances where significant intertemporal linkages are present. Put it this way: The more complex their environments are, the less likely they are to come to grips with that complexity effectively. As we move from the Prisoners' Dilemma of Figure 1a to the games in Figures 1b and c and then to the fourth and least specified treatment with which this essay began, it is increasingly unlikely that the players will achieve anything like efficient cooperation.

Efficiency, I assert, is a likely outcome only in a simple and transparent environment. (See Roth and Erev 1995.) If so, this will not have escaped the notice of those who design or, at least, influence economic institutions: To the extent certain features of dynamic decision problems make the problems complex – perhaps too complex for the wits of boundedly rational individuals – and to the extent that efficiency is a virtue for the institutions within which individuals are solving those problems, we will find that economic institutions are designed or at least evolve toward forms that avoid those complexity-inducing features. In other words, the net result of studying dynamic decision making by boundedly rational decision makers may not be – I assert, will not be – a universal set of models, heuristics, and procedures by which all dynamic decision problems can be studied. Instead, it may be a better understanding of what makes dynamic decision making complex, and (thus) why economic institutions are shaped the way that they are. If this is what we learn, it will be plenty.

References

Larry E. Blume and David Easley (1982), "Learning to Be Rational," *Journal of Economic Theory*, Vol. 26, 318–39.

Margaret M. Bray (1982), "Learning, Estimation, and the Stability of Rational Expectations," *Journal of Economic Theory*, Vol. 26, 340–51.

In-koo Cho (1996), "Learning to Coordinate in Repeated Games," mimeo, Brown University.

David J. Cooper and Nick Feltovich (1997), "Selection of Learning Rules: Theory and Experimental Evidence," mimeo, University of Pennsylvania.

Glenn Ellison (1997), "Learning from Personal Experience: One Rational Guy and the Justification of Myopia," *Games and Economic Behavior*, forthcoming.

Ido Erev and Alvin E. Roth (1997), "Modeling How People Play Games: Reinforcement Learning in Experimental Games with Unique, Mixed Strategy Equilibria," mimeo, University of Pittsburgh, forthcoming in the *American Economic Review*.

Frank M. Fisher (1989), "Games Economists Play: A Noncooperative View," *Rand Journal of Economics*, Vol. 20, 113–22.

Drew Fudenberg and David Levine (1993), "Steady State Learning and Nash Equilibrium," *Econometrica*, Vol. 61, 523–46.

Itzhak Gilboa and David Schmeidler (1995), "Case-Based Decision Theory," *Quarterly Journal of Economics*, Vol. 110, 605–39.

Itzhak Gilboa and David Schmeidler (1997), "Act-Similarity in Case-Based Decision Theory," *Economic Theory*, Vol. 9, 47–61.

Sanford J. Grossman (1976), "On the Efficiency of Competitive Stock Markets Where Traders Have Diverse Information," *Journal of Finance*, Vol. 31, 373–84.

Sanford J. Grossman and Joseph E. Stiglitz (1976), "Information and Competitive Price Systems," *American Economic Review*, Vol. 66, 246–53.

Martin F. Hellwig (1980), "On the Aggregation of Information in Competitive Markets," *Journal of Economic Theory*, Vol. 22, 477–98.

Ehud Kalai and Ehud Lehrer (1993), "Rational Learning Leads to Nash Equilibrium," *Econometrica*, Vol. 61, 1019–45.

Ehud Kalai and Ehud Lehrer (1995), "Subjective Games and Equilibria," *Games and Economic Behavior*, Vol. 8, 123-63.

274   **David M. Kreps**

David M. Kreps (1990), *Game Theory and Economic Modelling*, Oxford: Oxford University Press.
David M. Kreps (1992), "Static Choice in the Presence of Unforeseen Contingencies," in Das Gupta, Gale, Hart, and Maskin (eds.), *Economic Analysis of Markets and Games*, MIT Press, Cambridge, Massachusetts, 258–81.
David M. Kreps (1998), *Dynamic Choice in Ambiguous Circumstances*, The Morgenstern Memorial Lectures for 1997, mimeo, Stanford Universty.
Albert Marcet and Thomas J. Sargent (1989a), "Convergence of Least Squares Learning Mechanisms in Self Referential Linear Stochastic Models," *Journal of Economic Theory*, Vol. 48, 337–68.
Albert Marcet and Thomas J. Sargent (1989b), "Convergence of Least-Squares Learning in Environments with Hidden State Variables and Private Information," *Journal of Political Economy*, Vol. 97, 1306–22.
Ramon Marimon, Ellen McGrattan, and Thomas Sargent (1990), "Money as a Medium of Exchange in an Economy with Artificially Intelligent Agents," *Journal of Economic Dynamics and Control*, Vol. 47, 282–336.
Paul N. Milgrom and John Roberts (1991), "Adaptive and Sophisticated Learning in Repeated Normal Form Games," *Games and Economic Behavior*, Vol. 3, 82–100.
Michael E. Porter and A. Michael Spence (1982), "The Capacity Expansion Process in a Growing Oligopoly: The Case of Corn Wet Milling," in J. J. McCall (ed.), *The Economics of Information and Uncertainty*, Chicago: The University of Chicago Press, 259–316.
Roy Radner (1982), "Equilibrium Under Uncertainty," in K. J. Arrow and M. D. Intriligator (eds.), *Handbook of Mathematical Economics*, Vol. 2, Amsterdam: North-Holland.
Alvin E. Roth and Ido Erev (1995), "Learning in Extensive-Form Games: Experimental Data and Simple Dynamic Models in the Intermediate Term," *Games and Economic Behavior*, Vol. 8, 164–212.
Thomas J. Sargent (1997), The *Conquest of American Inflation: Ideas or Regressions*, The Marshall Lecture for 1997, mimeo, Hoover Institution, Stanford University.
Amos Tversky and Daniel Kahneman (1981), "The Framing of Decisions and the Psychology of Choice," *Science*, Vol. 211, 453–8.

Printed in the United States
By Bookmasters